WORKING RESEARCH
Strategies for Inquiry

WORKING RESEARCH
Strategies for Inquiry

TIMOTHY J. HIRSCH

University of Wisconsin-Eau-Claire

Prentice Hall
Englewood Cliffs, New Jersey 07632

Library of Congress Cataloging-in-Publication Data

Hirsch, Timothy J.
    Working research : strategies for inquiry / Timothy J. Hirsch.
      p. cm.
    Includes bibliographical references and index.
    ISBN 0-13-950973-9
    1. Research—Methodology. 2. Problem solving. 3. Technical
writing. I. Title.
    Q180.55.M4H57 1992
    001.4'2—dc20
                                       91-20206
                                         CIP

Acquisition Editor: Tracey Augustine
Production Editors: Fred Dahl and Rose Kernan
Marketing Researcher: Linda Bennani
Copy Editor: Rose Kernan
Designers: Fred Dahl and Rose Kernan
Prepress Buyer: Herb Klein
Manufacturing Buyer: Patrice Fraccio
Supplements Editor: Ann Knitel

Printed in the United States of America
10 9 8 7 6 5 4 3 2 1

ISBN 0-13-950973-9

Prentice-Hall International (UK) Limited, London
Prentice-Hall of Australia Pty. Limited, Sydney
Prentice-Hall Canada Inc., Toronto
Prentice-Hall Hispanoamericana, S.A., Mexico
Prentice-Hall of India Private Limited, New Delhi
Prentice-Hall of Japan, Inc., Tokyo
Simon & Schuster Asia Pte. Ltd., Singapore
Editora Prentice-Hall do Brasil, Ltda., Rio de Janeiro

CONTENTS

PREFACE
FOR THE
INSTRUCTOR

My great-uncle Sebastian crafted wooden boards and timbers into houses, some with seven rooms and living space for twelve people, and some so tiny I could carry them around in my pocket. He did all his carpentry work with eleven tools—a hand-saw, an auger with bits, a draw knife, two planes, a wood chisel, a screwdriver, an ax, a rule, a square, and a claw-hammer. In 1960, two years before he died, he added a new screwdriver with a Phillips head. "I may be eighty-six years old," he said when people commented on his new tool, "but I'm not too old to keep up with the times."

From Sebastian I learned the potential for work imbedded in a few basic tools carefully chosen, kept sharp, and handled with skill. His hand-saw now rests on the shelf behind my computer work table, the handle burnished to a golden patina, the teeth still sharp. I put the saw there to remind me to stick to the basic tools of research—What is "research?" How do we formulate research questions? How do we identify what information we need? How do we find that information? How do we process information? How do we organize and record our findings?

With this chest of basic research tools, you can teach fundamental research skills to your composition students. With your guidance, each student will become familiar with the tools and develop her or his research prowess by answering a significant question. The skills they develop will transfer to other, more complex, research applications, both in school and out.

This text is based on the premise that, before anything else, "research" provides systematic strategies for inquiry and critical thinking. To highlight the importance of the "search," I have concentrated on research which begins with a question. To underscore the importance of thinking through evidence in a systematic way, I have presented an approach which requires critical thinking. I want your students and mine to comprehend the richness of the resources available to them—libraries, people, their own powers of observation—when they develop systematic habits of inquiry and thought.

This text will help students see that genuine research begins with an important question shaped and limited by the relevant existing conditions, and by the criteria they choose as the balance points for their judgments. Once they have identified the specific information they need to answer their questions, they will learn how to find it with more purpose and energy.

In this text I explain each step in the research process, using examples from student work to illustrate how it's done. The three complete papers included in this text provide student researchers an opportunity to see how their work on the early stages lead to successfully completed projects.

Like my great-uncle, I hope I am not "too old to keep up with the times." Therefore, I have added guidance for the use of a couple new basic tools such as on-line data-base indexes (now often used in college and university libraries), copy machines, and word-processing equipment.

Thank you for choosing *Working Research* as your text. If you have suggestions which will help me make it a better text in the next edition, please call me or send me a note.

I developed the concepts and materials for this text over a period of twenty years, so I am sure that I have forgotten many of the people who have contributed insights, ideas, or resources. I owe them my gratitude. I especially want to thank LuAnn Fletcher, Paula Weiler, and Elizabeth Ryan who contributed the sample papers included in the text; Jessie, Pete, Sally, and Richard whose work I also use as illustration; and all of my composition students whose research papers have helped me understand the research process. Karen Welch (UWEC English Department) used an early draft of the text with her composition classes, and her comments and suggestions were very valuable. Eugene Engeldinger (Director of the UWEC Library) provided assistance on the sections which deal with bibliographies and the use of the library. Maria Szarska, Jenny Arneson, and Patricia Zwiefelhofer also provided assistance with technical materials. David Hirsch, a college student and my son, gave me many practical suggestions and helped me prepare the manuscript. Nan Dougherty and Jan Kippenhand, colleagues and friends both, supplied advice and assistance at critical moments, and Rose P. Kernan, the Production Editor, has earned my lifelong regard and appreciation for her expert work and energetic support. To those and all others who have helped me become a better teacher of composition, thank you. Everything good about this text grows out of the help others have provided me. All the blunders, big and little, are my own.

PREFACE FOR THE STUDENT

This text will help you develop a systematic approach to research. To learn the process, you will begin with a serious question which you need to answer in the immediate future. After you describe the relevant existing conditions, you will select the factors you want to take into account as you look for information to answer your question.

Using the process outlined in this text, you will go beyond paraphrases and quotations. Although you will learn how to find and incorporate information from other sources, you will do your own thinking—your own translations, your own interpretations, your own analyses, your own comparisons, your own evaluations. You will learn how to apply the research process to other questions—personal, academic, business, community. You will develop a strategy for systematically finding information and thinking through important decisions.

Using three complete papers and other illustrations from student work, this text will lead you step by step through the process. Good luck! Write me a note with your suggestions about how you think the text could be better in the next edition.

WORKING RESEARCH
Strategies for Inquiry

CHAPTER ONE

SETTING OUT

RESEARCH: AN INTRODUCTION TO THE PROCESS

An Overview

This textbook is designed to help you review some basic questions about "research." What is it? Why do we do it? How can we do it better? I hope that, when you finish this book, you will be able to see that the ability to carry on systematic research can be one of the most important tools you can use to create for yourself a healthy, happy, more fulfilling life. The ability to do research well will also make you a more valuable employee, and a more responsible and productive member of the communities in which you live.

As a college student, you have many significant, sometimes even life-changing, decisions to make: What should my major be? Should I transfer? Where? Where should I work this summer? Where should I live next year? How can I pay my tuition? Should I buy a car? Am I getting more serious with my girlfriend (boyfriend) than I want to be at this stage in my life? What kind of birth control should I use? Should I marry Sam in June? Should I continue on the swim team? When you ask these and a thousand other questions, you will find the best answer more easily if you do research.

In addition to your own personal decisions, you have decisions to make on behalf of others. Perhaps you are the one who decides where the ski club will go for its Spring skiing trip? Maybe you are on the staff of the school literary magazine: Should you go to four issues a year or stay with two? Perhaps you make (or influence) family decisions: Should my family move to a new apartment, buy a house, or stay where we are? Some of you already are responsible for business decisions about facilities, inventories, personnel. And all of us have an obligation to participate in local, state, and national community decisions. You can improve the

2

quality of your decision making, both for yourselves and for others, if you learn to use research.

Begin with a Question. You may wonder, "How can I research questions like that? They're so specific." In fact, such questions provide significant advantages as research questions. First, on such topics, you begin with a question—an important first step in any genuine research. Some textbooks on "research paper" projects ask the student to begin with a "topic," or with a "thesis statement." When one begins with a "topic" the inevitable result will be report writing rather than research. In good report writing you collect, select, translate, and transfer information from several sources into one compact coherent source. The ability to "report" is an essential skill and an important ingredient in genuine research writing, but it does not provide much opportunity for the writer to incorporate his or her own higher level thinking skills into the project. What one usually gets from a "topic" beginning, is a voiceless patched together paper—"Pap, pastry, and plagiarism," as one of my colleagues calls it.

Beginning with a "thesis" throws even more serious hurdles between you and genuine research. If you begin with a thesis statement, you will be tempted to search for and select only information which supports your initial thesis. But if you begin with a serious, genuine question, the research process retains the incentives which come with a "quest" for information. Your eagerness to find information will lead you to search for answers rather than for support for a predetermined position. If you begin with a thesis, you will find it more difficult to present a balanced, unbiased examination of the evidence. Begin with a question.

Your first step, then, is to begin with a question of critical importance to you. The answer to this question should lead to action. It should be a question which leads to a choice rather than to the simple accumulation of information and opinions about a topic. After the question is established, you will define your "givens," and establish the criteria you are going to use to answer your question.

Identify Givens and Establish Criteria. You can immediately see that a topic like, "Divorce in the 1980s," cannot lead to any genuine research; it will be a report. You can also see that a question like, "Should people get divorced?" (or married) is much too general. There are too many variables. It's impossible to answer that question for everyone. But it is possible to answer it for oneself. If you limit the scope to one specific set of circumstances (the "givens"), and then identify the factors (criteria) most important to you, you will automatically limit the scope to a level which permits you to do genuine research.

Because everyone has a unique set of "givens" and "criteria," two or more students asking the same question ("Should I transfer from the University of Wisconsin—Madison to the University of Minnesota—Minneapolis?" for example), will write entirely different papers. For one, distance from home may be an important factor; for another, an opportunity to study architecture and design might be the most important criterion. Opportunities for plagiarism of all kinds are dramatically reduced. In fact, this kind of topic makes plagiarism unthinkable. I am sure you are not interested in making up or copying the answers to important personal questions.

Search for Sources. Once you have refined your question, added the "givens," and identified your criteria, you are ready to search for information outside your own personal memories. Many guides to "research" paper writing begin with a unit on using the library. Some textbooks actually call this assignment a "library" paper, perhaps a more accurate and descriptive title. In this text, we will try to identify our information needs before we work in the library.

A good library can be a profoundly valuable resource, and everyone should know what's there and how to find it. I think that's more likely to happen, however, when we have a compelling need for information, an important question to answer. Other students who have asked, "How can I research a question this personal?" have usually been surprised by how many relevant sources they were able to find in the library. For example, at least one of my students each year wants to ask, "Should I marry Joe (Mike, Sally, Sam) in June as we planned, postpone until the following June, or call the whole thing off?" The last student who asked such a question found for her working bibliography over seventy-five potentially useful sources in her college's library. In her final paper, she cited nineteen printed sources. These sources provided her with information about problems faced by couples who have different religious backgrounds (she is Lutheran and he is Catholic), about the divorce rates of married U.S. Navy personnel (her fiance is in the Navy), about the problems faced by professional married women (she plans to become a physician), and so on. The library almost always provides important information.

If we emphasize the library too much, however, we often ignore other important sources of information—personal observation, interviews, letters. How does a biologist carry on his or her research? A chemist? A physicist? Very often they depend on direct personal observation. They establish a controlled activity in their laboratories, and using instruments to augment their capacity to observe and record, they simply watch carefully and write down what they see. That's one kind of research we often neglect in the English classroom. For example, Pete wants to answer the question, "Should I continue to live in the Towers dormitory next year or should I move to 611 Water Street with John and Fred?" What kind of research should he do? Certainly he will find relevant material in the library. But he also needs to record his own controlled and careful observations. He needs to take a tape measure and visit the apartment on Water Street. He needs to be there to see what happens in the morning when they all need the bathroom at the same time. He needs to look in the refrigerator. He needs to go shopping for groceries with them. All of these things are research, research which will provide him "hard evidence."

Peter also needs to use the interview as a way of getting information he has no access to either through library sources or direct experience. He can talk with university housing officials, with Fred and John's neighbors, with Fred and John, with his parents, with his present roommate, with people from the utilities offices, with the landlord at 611. . . . Perhaps someone in the counseling services can direct him to information about the relationship between off- or on-campus housing and academic performance.

Evaluate Your Sources. No matter where it comes from, borrowed information requires examination before you accept it into your research. Traditionally at this stage in teaching a research project, teachers remind students to assess the validity of their sources by looking at the authoritativeness of authors, the currency of dates, the reputations of publishers. There are even more important questions: Does the information help answer your question? Does the information stick to the issues or does it draw on propaganda techniques, logical fallacies, or other emotional appeals? Most important of all, does the information provide "hard evidence" rather than an already thought out judgment higher on the taxonomy of thinking levels?

Insist on Hard Evidence. As much as possible, I encourage you to avoid the opinions of others, and instead, search for as much *hard evidence* as you can. Then you will be better able to do your own thinking. When we get to this point in the text, you will be introduced to a "taxonomy" of knowledge. Good thinking usually begins with hard evidence which sometimes needs translation. We interpret the evidence, we analyze it, we compare it, we apply it, and we use it to evaluate our options. In other words, we think our evidence through from hard evidence to evaluation.

These will not be new concepts. With this text, I simply want to remind you that judgments require a foundation of thinking based on some kind of verifiable, almost unchallengeable evidence. That's the kind of evidence you need from your sources. For example, if Fred (in the example above) wants to know whether or not he can afford to live in the Water Street apartment, he needs to have more "hard evidence" than Peter or John's estimate. Nor should he accept his father's insistence that he'll "end up spending almost twice as much as he thinks." Instead, he should carefully gather "hard evidence," then do his own calculations, comparisons, and evaluations.

As you gather information, you need to remind yourself again and again— "Look for hard evidence." When you learn to accept only verifiable hard evidence (or as close to it as possible), you will seldom have difficulty with poor paraphrasing or other kinds of technical plagiarism. If you can learn to delineate evidence levels as you collect information, you usually do not need to borrow the thoughts of your sources; you will do your own thinking. In addition to developing a system to collect information, you need to hone your ability to distinguish valid evidence from unsupported judgments.

Organize the Paper by Criteria. The "question" approach to research has an additional advantage: organization is relatively simple. If you begin with a question, establish the givens, and then identify the important criteria, a rational pattern of organization has already been established. Each criterion can be treated as a sub-question to the primary question. For example, Peter (from the example above) would have criteria like cost, convenience, available space, privacy, study conditions, and freedom. His paper might be organized by handling the least important criterion first and working through to the most important. Each would be a sub-section of the paper for which he would reach a sub-conclusion.

Once you have a first draft, work it through several revisions. Ask yourself, "Would I have more confidence in my project if I added a section? Would more detail make this paragraph more clear? Can I refine the language or the sentence structure? Would the organization be more clear if I moved things around or if I cut? When you think it's ready, polish and edit, and submit your project for evaluation.

BENCH NOTES: OVERVIEW

SUMMARY

Begin with a question of vital importance to you. Answer the question using the best information available, and employ a rational, systematic process. If you follow these guidelines, I guarantee that your teacher will enjoy reading your paper.

I hope that your success on this project demonstrates to you that you can use research to take control of your own life. When you have confidence in a strategy for carrying on research, the process becomes an important ally rather than a formidable task. You will begin to see other questions—personal, professional, community—which might be answered by an application of the research process.

TOOLS FOR THE RESEARCH TRADE: KEEP A PROCESS LOG

The Tradition

Trembling with excitement and a little wobbly, the seventeen-year old student climbs out of the Cessna 150, safely down from his first flying lesson, a birthday gift from his mother. Smoothly professional, nonchalant and a little bored, the captain of the 747 just in from Geneva stops in the airline flight room to finish up her post-flight paperwork. Though home from very different fights, both pilots will enter the flight into their flightlogs.

Like many others, pilots keep a log of each flight—where they flew, when, with whom, any remarkable episodes during the flight, special procedures performed or practiced, unusual weather—a cryptic but remarkably complete record. Physicians and nurses keep charts on their patients. Policemen write reports on every accident or robbery they investigate. Architects and lawyers log the time and specific tasks they perform for their clients.

The Purpose

These logs provide an essential record for many purposes. The pilot's logbook is his or her official record of experience and the currency of his or her credentials. For the lawyer and architect, the log provides documentation for the bills submitted to their current clients and a basis for the estimates they send to prospective clients. The records they have of past experience make it possible for them to estimate with remarkable precision how long a complex problem will take and what problems to expect.

As writers, we too can learn from keeping a writing log. From the record of your experience on the paper you are writing for this class, you will be able to estimate with precision how much time a similar project will take you in the future, and what problems to anticipate.

A Sample Format

By writing in your log at the end of every work session, you will find it easier to keep on track, plan you work sessions, and see clearly what you still have to do. I recommend a format like the following:

PROCESS LOG				
ENTRY #				
DATE	TIMES BEGIN / END	SLIPPAGE TIME (Subtract)	TOTAL TIME ON TASK	STAGE OF RESEARCH ENGAGED
WORKSITE	TOOLS USED		PROGRESS	PROBLEMS
COMMENTS/OBSERVATIONS/PLANS FOR NEXT SESSION				

Each time you work on your paper, complete a page of the log. Number the entries in sequence, beginning with Entry #1. Enter the times you begin work and when you end. Also enter "Slippage Time" (the minutes you lost to distractions, to equipment breakdown, to breaks). Then calculate total "Time on Task"—time actually spent working. Describe briefly the stage of research (questions for outline, working bibliography, taking notes, drafting). Note the place where you worked (library, dorm room, classroom) and the tools you used (periodical indexes, copy machine, on-line data base). Describe the problems you faced and the progress you made. In the larger open space at the bottom, describe your insights, your feelings about how your research project is going, or anything else you want to write. Finally, at the conclusion of each working session, save a couple of minutes to review what you have already done and what you still have to do. Enter a brief description of what you intend to work on during the next session.

As you work through the stages of your research, you will find excerpts from the "progress and problems" section of the "process log" Paula Weiler kept while she worked on her paper, "A Runner's Question," one of the sample papers in this text.

With each stage of the research process, I have also included the approximate amount of time you can expect to spend on that stage. I have arrived at these time estimates by examining the "time on task" sections of several hundred Process Logs of my students over the last five years. These times should help you plan the amount of time you need to allocate to each step.

BENCH NOTES: 'KEEP A PROCESS LOG'

SUMMARY

Most professionals who work with projects—tasks which require a many stage process—keep a log to help them see exactly where they are in the process. You will be more comfortable throughout your project if you keep one too. It will help you plan your tasks and your time.

ESTIMATED TIME NEEDED

For each section of the text, the "Bench Notes" will include an estimate of the time you need to perform the steps in the research process described in that section. I arrived at these estimates by examining several hundred Process Logs for projects similar to those represented by the samples in this text. The amount of time needed will vary if you are working on either a more or a less extensive project.

Schedule from two to five minutes for each log entry.

PRACTICE AND APPLICATION

Among the Bench Notes you will find suggestions for ways to practice the skills presented in the section and advice about how the skills can be applied in other situations.

Select a typical school day and maintain a process log for the entire day. Analyze the log for slippage, for your most productive times, for tasks which seem to take much longer or much less time than you expected.

BENCH NOTES *continued*

KEY TERMS

Process: All of the activities (often organized into steps or stages) which one goes through to complete a specific project.

Slippage: Time (and sometimes other things like money) lost to distractions, broken equipment, anything which takes one away from "time on task."

Time on task: The actual amount of time devoted to work on a project. Total time engaged in the process minus slippage.

TOOLS FOR THE RESEARCH TRADE: USE A COMPUTER

Why and When

Pens, pencils, chalk, ball point pens—all these hand-writing tools, when they were developed, provided tremendous new flexibility and speed to the transference of human thinking to a written form. But now, in comparison to the tools we have available today, those handheld devices seem as slow and clumsy as chiseling in stone must have to the first user of the quill pen. Contemporary personal computers supported by word-processing programs, and many new typewriters, make it possible for us to record our thoughts in writing much more quickly than we can with a pen or pencil. Even more importantly, these new tools make it possible for us to correct and revise our work much more conveniently.

Many of you already use computer equipment and need no instruction or encouragement. But if you know nothing about these new writing tools, learn as soon as you can. Take a class, get a friend or relative to teach you, read instruction books, and practice. Many schools have computers in convenient places where you can use them free of charge. Perhaps your instructor will schedule a session or two in a computer laboratory and teach you some of the basics. Because of the many different types available, I'm not going advise you about specific hardware or software. Instead, I am going to urge you to use the latest technology available on your campus.

Whatever hardware and software package you use, I promise that you will be able to write, save what you write, correct errors, revise, format, and print—all light years more conveniently and faster than you can with a pen or pencil, or even than with a traditional typewriter.

All systems include a typewriter-style keyboard through which you transfer your thoughts onto an electronic page. Because your writing is stored electronically rather than mechanically in ink or graphite, you can easily change it. You can correct errors, move materials around, add, delete, change format, margins, page numbers, almost anything you want. You can make multiple drafts without the burden of recopying.

As You Compose

Especially if you type moderately well, you will be able to put down your thoughts much more quickly than you can with a pen or pencil. When I time myself writing with a pen as fast as I can, I average around forty words per minute, and I'm exhausted when I stop. When I type as fast as I can, even though I'm not a good typist, I can average over fifty without difficulty. Although I have not measured the energy expended, I know that I find writing by hand much more tiring than typing on the computer keyboard. What's more, I can read what I have typed, but I myself have serious trouble reading what I have written by hand.

For most people composing on an electronic slate goes faster for another reason. When writers print or write in long hand, they generally spend more time "rehearsing" before they commit their sentences to paper. On a computer, because you know how easy it is to erase and re-write, you will do more rehearsing directly on the keyboard. You will be able to commit your thoughts into prose more quickly, more freely, because the investment in effort is not as great, and the penalty for error, minimal.

Most people working on a computer do much more revision and correction as they compose than they would on paper. Again, it is so easy to back up, erase, and try a different sentence or usage option. Typographical, punctuation, and spelling errors are easy to see and correct on a computer.

As You Revise. Once you have a draft underway, you can add entirely new materials, delete sections, expand, rewrite sentences, change single words, or modify what you have written in any way you like. With a pen, pencil, or standard typewriter, once you have a draft down on paper, anytime you change more than a word or two, you usually need to recopy the entire draft. Before the word processor, many people tolerated the weaknesses in their drafts to stand unchanged simply because they had no time or inclination to re-copy.

With a computer, you can go through many drafts without a great investment of time or tedium. All the changes take place electronically. In this way, the computer works especially well with a process approach to writing. Even with a computer, however, revision does not take place automatically. Writers need to practice revision just as they do other steps in the writing process. A computer simply makes it easier to change what you want to change when you know what it is.

During the Final Draft. When you are satisfied with the text of your paper, you can use the features of your word-processing program to help you clean up any last errors, incorporate last second insights, and set up the final draft. Every program I've seen permits you to set and change margins, spacings at top and bottom, and page breaks. Many also include a spell-checker which identifies for you any word not matched in its dictionary. Some permit you to change the font style or size, use bold type, italics, or graphics. A few even analyze the syntax and style of your text and tell you such things as how many words you have per sentence, or how many "to be" verbs. In the next several years such programs will become more and more sophisticated and routinely part of composition classes.

As You Print. While you work on your computer text, it is stored on an electronic slate where you could make changes easily. When you have got it just the way you want it, you can transfer it from electronic memory to "hard" copy—printing on a paper page.

One day last year I walked past the benches outside one of the computer laboratories on our campus and met one of my composition students sitting on the bench, drinking a cool beverage, and watching the people walk by. He had—for him—a remarkably beatific smile on his face.

"Hello, Jake," I greeted him. "You look happy."

"You bet," he responded. "As I sit here enjoying the view, in there"—he pointed inside the computer lab—"my research paper is printing."

I understood his feelings. If you hand write or type early drafts, at some point, you have to type (or hire to be typed) the final draft. If you have used a computer, the machine does the final draft almost by itself. Like Jake, I thoroughly enjoy those moments when my work on a text is done and I can sit back and let the printer make the final copy.

After You Print. Let's say you have your paper all finished and you look it over one last time. On page ten you find a completely garbled sentence, maybe even a critical paragraph missing. If you have typed, it's time for panic. If you have been using a computer, a few minutes of work on the text, and you can print again the page or pages affected by the correction.

Once you have your "hard" copy, you can quickly make a back-up copy of your working diskette for security, and save the manuscript in a small, easy to store electronic format. As I worked on this textbook, I kept the entire manuscript on two disks.

Warnings

Whenever you write using a computer and a word-processing program, you encounter a couple hazards you don't face with paper and pencil. Years ago, when students came to class without a required paper, they used to say, "My dog ate it," or "My baby sister flushed it down the toilet." Now the favorite excuse has become, "I lost it in the computer."

I know from experience that sometimes the "I lost it in the computer" excuse is valid. On the third day after I began using my current machine, I lost fifteen pages—an entire day's work, completely evaporated.

Save Often. To avoid the despair which comes with "the computer ate it" blues, learn to use your system well enough so that you can *"SAVE" OFTEN.* Learn how to "save" and get in the habit of saving at least every ten minutes.

Paula's Log, Entry # 35

Tonight I worked on my paper in the computer lab in my dorm. I'm making real progress—two major sections nearly complete. I'll explain that 45 minutes of "slippage." Marjorie, a really nice girl from across the hall, was working on the machine next to mine. We were both clicking away when all of a sudden she started shouting, "No. No. No. What's going on here? Come back. Oh [expletive deleted]." She had been working four hours on a paper for her psychology class and was running the "Spell Checker." Suddenly everything disappeared. It was only her second time on that machine and she didn't know how to find the file where she had been saving her work. I tried to help her retrieve her paper, but no luck. Finally we got "Hacker" Jeff out of bed to see what he could do. He found it for her, but he called Marjorie several names—the most mild was stupid. Marjorie was so glad to get her paper back from the void that she tried to kiss him in spite of the names he was calling her. It's hard to work when that kind of drama is going on around you.

Make a Backup Copy. Warning number two: *MAKE A BACKUP COPY.* The masterpiece you have recorded on the computer's electronic slate can be scrambled into magnetic chaff without too much trouble. Heat, magnets, rough handling, mysterious gremlins, all can quickly disturb the data on your disk and ruin your paper. Establish a habit of making a backup copy at the end of each working session.

Do Not Depend Too Much on Your Computer. Warning number three: *DO NOT DEPEND TOO MUCH ON YOUR COMPUTER.* Over the years as a teacher, I have noticed that students who drive a car or take a bus to class are more often late than people who walk. One of my colleagues leaves his house exactly nineteen minutes before his early morning class. On his way to school, he passes through nine stop and go lights. He has calculated the average number of times he gets a red light, and the average length of time he has to wait. If his usual parking space is open, he arrives in his classroom two minutes early. About once a week he turns up late—he had one more red light than average; his favorite parking spot was gone; he had to stop to buy gas; the traffic was slowed down by the fog or ice. He has not allowed for slippage—distractions, little glitches in the system, problems with the machinery.

Allow for Slippage. When you work with a computer, especially until you master the program, you will find yourself taking much more time than you expected trying to get your program to print, fixing page numbers, margins, page breaks. Sometimes when we work with computers we become like the hare in the "Hare and Tortoise" tale. *ALLOW FOR SLIPPAGE.*

BENCH NOTES: USE A COMPUTER

SUMMARY

If you heed the few simple warnings, you will be a much faster, more efficient writer when you use a computer with a word-processing program.

As you draft, your thoughts become transcribed into words more quickly with less effort. You can make corrections and changes without the tedium of recopying the entire text. You can add, expand, delete, revise, or completely re-write. You can check your spelling, set the format you want, and then, sit back and watch your printer do the work. Use a computer.

PRACTICE AND APPLICATION

The next time you write in long hand, time yourself to see how many words per minute you write. If you process words on a computer, time yourself again. What is the difference? If you do not type or use a computer, find out what resources your campus has available to help you begin.

KEY TERMS

Hardware: The mechanical and electronic equipment used for computing.

Software: The electronic programs which enable computer hardware to organize and shape information. Most programs are designed for specific computing tasks. Word-processing programs, for example, enable users to devote a computer to writing processes.

Word Processor: A combination of hardware and software set up for writing—composing, revising, editing, printing.

Stylus: A device which permits humans to transfer the words in their brains to words on a page—a pencil, a computer keyboard, a piece of chalk.

Electronic Slate: A metaphoric description of the way words are stored in word processors. While markings of chalk store the words on a slate chalkboard, the words in a computer are stored as electronic signals.

Save: The signal sent to a word processor if you want to keep what you have written. The words entered into a word processor are stored in a temporary state. If the user wants to keep them, he or she must signal the word processor to ''save'' them.

Backup Copy: An additional electronic copy of what you have written. The devices (usually disks) on which information is stored are vulnerable to damage. If you have no ''backup'' you could loose weeks of work in seconds.

EXHORTATIONS/KEEPING ON TRACK

Beware of Distractions

Working through the stages of any long process requires tenacity, the ability to grab hold and hang on until the absolute end. Sometimes critics of education assault certain academic programs because they require (and encourage) more tenacity than brilliance, more endurance than insight. In part, I agree. I believe, however, that brilliant insights almost always appear only after someone has tenaciously hung onto a problem, thinking it over and worrying about it for a long time. "Tenacity" and "brilliance" are not mutually exclusive, but a team which work best if pulling together in the same harness. Simple "endurance" without insight grinds on into meaningless tedium, but insights without sufficient endurance to clarify and communicate flash impotently and go out.

On long and complex problems like your research paper, you not only need to think clearly, you will also need to endure, to keep tenaciously on the track. Those who expect to rely primarily on their brilliance will not do well. Those who go numbly through the steps without engaging the full capacity of their brain will not do well either. In this chapter I want to give you some advice on how to keep the fire up, how to grab hold and hang on when you get tired.

While working on your research project, if you feel moments when you want to throw it all away, you are not alone. Everyone feels periods of frustration during long writing projects. In fact, it's an inevitable part of the process. Often you won't be able to see how it will all come together; maybe you have not been able to get a specific piece of information you were counting on; maybe you have written ten pages and they all seem irrelevant or gibberish. To be a successful writer you absolutely must learn to handle the anxiety and frustration which swirl around a long project.

Be Tenacious

Schedule Short Breaks. What do professional writers do when they get frustrated, when nothing seems to be coming together? We read and often hear about how professional writers, stuck for some reason, take a break, work in their gardens, chop wood, go for a walk on the sea-shore, or play with their dogs. All true, but professional writers usually take these breaks only after many hours of intense work, not after a half-hour of sharpening pencils. And the breaks they take do not extend into week-long vacations from their projects. Through experience, professional writers know that a short break from their desks to do physical work or play helps them when they come back. But come back they must, and soon.

Those magical moments of insight when the solutions come in a flash to the thinker as she or he sits under a tree or paddles in a canoe come only after he or she takes a break from long hours and intense direct concentration on the project problems. If the long and intense concentration is not invested first, you can be absolutely certain that the insights will not come. You must make the investment first, third, and last. The insights come second.

When anxiety and frustration arrive, as they inevitably do, try to accept them, become familiar with them, treat them as allies in your project. And continue working with these new allies at your elbow, at least for an hour or two more. If nothing still seems to be working, then take your break—go for a walk, play a game, watch television, talk with friends—an hour or two at most. But come back to the project again, or your rest will have been wasted. Once you begin a long project like this one, take no more than a weekend away from working on it. Keep the materials and the problems always fresh in your mind, or you will find it very difficult to pick it up again. Once you have your outline ready, take a copy with you during the day. If you have a few minutes waiting between classes, or in line for lunch, take it out, look at it, think about it.

Work on Another Section. When you have a long and complex project, you can usually find some little tasks to be done which you know you can do. When you get stuck on one part, go on to some other part of the project, something easy for you. For example, Paula's log shows that she had trouble drafting the section of her paper devoted to the psychological effects of going out for track. After several frustrating hours of working on that section, she changed tasks and worked on rewriting her outline. Once she had decided to move the "Am I Good Enough?" section to an earlier point in the paper, she knew she would have to re-do her outline sometime, but she hadn't gotten around to it. Now, blocked by the seemingly unsolvable problems in Section Five, she tackled the outline because she knew exactly what to do with it. Then, coming back to Section Five, she had new confidence and she made better progress.

Paula's Log, Entry # 40

Complete frustration. Until today my paper had been going so well. I can't believe I spent an entire Sunday afternoon and accomplished nothing. The first three major sections just seemed to fall in place. But this section on "psychological" effects just won't go. I can't pull it together, and time is running short. I felt so righteous this morning giving up the canoe trip to work on my paper, and now I'm exhausted and I accomplished nothing. I wasted the day. [Expletive, expletive, expletive—all deleted].

Find a Secure Place to Work. Your work on this long project will go better if you can find a secure, quiet place to work. Most people work better on long projects when they have a place where they can safely leave the bits and pieces lying around.

This secure place need not be the place where you do most of our actual work, but it should be the place where you can go to think over the "big picture."

This place doesn't have to be large, but the smaller it is, the more neat and orderly it has to be. That means, for most of you living in dormitories, you probably will need to spend some time each time you work on your project making sure that everything is neatly in order. Over the years I have taught the research paper assignment, I have heard many horror stories about note cards lost, computer disks destroyed by spilled soda, and once, an entire project—rough drafts, notes, final copy, everything—blown off the pedestrian bridge into the river. I wouldn't have believed it, but I saw it happen.

I recommend a box, a file drawer, at least a special folder, where you keep everything—EVERYTHING—or at least copies of everything, all neatly together. As soon as you have a section completed, make a copy, and keep it in a separate place from your original. If you are using a word processor, print a hard copy and make a copy of the diskette as well.

Note and Reduce Work Avoidance Activities. I recommend that you note in your research log every time you get up from your work just to escape the strain of hard thinking. A lucky few of you may have had lessons on how to identify and neutralize work-avoidance patterns. The rest of us have to struggle with work-avoidance urges on our own. The struggle doesn't get easier with age, either, I'm afraid. Right now, a hundred little demons are urging me to stop, have a cup of coffee, check to see if any tomatoes are ripe, fix that door that's stuck, call the barbershop. . . .

While you work on a project like your research paper, no boss, teacher, parent, or coach, stands over you forcing you to work. Whenever you want, you can stop, get up, turn on the television, get a drink. You might feel an irresistible urge to eat something, so you go out for a snack, or you remember that you haven't talked with friend A or B about his or her weekend yet, so you visit for five minutes—or an hour. Maybe your typewriter needs a new ribbon, the light needs adjusting, the wastebasket needs emptying. Your music machine needs a different tape, or the room is too cold or hot. Most of us have no trouble thinking up excuses why we can't work right now. Some writers fantasize about being put in jail so that they could be freed from all of these temptations, but even in the most simple cell, writers have always found distractions tying to lure them away from the difficult chore of writing.

Sometimes during your project, everything will hum along. You will know what you want to write, and the words will seem to flow. You will be so engaged in your project that you will not even notice that lunch hour has passed, or that you worked right through your favorite soap opera or the football game. For every hour like that, however, you will necessarily have to invest three of the kind where the slightest excuse to stop working seems overwhelmingly attractive. If you want to do well on this project, you need to show your strength: resist the work avoiders.

Avoid Procrastination

All of us succumb occasionally to short-term distractions from our projects. Don't feel guilty about it. But when you find yourself putting off your work too often, you will soon be in deep trouble. If you find yourself procrastinating, get help immediately. Procrastination is academically fatal.

Get an Early Start. As soon as you can after you learn about an assignment, get started on it and work on it steadily through to your projected completion date. Every long project can be divided into parts. The research project you are working on for this class has already been divided for you, and deadlines established. Keeping on track is more difficult when you are given an assignment and then left on your own to divide the process into steps and establish a calendar. You absolutely must do it.

Be Realistic About the Demands of the Task. Perhaps you can begin and complete a 500-word essay in the evening before it is due, but a longer project requires many steps. If you add up all of the time required for each step of a project like the one you are doing now, you can see that one evening's work does not touch it.

By reading through several hundred "Process Logs," I have estimated the range of times you will need if you prepare a research project similar to the samples included in this text. Paula and Elizabeth both spent close to eighty hours on their projects, and LuAnn spent about seventy. The hours shown on the chart below are the times actually engaged on the project; "slippage time" has been already subtracted.

Even if you are brilliant and organized, and can manage your project in the minimum time, you need to plan on at least a full work week plus one day to complete your project.

Stages	*Hours*
Selection and Clarification of the question	
Identify givens, select criteria, produce outline	3 to 5
Research—finding sources, taking notes, designing observations, conducting interviews	25 to 44
Writing it down, rewriting, introducing sources, working through the evidence, reaching conclusions	15 to 24
Preparing a final draft—polishing, preparing final copy	5 to 10
Totals	48 to 83

Note. The times above are for a project as extensive as those represented by the sample papers. In some cases, your teacher may not want to concentrate so much of the term work on a research project. She or he may prefer a shorter paper which concentrates on a more focused question. If that's true, ask her or him to help you arrive at times more realistic for your situation.

Some students might think they could work forty-eight hours all in one stand. If you go in for such adventures, I recommend you try a triathlon or a swim across Lake Superior instead. The human brain and body does not function well without regular sleep. Research at the University of Minnesota and other places shows, without a doubt, that "all-nighter" projects result in grades far below average in the class, and significantly worse than the same student's performances in projects where the effort was spread out over a longer time with periods of normal sleep between.

Chronic Procrastinators Need Help. If you are the kind of person who procrastinates because you think you "write better under pressure," I recommend that you visit a counseling center. Many schools conduct special seminars for chronic procrastinators, and those who deliberately put off projects to let pressure build before they begin, top the list of those who need help.

Allow for "Slippage." It is true, working with a deadline can be exhilarating. The pressure of knowing that we have only X amount of time might help us keep on track once we begin. In your lifetime, you will face many such deadlines even when you scrupulously plan your schedule and start on time. Please save your special efforts for genuine emergencies, however. Whenever possible *allow yourself some "slippage."* What if you get sick, for example? The university health service where I teach told me that the probability of a student being sick enough to miss classes ranges each day from about 2% at the beginning of the semester to almost 8% near the end. What if you have an unexpected chemistry test? What if your typewriter breaks down, you have trouble with your computer, you have a fire in your room? What happens if you get an invitation to fly to Paris on the Concorde? What if you just don't feel like working? If you start your project early and keep up, you will have room to fit those things in—"slippage" time. If you try to do the whole thing during the last week, the slightest glitch will make it impossible.

It is especially important to allow "slippage" time when you need to depend on others. If you ask someone to mail you information, allow at least six weeks, and follow up your letter with a call. If you need an interview with someone, allow for the possibility that he or she might need to postpone the interview until a later date. Start everything twice as early as you think you need to. My great-uncle, a carpenter, had a rule of thumb: "Everything takes twice as long and costs twice as much as you expect." During research and writing tasks, the rule works almost infallibly—estimate how long it will take, and then double it. If it takes less, then you have a reason to be pleasantly surprised.

Don't Expect (Or Wait For) Perfection. Ironically, people who like things done well often find themselves waiting too long before beginning a project. If you have high expectations for yourself, you might find the early stages of a long and complex project painful. Because our first efforts are necessarily crude and irritatingly unsatisfactory, we might want to avoid the beginning. We would prefer to begin with the concert rather than the first read-through. To get to the concert, however, we need to rehearse; to get to our final drafts, we need to begin with rough drafts. Do it. Get started. With a long and complex project, you absoluteiy cannot wait until you have the entire work composed in your head before you put it down. Get going. If you want to be as good as you imagine yourself, learn to suffer with the awkward fumblings at the beginning. If you procrastinate because you are a perfectionist, again, I recommend that you visit your school's counseling center to see if they are offering a seminar for procrastinators.

Procrastination Leads To Misery

Any evening in any home, apartment, or dormitory where students live, I am sure you could find examples of common procrastination which, if continued, will quickly make life miserable for the practitioners. Very soon a mountain of tests and paper deadlines will loom over their heads. Teachers will become unreasonable about extensions, and parents, friends, and even roommates will become nags.

A Case Study. Let's look into one of these rooms for a peek at a case study. It's a Tuesday evening, and we see a college freshman, Sally, returning from supper about 6:00. She says "goodbye" to her roommate who leaves to go to the library. Sally figures that she has about two hours of homework due for the next day, and she has two long-term projects she could be working on, and maybe, if she were really ambitious, she could be reviewing for the Math test on Friday. She figures she'll put in the two hours on the homework due, and maybe an extra hour on the longer projects—that's three hours.

"Let's see," she thinks. "It's six o'clock now. I'll start my studying about 9:30. By 12:30, I'll have my three hours in. Nobody human goes to bed before 1:00 anyway. I'll go watch TV for an hour."

On her way to the television lounge, she meets Kelly who invites her to join a softball game. Sally plays softball for about an hour, and then joins the others for a beverage after the game. Getting back to her room at 8:00 she feels sweaty, so she takes a shower. At 8:30, she begins the hour of television she had allotted herself for the evening. She watches a half-hour sitcom, but the next show she watches is an hour-long show, so she can't quit in the middle, and stays only a half-hour longer until 10:00.

When the 10:00 news comes on, she thinks, "time to get to work," and heads back to her own room. Passing Dawn's room, she smells popcorn, and she sticks her head in. She stops in for a minute—well, twenty minutes—to find out how Dawn's weekend went with her new boyfriend. She gets back to her own room about 10:30 and sits down with her books. The phone rings. It's Mark, a friend from home who just broke up with Sally's best friend, Mary. They talk for twenty minutes and Sally's ready now to study—11:00. She picks up her philosophy book to read the chapter on David Hume. Her eyes droop, and she feels a little sleepy.

"I'll just lie down for fifteen minutes and get right back at it." She sets the timer on her digital watch to go off at 11:20 and immediately goes to sleep. She sleeps through the timer, but she wakes up at 12:00 when her roommate comes in from the library. Sally gets up and goes out to get a diet coke while her roommate gets ready for bed. When Sally gets back, her roommate is in bed already sleeping—12:30. Sally starts on David Hume again, this time getting through eight pages. When the words begin to blur again, she turns to her math. She does the first two of the ten problems assigned, but she can't get the third one. She gets up to go ask someone for help, but it's after 1:00 and she thinks maybe it's too late. "I'll do them in the morning."

At 1:15 she begins the five-hundred word essay due in English the following day. She knows that she has been able to write four to five hundred words for in-class writing exercises, so she had allocated about an hour for this assignment. "Where did the time go?" she wonders. "I've been studying since 10:00."

Sally makes several stabs at the essay, but nothing seems to come. Finally, at 1:45, she has what seems to be a coherent idea, and she begins writing rapidly. At 2:30 she stops. "I'll copy it over in the morning," she says to herself, and she goes to bed.

In the morning, Sally's roommate gets up at 7:00 and goes to breakfast at 7:30. She studies until 8:30 when she wakes up Sally.

"It's 8:30, Sally. Aren't you going to your 9:00 class?"

"No, I guess not. I was up late last night writing a paper for English."

Does Sally's story sound familiar?

If she continues this pattern, Sally will be behind in all of her classes, and even when she has her work finished, she will not be satisfied with the quality or the grade. And what will she do about her term projects?

What Can Sally Do? What can Sally do? I suspect it's unlikely for us to expect Sally to emulate her roommate entirely (perhaps not even healthy—her roommate might have another kind of problem, much more rare), but she needs to be at least a little more like her. If she can't spend six hours at the library, perhaps she can spend three. But she needs to make those three hours productive hours. Instead of scheduling her work for the end of the evening, she needs to schedule it early, before she has her recreation. If she had worked from 6:00 until 9:00, Sally would still have plenty of time for television, friends, and sleep.

She also needs to work in an environment less likely to distract her, someplace like the library.

If you have trouble scheduling your time, find out if your university has a "Study Skills" program or center. The people who work there will help you examine your work habits and help you make more efficient use of your time.

Your school may also have a "composition laboratory," usually free, a place where you can go to meet with a tutor who will help you with your writing.

BENCH NOTES: EXHORTATIONS

SUMMARY

Procrastination is the absolute clear winner in the list of causes for failing grades on research projects. Long and complex projects require an early start, planning, and sustained hard work. When you find yourself distracted, note the source and avoid it as much as possible. Work through your frustrations. Be realistic about how much you can get done in a given time period. Build "breaks" into your work schedule and allow for slippage—breakdowns of equipment, interruptions, emergencies, rare opportunities. Do not wait for perfection and inspiration to find you. Search for them in the hard work and details of your project.

ESTIMATED TIME NEEDED

Remember my great-uncle, the carpenter, who used to say, "Everything takes twice as long and costs twice as much as you expect." That's how he arrived at his estimates for building. If he thought the project might take two days and cost $600, he told the customer, it would take four days and cost $1,200 to "get the job done right." Even then, he insisted, he sometimes went over the estimate.

Using my great-uncle's rule of thumb as a guide, I recommend that you plan for at least as many hours of "slippage" as you do for work. Thus, if you schedule sixty hours for work on your research project, and then you add sixty more hours for slippage, you'll probably come out right. Don't forget to include slippage time in your log. For example, you may be in the library ready to make photocopies and you discover that you don't have change, and then, that the change machine in the library is empty. If you take twenty minutes to find change, record that in your log: "Slippage time (20 minutes)—went to student union to get change."

PRACTICE AND APPLICATION

Collect proverbs and slogans which warn against procrastination and distraction. Memorize them all so that when you are tempted, you can recite them to yourself, or out loud if the setting allows. Put your favorite on a big poster where it will always be visible. Do all of this with a touch of irony, of satiric self-deprecation if you need to, but remember that the ability to hold tenaciously to a task is absolutely prerequisite for achievement.

KEY TERMS

Exhortations: Efforts to persuade or encourage someone to do well.

Work-Avoidance: Anything we do to escape the discomfort of work—sharpening pencils, eating, drinking, playing games, watching television. . . .

Procrastination: Putting off until sometime later a task which could just as well be attended to now. A common pattern of behavior among students because they often work without direct supervision.

CHAPTER TWO

DESIGNING THE PROJECT

BEGIN WITH A QUESTION

ESTABLISH GIVENS

SELECT YOUR CRITERIA

PRIMARY AND SECONDARY AUDIENCES

BEGIN WITH A QUESTION

Why a Question?

''Show, don't tell,'' your composition teachers tell you time after time. So I'd like to begin with an example.

Meet Paula. When I first met her, she was a student in my composition class. She usually wore her carrot red hair in a thick french braid, and she often came to class in sweats and running shoes. The many freckles on her nose and cheeks stood out firmly on her light skin. When I first saw her sitting in her desk, I thought she was shorter, but when she stood, I realized that she must be at least five feet nine— long legged but short in the torso. One noon hour, about the third week of the semester, I walked past the Nautilus center in the physical education building and saw her lifting weights. After that, I noticed that she had better muscle definition than anyone else in the class. Although I did not ask, I began to infer that she was an athlete of some kind.

I wasn't surprised, then, with the question she chose for her research paper. I had explained to the class that research begins with questions, and that the most fundamental questions are those which we ask about how to live our own lives. I asked them to make a list of decisions that they had to answer in the next three years and to underline those which worry them the most, the ones they lie awake at night turning over and over in their minds. Paula had five questions on her list, but she had underlined only one: ''Should I try out for varsity track?''

Without hesitation, I approved her topic. The final draft of the paper appears in this text.

If you are like Paula (and most students), you are in a stage of your life when you have many important unanswered questions: What should my major be? Where should I live? Where can I find the money I need? How can I find the right mate? Although the process of performing research can go far beyond your private concerns, these personal questions are a good place to begin. I want you to see that research can help you answer such questions, and I want you to learn one approach to research which you can modify and apply to other questions. The final unit in this text suggests a variety of ways you can transfer this process to other applications, both in school and out.

Are you responsible for recommending an answer to a decision faced by a group? Are you president of a club? Editor of a publication? Parent in a family? Manager of a store or other business? You can extend your value to other people and organizations by asking an important community question.

What Kind of Question?

Step one, then, is to think over the problems you have and the questions you need to answer in the next several years, selecting one you would like to research. Recently one of my students, Jessica, wrote her paper on the topic "Should I Marry Michael Pozarski In the Summer of 1989, Postpone Our Wedding, or Call the Whole Thing Off?" I don't know if she lost sleep over this question or not, but it certainly was important to her. I know that some of you wonder how you can research a question like that—where will you find materials? Jessica's bibliography included twenty-seven valid sources of information, both from library and community resources. All of them helped her reach a decision. She could have found many more. Clearly, she benefitted more from doing her research on this important question than she would have on a topic like "UFO's" or "Computer Crime?"

I remember painfully the "research" paper I wrote as a freshman in college. The topic was, "A True Liberal Arts Education." I wrote twenty-five pages and quoted liberally from Alfred North Whitehead, John Henry Newman, John Dewey, and Aristotle. When I reflect on that paper now, I identify with my teacher and imagine her despair over having to read papers like mine. I remember how upset I was then to have received only a "C" on it. I now realize that the grade was no doubt too generous.

I can see now that my paper had been much too general. First of all, I began with a topic instead of a question. I also had the strange notion that one could define a "true" liberal arts education in absolute and final terms. Of course, in retrospect, I realize that the *best* liberal arts education for me in the early 1960s would be quite different from anything Cardinal Newman might suggest from his perspective in the middle of the 19th-century England. What I wanted and needed were quite different from what Aristotle needed, and the resources I had available were far different even from those John Dewey might have had available at the University of Chicago or Columbia University. My paper would have been much better had I asked the question: "What would be the best education for me?"

Certainly Whitehead, Newman, Dewey, and Aristotle can help clarify what one wants in an education. Such background and theoretical resources are essential.

However, it is never enough simply to quote an authority—whether it's John Dewey or even the Bible.

Had I made the question personal, I could have grounded it in specific existing conditions: my high school record (not outstanding), the amount of money I had available (none), my level of sophistication (I had never been out of Wisconsin), my will to succeed (enormous). By limiting the question to my education instead of everyone's, I could have identified with more precision exactly what I wanted out of a liberal education. In other words, I could have identified the criteria relevant to my decision: cost, location, social environment, access to learning resources, curriculum, preparation for employment, extracurricular activities. Then the question, "What would be the best education for me?" could have become even more specific, perhaps something like: "Should I continue at Northland College or transfer to the University of Minnesota—Duluth?"

For the last several years, *U.S. News & World Report* has attempted to select "America's Best Colleges." The magazine's rankings suffer from a similar difficulty—"best for whom?" As the text of the article suggests, any ranking depends on the criteria one uses, how those criteria are defined and measured, and in what priority order one places them. In short, it's impossible to select any school which would be right for everyone. The criteria prospective students choose, and how much emphasis they place on each, depends on who they are, where they live, and all of the other conditions which make each of them unique individuals—the "givens."

Paula's Log, Entry #1

My first entry. I can't believe we can write on such personal topics. My roommate, Jane, can't believe it either. In her class, the teacher provided a list of topics, and Jane chose "Subliminal Advertising." Sounds interesting, but I think I'd rather do something really important to me.

Your own question should permit you to use the research process to reach a conclusion and take some action. After going through the research steps, Paula answered her question with a new confidence that came from knowing that she had reached her decision through a systematic, thorough examination of all of the available evidence. If she had begun with a topic like, "Women in Intercollegiate Track Competition," or "Women Sprinters," she might have collected interesting and perhaps relevant information, but the report which resulted would probably have brought her actually no closer to deciding: "Should I try out for varsity track or not?"

A "thesis" approach would have been even less helpful. If she had begun with assertions like, "Running Builds Character," or "Universities Should Invest

More in Women's Athletics,'' the process of "proving" her thesis would have directed attention away from her own situation rather than help illuminate it.

In Jessie's case, had she begun with a topic like, "Wives of Military Men,'' or "Commuter Marriages,'' she might have learned something relevant and interesting to her, but her research would not lead her to a decision. She would not have much opportunity to relate the information to her own genuine question—"Should I marry Mike next summer?''

Sometimes books and teachers instruct students to develop a "thesis statement'' (instead of a question) and then carry out "research.'' Although that might sometimes work, I think it's very hazardous. Once you develop a thesis, no matter how carefully you try to be open-minded about it, you will be tempted to search for information which supports your thesis. Instead, research should aim for the truth. If we begin with a thesis, we confuse the goals of persuasion or argument with the purposes of research. If you are after the truth, begin with a question and sustain that question until the final conclusion of your paper. If you already know the answer to your question before you begin your research, find another question.

The "question'' approach to research is a variation of the "scientific method.'' In the most simple and ideal situations, the scientific method begins with a question, usually about some unexplained natural phenomenon. After an investigation of the mystery, the researcher comes up with an hypothesis, or a tentative solution to the question. For example, if my car won't start, I look it over and formulate one hypothesis, test it, and if that doesn't turn out, I formulate another and test it, continuing until I discover the solution or am forced to give up. An important part of this process, even before I formulate my first hypothesis, requires identification of verifiable existing conditions. For example, what is the temperature outside? If it is minus thirty degrees Fahrenheit, I will certainly take that into account in my hypothesis. These existing conditions we will call "givens.'' These "givens'' are important to your research as well as to scientists. A question like, "Why don't cars start?'' would be far too general. I can only ask, "Why doesn't this car start this morning?'' Eventually, perhaps, by adding the results of many such specific questions together, we might be able to move on to a higher level of generalization, and deal with all cars in general.

Make the Question Specific

Paula did not want to ask whether all college women should participate in intercollegiate track; she wanted to know whether she—Paula—should. Jessie didn't want to know if people in general should get married; she wanted to know if she should marry Mike the following summer. Some questions, like Jessie's and Paula's, seem to have "yes or no'' answers. Others might enable you to select among two, three, four, or more options. Please remember, however, that both Paula and Jessie are also choosing between options. If Paula decided not to participate in track, by making that choice, she selected for herself the results of that decision. To use a different example, if someone asks, "Should I drop out of school at the end of this semester?'' he or she must also consider what he or she will do instead of going to school—work? Where? Be a bum? Where and on whose money? Paula's question, therefore, also includes a consideration of what she will do if she does not go out for track.

BENCH NOTES: BEGIN WITH A QUESTION

SUMMARY

In this book I am going to make a distinction between "research" writing, and "report" and "persuasive" writing. In report writing, you summarize or paraphrase what someone else thinks about a topic. In persuasive writing, you begin with a notion of truth, and you look for information, which supports that notion. Both kinds of writing are useful and I hope you learn how to use them, but this book will concentrate on "research."

In research writing, your goal is to discover as much of the truth as you can about an important question. I recommend, for this first attempt at research, that you begin with a specific question about which you have been worrying, perhaps even losing sleep. I also hope you select a question which—once you answer it—will permit you to take action. Research can help you see the truth a little more clearly, and knowing a little more about what is true, you will be better able to steer your life on a happy and productive course.

As you work on your project, keep in mind your audiences—anyone affected by the outcome of your question, others who might be interested in your question for either personal or intellectual reasons, classmates interested in learning more about the research process, and, of course, your teacher.

ESTIMATE WORK TIME

In the last chapters, you were introduced to the "Process Log." In your log, you will note the amount of time you spend on each step in the research process. Using the "Process Logs" of many students who have gone through these steps in the past, I have projected an estimate of how much time you will need to complete each step. For example, I estimate that finding a workable question will take you from one to two hours. However, some of you will have your question in fifteen minutes, and others will require four or more hours and a conference with their instructor before settling on a question. The amount of time needed by each person for each step in the process will vary. In each "Estimated Work Time" section I have simply provided average times.

The time needed for each step of the process will also change when the scope of the project is either expanded or reduced.

PRACTICE AND APPLICATION

Most of you will be using the research process outline in this text to answer a question important to you personally. I hope that you transfer what you learn about the process to other personal questions, to research assignments in other classes,

BENCH NOTES *continued*

and to the business and community questions you help resolve as an out-of-school adult.

To help you see the opportunities for the transfer of your research skills to other situations, I will ask you to imagine additional applications as we go through the process. When you have finished this chapter and selected your own question, I want you to devise eight or ten more questions similar to the following:

Community Decisions (made by elected officials):

1. On which of five available sites should the our small town build its new outdoor swimming pool?
2. Which of the three routes proposed for a Highway 53 bypass around Eau Claire should the City Council support?
3. Should the state of Wisconsin lower its legal drinking age to eighteen?

Business Decisions (made by company owners and mangers):

1. Should the RCA recording company begin the phase-in of digital tape technology?
2. Should the retail clothing chain Benneton's expansion be directed more toward the downtown district or toward the suburbs?
3. Should Kinko's Copy Center on Water Street install a new color copier?

Academic Research (judgments reached by academic researchers):

1. Which standardized test is the best predictor of success in college?
2. Should broadcast media be prohibited from reporting the results of exit polls until all of the voting places have been closed?
3. Should the new edition of the anthology of American Literature include an additional work by Kate Chopin or by Thomas Woolfe?

KEY TERMS

Question approach: Research which begins with a need to find an answer to an important question. The researcher looks for information to answer the question.

Thesis approach: Research which begins with a general statement assumed to be true at the beginning of the project. The researcher looks for information to support the initial thesis, modifying it if the evidence is clearly contrary. Usually research which uses a thesis approach culminates in a persuasive final paper.

BENCH NOTES *continued*

Persuasion: Writing which attempts to convince the audience that the writer's assertions are true.

Topic Approach: Research which focuses on the exploration of a limited topic of interest to the researcher. Using primarily library resources, researchers learn as much as they can about the topic. A topic approach usually leads to a report paper.

Report: Writing which provides as much information as possible on a limited topic, usually in the form of paraphrase, summary, and direct quotation.

ESTABLISH GIVENS

Identify Existing Conditions

Once Paula had decided to research her question, "Should I try out for the varsity track team in the spring," she began the next step in the process—identifying the "givens." Givens are all of the conditions relevant to the question which will not change during the research process. For example, for Paula, it was a given that she would continue in school at the same institution. Her performance in track up to this time, her injury history, the performance levels of other runners in the school conference, her level of physical training—all were givens. She also identified other related conditions as givens—her academic record, her need for financial resources, her experiences with stress, and her ambition to excel.

> #### Paula's Log, Entry #2
>
> My question was approved. I'm excited about learning more about it. I thought I had definitely made up my mind to stay away from track, but here I am considering it again. As my roommate says, "Good ideas just naturally pop out of my brain because they can't stand the mess inside."

Notice that some of the givens are physical conditions and others might be described as emotional conditions. For example, Paula might mention her bone and muscle structure as a physical given, but her desire to excel is a "given" attitude. Jessie identifies a specific man in her question. Although her affection for Mike is, in part, irrational, emotional, it remains a given, assumed to remain constant in the course of the research process. Once you have your question, write down as many of the relevant givens as you can.

Each Situation is Different

A question appropriate for one person obviously is not appropriate for most other people. Clearly I would never ask if I should try out for a varsity track team. I've never lost even ten minutes sleep over the question; the givens in my life do not lead me to consider it—I am not a student, somewhat overweight, slow of foot, and not even slightly interested in running fast at my age.

Annually since 1981, Richard Boyer and David Savageau have published *Places Rated Almanac: Your Guide to Finding the Best Places to Live in America.* Early in the book, they acknowledge that all people live in different circumstances, and have different needs and desires. Thus they provide their readers with an opportunity to complete a "Preference Inventory" which is designed to help the readers establish their own unique "givens" and to establish a priority ranking for the criteria different from the one used by the authors. They make it clear that the "best" city will always depend on the unchangeable conditions faced by people who make the judgment.

Even in situations when students ask similar questions, the conditions (the givens) make each research project different.

Be Frank

Sometimes the "givens" include personal information, and thus this step of the process sometimes requires introspection and frankness. For example, last semester a young man started his paper with the question, "Should I transfer to the University of Wisconsin—La Crosse or return to UW—Eau Claire next year? Among his givens, he included his academic interests and aptitudes, his current status in school, and so on. He did not mention, however, that the love of his life was a student at UWLC. Certainly that would be one of the most important givens in a question like his. Be as honest with yourself as you can. If you do, then such information will assume a legitimate place in the research process, and you will be able to see its relative importance more easily.

Paula's Log, Entry #5

When I read my "givens" to my reading group, they told me I was trying to be "coy." "Modesty has no place in research," Phil said. (He's my favorite in the group. A little pompous, but smart and cute.) I guess I have to get over the embarrassment of writing about my own achievements—and fears.

At first, Paula was reluctant to describe as "givens" her track records—she was first in the state in the two hundred meter and second in the one hundred meter dash in her senior year of high school. Eventually, she understood that the results of her research require getting behind such obscuring tactics as modesty. She also was reluctant at first to acknowledge how much she craves to be the "best" at something. She thought of such competitiveness as unbecoming and was ashamed of it. Finally, she was able to say, "I love to win. That's part of me, at least at this stage of my life." That attitude then entered the givens column.

If you are careful and frank as you identify and describe the givens you consider important, you will find it much easier to shape the criteria (see the next section) you take into account as you go ahead with your research.

Careful alignment of your givens also permits you to further narrow your question. Jessica had already narrowed her topic to consideration of one potential husband. Until she reviewed her givens, however, she had not included the three options she considers in her research. After reviewing her givens, Paula was able to refine her question by identifying the events for which she would train and try out— one hundred meter and two hundred meter sprints—by far her best events in high school.

BENCH NOTES: ESTABLISH GIVENS

SUMMARY

Once you know what question you want to explore, you need to write down your "givens"—every established condition you know about the question, unlikely to change during the stages of your research. Describe these givens as completely and frankly as you can, drawing out with especial care any conditions which might be obscured by embarrassment or fear. Keep in mind that the conditions of each person's life are different from every other person, so even if your question seems similar to someone else's, the different "givens" make the question and, thus, the research project different. Read over the "givens" sections of the sample papers and write the first draft of the "givens" section of your paper.

ESTIMATED WORK TIME

Plan to spend between one and one-half and two and one-half hours on this step, including an hour or more for drafting the "givens" section of your paper.

PRACTICE AND APPLICATION

Again, I want you to transfer the research process you are learning to other questions. Using either one of the questions I provided you in the "Application" section of this chapter, or one of the questions you developed, compile a list of probable givens. For example, if I choose the question, "On which of the five available sites should our small town build its new outdoor swimming pool?" my list of givens might include some of the following:

1. The city has allocated $1,530,000 for the construction of a new outdoor pool. They have an additional $98,000 available for site preparation and landscaping.

BENCH NOTES *continued*
---

2. The city owns five properties which might be suitable for the pool.

3. Ten years ago, the city commissioned an architect to design a pool. With minor changes, the city, after consulting with the architect, has decided to use the existing design.

4. The pool will be open each year from June 1 to September 1.

5. The city Parks and Recreation Department has the personnel and equipment resources to staff and maintain the pool.

If I were responsible for deciding whether to use a work by Chopin or by Woolfe for an anthology, my list of givens might include some of the following:

1. We have room for a work of about eighteen pages.

2. Both wrote fiction, and both wrote stories about eighteen pages long.

3. Thomas Woolfe was male, Chopin was female.

4. The last edition of this anthology included four works by a man for every one work by a woman.

KEY TERMS

Givens: All of the known conditions relevant to the research question which probably will remain the same during the research process. For example, I might know that I want a dog, that I hunt quail and pheasant, that the dog must live outside, that I have a fenced in space forty feet by twenty feet, and that I have $200 a year to spend on it.

Criteria: Standards of judgment selected by the researchers as the basis for a search for information, and for the decisions (once information becomes available) they want to make. Conditions, circumstances, or factors relevant to making a valid judgment. For example, to choose one breed of dog over another, I might select as my standards of judgment such factors as, bird hunting ability, ability to live outside, probable costs of care and feeding.

SELECT YOUR CRITERIA

Relate the Criteria to the Givens

After Paula defined the givens relevant to her question, "Should I try out for the varsity track team in the spring?" she was better able to select her criteria—the factors she intended to take into account.

In most cases, your criteria will grow out of your givens. For example, Paula identified her natural speed and her success in high school track as givens. However, she remained uncertain about her ability to compete in intercollegiate track. She needed to do research to find the answer. "Am I good enough?" became one of her most important criteria.

Once she began to list her criteria, she put down health as her first and most important consideration. As part of her "givens" she mentioned that during the last week of competition in high school she suffered a stress fracture to a bone in her foot. Unaware of the seriousness of the injury, she continued to run on it, and a week after her last meet, she needed crutches to get around. She also experienced menstrual irregularity during the most intense months of her training, and she had heard rumors that female athletes suffer more often than non-athletes from bone diseases once they stop training. Paula was interested in both the long-term and the short-term affects of training and competing in her sport.

Next on her list of criteria she put "time." She wanted to know exactly how much time training and competing would take, and whether she could afford to lose that time from her studies, her part time job, and interaction with friends and family.

As her third criterion she put down "competition." She worried whether or not she could make the squad, whether or not she could do well enough in inter-collegiate competition to help her team, and whether or not she might win occasionally.

She was also interested in how involvement in track would affect her relationships with friends and acquaintances—would her social patterns change if she made the team? Would she have opportunities to meet people from other schools? Would she have to give up her plans to go skiing in Utah during Spring break?

For her final criterion she listed "psychological, emotional and mental satisfaction." She hesitated with that one because she was afraid it would be more difficult to research than the others. Perhaps her fears were justified. But even if hard evidence on this topic is hard to find, she was better able to address the questions which grow out of this criterion when she had a *little* information than if she had had none at all.

In the *Places Rated Almanac*, Boyer and Savageau identify "living costs, jobs outlook, crime, health, transportation, education, the arts, recreation, and climate," as their criteria for identifying the "best places to live." In its ranking of "America's Best Colleges," *U.S. News & World Report* uses "selectivity, reputation, faculty, resources, and retention," as its criteria. *Consumer Reports*, in its "Annual Auto Issue," encourages consumers to consider "safety, cost, the dealership, the optional equipment, size and space, the warranty, the performance, the operating expenses, and the frequency of repair required for earlier models of the same car. Of course, if you were choosing a place to live, a college to attend, or a car to buy, your criteria would be different. You would select criteria which develop out of your "givens." As Boyer and Savageau insist several times in their *Almanac*, "the best strategy is to focus on *your* own preferences and needs" (39).

Your "own preferences" might be less important, of course, if you have a family who goes with you if you move. If you do your research project on a question like, "Should we move to Toledo, to Phoenix, or stay in Des Moines?" list among your "givens" the number of people, ages, and commitments of the other people in your household. And to determine your criteria, consult with them.

Whenever you work on a question for a larger community, for a business, or for an academic audience, your criteria will reflect the "needs and preferences" of everyone affected by or interested in the outcome. If you are asked to recommend a site for the new city swimming pool, for example, your criteria will reflect the values and concerns of the entire community. If you are selecting a site for a new factory of store, your criteria will reflect the business needs of the organization for whom you are doing the research. If you are selecting works for inclusion in an anthology of literature, your criteria will reflect contemporary critical trends and market analysis.

Again, Be Frank

Some time ago one of my students, Richard, did his research on the question, "Should I buy a new Pontiac 6000, a used (two-year old) Volvo Station Wagon, or a Jeep pickup truck with a topper (a small camper over the box)?" In the givens section of his paper, he described himself as a person who likes to hunt and fish and who sometimes needs to haul lumber or an outboard motor. He had been out of high school for four years working in the meat department of a local supermarket and he had saved enough money to pay cash. Among his criteria he included such factors as frequency of repair required, expense of operation, versatility, ruggedness, and so on. Although the Volvo wagon was a close second, he concluded that the pickup truck would be right for him. I was happy with the paper and he did well in the class.

The following summer on one sunny afternoon, I was walking along a street near the university and a bright red sports car came roaring up and stopped next to me. I thought, who's this? (I had heard that one of my colleagues was having a mid-life crisis; maybe he had bought the sports car as proof.) But no. Richard from my composition class leaned out the window. "Hey, Professor Hirsch, do you want a ride in my new car?" When I saw it was Richard, I was surprised, but I got in with him. I noticed the white leather seats and the genuine wood dash. "Like it?" he asked.

"But Richard," I stammered, "I thought that you had decided on the pickup."

"Well, I had," he answered. "And I would have bought it, too, but I thought maybe I needed something with a little more sex appeal."

"Why, then, didn't you include 'sex appeal' as one of your criteria?" I asked him in my most pedantic tone.

"Can you research something like that?" he asked, with genuine astonishment. At that moment, I considered giving up teaching.

Try Research First

Some elements in a decision, of course, can not be "researched" very easily. Jessie begins her research by telling us that she loves Mike very much. She accepts (and so do her readers) her feeling for him as a "given." She has been frank with us about it, and she makes no pretense that she will research the question, "Do I love him?" In contrast, Richard did not even mention "sex appeal" in his paper, even though it turned out to be the most important criterion in his decision. He didn't even consider research on the question, "Which vehicle has the most sex appeal?"

Could he have done research on a question like that? Of course. First of all, he should have included the sports car among his options. Then he could have seen how it compared on the basis of his other criteria. He would have been considering "sex appeal" as a matter of course in the research, and he might have seen that single criterion in a more balanced way. He could have interviewed the specific women or woman to whom he wanted to project sex appeal. He could have conducted a survey of many women of the age and type he wanted to attract. He could have explored printed sources on the topic (our local library has at least two dozen which might have helped him assess the sex appeal of the vehicles he was considering). As it was, he bought the car on the basis of some vague impression that it would give him sex appeal.

Two years after he had given me a ride in his sports car, Richard drove into my driveway one summer morning when I was out trying to start the lawn mower. This time he was driving a pickup. He didn't offer me a ride, but he did confess that the sports car had not served his needs well—no place to store his fishing gear, much less his canoe or his cross country skis. The car had been very expensive to insure and to maintain, he said, and worse yet, it had not attracted the right kind of woman for him (although it had attracted some of the wrong kind). Then he grinned and handed me an envelope. "An invitation to my wedding," he mumbled, and then he drove off.

At the wedding, I met the bride. She is a competitive cyclist, and one day on one of her training rides, her front wheel hit a railroad track and she ended up with scraped arms and her bike unridable. Along came Richard in his pickup truck on his way back from fishing. I don't know if the truck had enhanced Richard's sex appeal or not, but I do know that they drove off in the truck for their honeymoon—a camping trip to Colorado.

Maybe if Richard had been frank about what was important to him in the first place, he wouldn't have had his three years of struggle with a car which did not serve his needs. Always ask yourself, "Is there some way I can research this question? That establishes the right frame of mind for intellectual work. Then you can begin to gather and shape information in manageable ways.

I hope you can begin to see the relationship between your givens and your criteria. The givens are those conditions which pre-exist and which you do not intend to research at this time, even though in another time you might. The criteria are the factors you intend to consider during your research. Sometimes two questions are closely linked and must be treated together. For example, Paula's question might be more complex if she didn't make the varsity but had a chance to run with the freshman squad. Then she might have to take the question in stages:

1. Can I make the varsity track squad?
2. If not, can I make the freshman squad?
3. If I make the freshman squad but not the varsity, do I still want to run track this spring?

Such questions get more complex, so we'll save them for a later chapter. For now, try to assume as much stability as possible among the givens.

Shape Your Criteria into Questions

Once Paula decided which criteria to research, she stated them as questions: How will training for and competing in varsity track affect my health? How much time will it take? Will I still have time to study, to work, and to be with my friends and family? And so on. Again, it's important to begin with questions because it reminds us to withhold judgment until we have collected all of our evidence and carried it through the evidence levels to evaluation.

When you finish this stage you will have a thesis question, a list of givens, and a list of criteria shaped into questions. Now rough-out a working outline for yourself like the ones in the sample papers. Please examine them carefully. You will probably revise your outline as you progress through your research, but you need a working outline now to help you identify your information needs.

Organize by Criteria

By identifying criteria, and by shaping them into questions, you have effectively divided your long, complex research project into manageable segments. While you work on the parts, however, it's important for you to keep in mind the relationship of those parts to your central question. An outline will help you do that.

Each of your criteria will be a major segment of your paper. Begin your outline by listing the questions you have created from your criteria? Now examine these questions and look for possible relationships from one to another. Are there some which will work better if they come early in the paper? Later? If no logical relationship presents itself now, perhaps one will emerge as you go ahead with your research.

Look for Prerequisites

Examine your criteria to see if any are prerequisite to any of the others. For example, Paula wanted to investigate first the question, "Am I good enough?" She reasoned that, if the the answer were, "No," there would be no point in continuing

---

Paula's Log, Entry #7

I guess I botched the "Working Outline." I had it organized into two big sections—one "pro" track and the other "con" track. I found out that doesn't work very well. I went to see my teacher and he explained criteria again. I think he thought I didn't pay attention the first time. I am still having trouble deciding what mine should be. I know I want to consider "health," but what else? Can "ambition to win" be a <u>criterion</u>? Teacher: Notice that I remembered the singular for criteria!

---

with the rest of her questions. She would start over on a new thesis question. Put any such qualifying questions early in your outline.

Organize by Degree of Importance

Perhaps some of your criteria are much more important to you than others. If so, you may want to organize your outline in the order of importance. Usually, in academic writing, one puts the least important first and leads up the most important last.

You can reverse this order if you prefer, but alert your audience. Tell them what you are doing. In her paper, after she had determined that she was "good enough," Paula organized from most important (health) to least important (social life). As you read through her paper, you will see that in each section she tells her readers how important each question is to her final decisions.

For Each Major Question, Create Subordinate Questions

Each of the major questions you shape from your criteria will have imbedded subordinate questions. For example, when we read Paula's question, "Am I good enough?" we immediately wonder how good she is. We also wonder what she means by "good enough." By asking that questions, Paula sets up a comparison (and possible contrast) between her performance and whatever performance would be "good enough."

By looking at her outline, we can see that she created sub-questions to make the comparison possible: "What are the record, average, and minimal performance levels needed to compete in our university conference?" This question makes it clear what she means by "good enough." Her next question is, "What were my best, average, and worst performances in high school?" If she answers both with hard evidence, she will have the foundation for a comparison.

Examine the Sample Papers

Look at the outlines for the sample papers and note the relationship in each between their criteria and the major questions they have in their outlines. Try also to see if you understand the logic used in each to create the sub-questions for each section.

BENCH NOTES: SELECT YOUR CRITERIA

SUMMARY

Your criteria grow out of your givens. You might think of your givens as your history, including your existing situation. Your givens have led you to a crossroad; you must choose one road or the other. The criteria are the factors you take into account to make the decision.

Each person comes to a crossroad with a different history, and with different concerns about which criteria to take into account. You select your own criteria. Try to be honest with yourself about what criteria you want to consider.

Your criteria form the backbone of your paper. Each criterion, shaped into a question, forms a major section of your paper. Under each major question, you ask sub-questions which will help you answer the major question.

ESTIMATED WORK TIME

Plan to spend from three to four hours for this step in your research. You will need at least an hour to draft your working outline, and another hour to draft the "criteria" section of your paper.

PRACTICE AND APPLICATION

After you have your own question fitted out with criteria, see if you can find some for a different question like the ones you created at the end of Chapter Three. An example: Once the City of Altoona had decided to build a new swimming pool, they needed to decide which of the five available sites would be best. At the end of Chapter Four, I listed some of the "givens" relevant to the question. Here are a few of the criteria they took into account as they explored the question:

1. We want the pool to be safely accessible by foot, by bicycle, and by automobile.

2. We want the pool to be in an area where the noise will not disturb people living nearby.

3. We want the pool to be as close to existing sewer, water, and utility resources as possible.

4. We want the pool to be as close as possible to other recreational facilities—picnic areas, playing fields, playgrounds.

5. We want the pool to be in a physically attractive environment.

6. We would like to use a site not likely to be needed soon for a new school, industrial park, or other essential municipal site.

BENCH NOTES *continued*

If you work with the Woolfe/Chopin anthology question, a partial list of criteria might look like this:

1. We want the work we choose to satisfy our standards for literary quality.

2. We want to have better gender balance among our selections.

3. We want the work to satisfy our space needs.

4. We want a work which is representative of the literature of the period.

Now it's your turn again. Take a question for which you have provided "givens" and add a list of "criteria." After that, create a full "question outline" for the question you have selected. As an alternative, begin with the question, "Which of the available five sites would be the best place for Altoona to build its new swimming pool?" and create an outline which the city of Altoona could use to research the question. Organize according to criteria.

PRIMARY AND SECONDARY AUDIENCES

Audience and Purpose

An early and often powerful reason for doing research will be an urgent need to know, a curiosity satiated only by answers. The authors of our sample papers all wanted answers for their own sake. LuAnn wanted badly to know whether she should continue in school or return to work. Paula really wanted to know if she should go out for track of not. Elizabeth suffered serious anxiety worrying about where to take her daughter for day care.

As they worked through their questions, however, they discovered that several other people were interested in their findings, either because they would be affected directly, or because their own curiosity was stimulated.

If you are typical, you have listened more than once to someone announce a decision which has changed your life? Maybe your parents decided to move, or maybe the school system changed so that you had to go to a different class or school. Maybe you didn't make the cut for the team or the cast for the play. Maybe your financial aid was cut. Maybe you didn't get the job, or maybe your fiance called it off. At such times, you were probably acutely aware of being an audience, of being out of control over a decision which will affect you.

Now, as an adult, you are yourself more often in a position to make decisions which affect the lives of other people. As you work on this paper, ask yourself, "Who are the people who will be affected by the outcome of my paper?" Once you have worked systematically through a question to its evidence-based, logical answer, you will want to share your conclusions with others who are affected, and with those who are simply interested.

Prepare a list of people to whom you will present you research—your *primary audience*. The list will include anyone who has an interest in the outcome of your research—parents, friends, roommates, employers, teachers. For example, Paula put her grandmother on her list, and after that, her high-school coach, the physician who treated her foot injury, the college sprinting coach, her mother and father, and her roommate. In my classes, I ask my students to think of the primary audience as their "Board of Directors." I ask them to imagine calling the "Board" together and presenting them with the finished product. How will they respond?

You will do your research to find answers, but you will present your findings in a written format so that your audience will be able to see the evidence and the thinking behind your decision. You will want them to respond to your paper by saying, "Yes, I can see how he or she arrived at this decision. I understand, accept, and approve her or his decision, and I support the action he or she will take as a result."

As you work your question through the research process, some bits of answer come clear. You'll put those bits together with other bits, and by the time you complete the process, you'll have the answer—firmly, confidently. You will be the expert, and you should be able to answer authoritatively any question your audience asks.

Some members of your audience may have strong prejudices, perhaps even conflicting prejudices. Paula's grandmother believed strongly that Paula should not go out for track; her high-school coach believed strongly that she should. Your job is to show all of them the results of your research in a balanced and objective way so that they can see how you established the questions, searched for information, and reached your conclusions.

In addition to your primary audience, you also have another group of people who have an interest in your decisions, but not as direct an interest as your primary audience. Included in this group will be your classmates, and other people who are interested in related topics. These people might want to read your paper, not so much because they are concerned about what happens to you, but because they are looking for information and procedures which they can use to answer their own questions. The other students in your composition class will be interested in your paper because, right now, they are all students of the research process. They will want to see how you went about it. These people will be your *secondary audience*." In my class, I call these people, "stockholders." Some teachers of composition speak about the several audiences for your writing as your *discourse communities*. That term, however, has more to do with shared assumptions about the forms of writing and research than with a special interest in the contents.

Your teacher is also one member of your audience. He or she is your ally on this project, however, a consultant who wants your project to be as successful as possible. He or she will be interested not only in the final product but in all of the steps you take during the entire process.

As you structure your question, look for information, and write your paper, remember that you will be presenting your paper to your primary and secondary audiences. They will expect you to be thorough and fair. Keep a list of your "Board" members near your work station and review it from time to time. You are working for yourself, or course, but you are also responsible to them.

BENCH NOTES: PRIMARY AND SECONDARY AUDIENCES

SUMMARY

Early in the research process, prepare a list of people who have an interest in the outcome of your research—your primary audience. They are the people who have a vested interest in the decisions you make.

Also identify a secondary audience, a group of people who might also be interested in your project because they have similar questions, because they are students of the research process, or simply because they are interested in the topic and the information you provide.

ESTIMATED TIME REQUIRED

It will take you about twenty minutes to make your initial lists. I recommend that you spend five minutes once a week or more reviewing the list, editing it as you go.

PRACTICE AND APPLICATION

Imagine that you were president of your school, and that, after studying the issues for years, you have decided to ban the use of alcohol beverages on campus. Who would you put on the "Board of Directors?" In other words, make a list of the people to whom you would like to explain your decision.

KEY TERMS

Primary Audience: The specific person or persons you have in mind when you undertake a writing project. The primary audience is different for each writing task. In this case, it will include anyone who will be affected by the outcome of your research.

Secondary Audience: Anyone who might read your paper because he or she is interested in the information you present or the procedures you used, or because he or she derives some intellectual or aesthetic pleasure from reading what you've written.

Discourse Community: Technical term used by composition theorists to describe the people who make up the audience for a specific piece of writing. A Discourse Community is a group of people who share assumptions about research and scholarly writing. In some cases, your work will reach more than one discourse community.

Purpose: What we hope to achieve by writing. Usually the purpose is a specific response from a specific audience.

Board of Directors: A metaphoric description of your research paper audience.

CHAPTER THREE

LOOKING FOR THE ANSWER

LOOK FOR HARD EVIDENCE

PREPARE FOR YOUR SEARCH

USE THE LIBRARY

TALK TO PEOPLE

STRUCTURE OBSERVATIONS—EMPIRICAL RESEARCH

LOOK FOR HARD EVIDENCE

Delineate Evidence Levels

If you have ever served on (or stood in front of) a jury, you know that not all evidence carries the same weight in a court of law. The U.S. legal system "delineates" very precisely between "strong" evidence and "weak" evidence. And so do each of us as we make choices in our lives. We constantly evaluate the relevance and reliability of everything we read, hear, and see. This sorting out is the part which requires our most rigorous thinking. When we seek to answer important questions, we want to be especially careful to employ a strategy for ranking the quality of information we uncover. Fortunately, here, too, we can draw on the experience of others who have analyzed this problem.

Perhaps you have read something about or by the hero of this chapter, Benjamin Solomon Bloom. When I was an undergraduate forced to read his work for class, my friends and I thought it great fun to emphasize the initials of his first and middle names. Now I consider the work we read, *Taxonomy of Educational Objectives: The Classification of Educational Goals: Handbook 1: Cognitive Domain* (1956) to be one of the most significant books on education in this century. If you are familiar with Bloom's "Taxonomy," you will see that the "Levels of Information" chart at the end of this chapter is a descendant of Bloom's work. In recent years since Bloom and his colleagues created their "Taxonomy," several others (I especially like the work of Carolyn Hughes of the Oklahoma City Public Schools, and Stuart Rankin of the Detroit Public Schools) have developed schema for describing levels of critical thinking (cognition). I hope you will be able to see the value of a systematic approach to the collection and examination of evidence more quickly than I did.

These "Levels of Information" will be important to you—both as you look for information to answer your questions, and as you record your findings in your paper. As often as possible, your research will begin with hard evidence. Your paper will be the record of your thinking from hard evidence through evaluation.

Whenever we "think," we identify what we already know, try to find as much additional hard evidence information as we can, and then, using what we know, we try to find the answers to those questions which remain unanswered.

Paula's Log, Entry# 9

I talked with my mom on the phone this morning and told her about my topic. She sounded worried, and she reminded me what an ornery [expletive deleted] I was when I had to use those [expletives deleted] crutches. I can just hear what Gramma will have to say: "Oh, honey, why would you even consider it, after all you've been through?"

As You Search, Note the "Level" of Information

Paula had her question, she had identified the "givens" relevant to the question, and she had defined the criteria important to her. Then she began looking for information to help her reach a decision. She wanted the decision to be hers, however, and no one else's, and she wanted to be certain she understood the thinking which had gone into the final judgment. Therefore she wanted to accept from other sources only hard evidence, or evidence as close to hard evidence as possible, and then do her own translation, interpretation, comparison, application, analysis, and evaluation.

For example, the student in charge of the Nautilus room where Paula trained told her every time she came in that she definitely should go out for the track team. He told her that intercollegiate sports would build her character, improve her love life, and help her get a job when she graduates. He offered her this advice in the form of a running patter of cliches, but with absolute indifference to supporting evidence. Of what value was his testimony to Paula's research? None whatsoever. The young man was simply passing on his own evaluation and did nothing to show the evidence (if, indeed, he had any) on which he had based the evaluation. The advice-giver's thinking might have been based on entirely different givens and criteria than those Paula had in mind.

Jessie told me that her roommate insisted she must be nuts to even consider marrying someone in the Navy. "You just can't trust a sailor," she told Jessie nearly every day she worked on her research. Could Jessie use her roommate's opinion? Of course not. She had given Jessie no hard evidence to verify, interpret, compare, analyze, or evaluate.

Once you begin to insist on hard evidence from your sources, you may be surprised to discover that it's not only neighbors and friends who want to jump directly to the evaluation level without providing the intermediate steps—hard evidence, translation, interpretation, comparison, application, analysis, synthesis, and evaluation. Twelve or fifteen years ago, I often had students who asked the question, "Should I smoke more marijuana than I do, less, or none at all?" The library had hundreds of sources on the topic, and everyone had an opinion. At that time, however, not much hard evidence had been accumulated on the effects of smoking pot, and most of the sources were useless. Some would say things like, "Smoking M.J. will rot out your brain and turn you into a pothead in no time."

Others would say things like, "Unless you smoke pot, you can't understand the true meaning of life. You can't really appreciate music, art, film, food, or sex without pot." In both cases, the authors were unable to provide hard evidence of any kind. Out of the many printed sources available, the students who researched this question were able to find only a very few which even attempted to provide and examine any hard evidence. Curiously, in recent years, when much more hard evidence is available, I rarely have a student interested in the question.

Paula's Log, Entry #11

I think I am becoming a more rational person because of this paper. I used to be more spontaneous. Now I can't even decide what to wear without identifying the "givens," and outlining the relevant "criteria." Let's see, should I wear the blue skirt or wear jeans? Givens—George Winston concert (cheap seats in bleachers), both skirt and jeans are relatively clean, maybe walk to "street" for refreshments later, sixty five to seventy degrees. Criteria: Comfort, appearance (what goes with the white cotton sweater?), conservation of clean items in wardrobe. Compute, compute. Conclusion: Jeans. I'm becoming a regular thinking machine.

Sometimes the important questions are those most difficult for which to find "hard evidence." The October 16, 1989 *U.S. News & World Report* evaluation of "America's Best Colleges" includes "instructional quality" as one of its criteria. The anonymous authors of the article acknowledge how difficult it was for them to assess:

> To measure Instructional quality, the most difficult of all the attributes to determine quantitatively, *U.S. News* used three subfactors: 1988–89 full-time students to full-time faculty ratios; percentage of 1988–89 faculty with doctorates; and the per-student instructional budgets, which reflect faculty salaries during the 1987–88 academic year. (58)

Anyone who has ever been a student can tell you the "subfactors" they chose have only a distant relationship to the "quality of instruction." We probably would agree with them that an evaluation of instruction is difficult to "determine quantitatively." It's probably not impossible, but *U.S. News* looked for the wrong kind of information. Not all hard evidence can be reduced to numbers.

"Faculty to student ratios" are often misleading because they usually do not take into account how much of the faculty time is actually devoted to instruction as opposed to other scholarly activities. Even "instruction" needs definition. For example, is academic advising part of instruction time? A doctoral degree (earned when and where?) might show something about the faculty members' preparation in their specialties, but it shows nothing about their ability to communicate and inspire students. And faculty salaries might show that the institution is willing to pay for the "best," but it might also show that many members of the faculty are near retirement age.

They probably chose the subfactors they use because the "numbers" are easily available and easy to use as basis of comparison among large numbers of schools. Other kinds of "hard evidence," student evaluations, for example, would have been more difficult to obtain and to compare with similar information from other institutions.

In your own research, look for hard evidence that genuinely relates to the questions you want answered, even if its more difficult to collect and to work with.

As you look, keep in mind this taxonomy. Before your accept information you find as valid evidence for your research, test it against the taxonomy of evidence levels which follows. You won't always be able to find "hard evidence," but come as close as you can.

Levels of Information Applied to the Research Process

"Hard Evidence" information is the kind of information that can be verified as true and valid by parallel observation or measurement. It is the raw material for the next levels of information. Example: We can time the performance of a sprinter over a measured distance in a given race.

Translation information is usually "hard" evidence information changed from one symbolic form to another. Examples: We can change meters to feet, minutes to seconds, kilos to pounds.

Interpretation is the discovery of relationships among segments of information. On this level we form generalizations and definitions, and we articulate both personal and community values and standards. Examples: After timing a sprinter on several different days in several different races, we can form a generalization about her performance level. If the sprinter has only run in races measured in yards, we use translation and interpretation to estimate her performance level in a hundred meter race.

Comparison is the process of considering one idea, object, or action next to another to see specifically how they are similar or different. Example: We can compare the performance records of one sprinter with another and the performance of sprinters with certain physical characteristics with others with different physical characteristics.

Application is the solving of a new problem using information and skills we have learned earlier in another situation. Example: From our experience doing this "research' project, we might be able to use the same process on an entirely different topic.

Analysis is the process of dividing big things into little things which we can more easily understand and handle. Examples: When we divide our research into "givens" and "criteria" we are using analysis. When we divide performance in a race into several stages (start, acceleration, pace, kick . . .) we are using analysis.

Synthesis is the use of familiar materials in the creation of a new solution to solve an old problem. Example: Most writing projects require large doses of synthetic thinking.

Evaluation occurs when you reach a decision that one thing (action, object, idea, procedure) is better than another within well defined circumstances (givens) and weighed against relevant criteria. Example: A runner decides that she would enjoy and benefit more from participation in competitive track than she would from recreational running.

PREPARE FOR YOUR SEARCH

Focus Your Information Needs

By the time you get to this chapter, you will have your approved question, your list of givens, and your list of criteria. Using your criteria, you will have shaped a working draft of your outline. Each entry on the outline will be a question. Now you need to find information to answer each question.

Later on you will examine each source more carefully to determine its final usefulness, but for now, you want to identify the *kind of information* and the *types* of sources you need to examine in order to find as many *specific sources* as you possibly can which might in any way help answer the questions in your working outline.

Let me illustrate with an analogy. Think about your search for information in the same way you might think about a search for new clothes. Your first task would be to examine your clothing needs. You might look over your closet's contents and decide that you need shoes, underwear, and a new winter coat. That's analogous to what Paula did when she decided she needed information about the performance times of college sprinters, the health effects of rigorous training, and the time commitment of working out.

Let's say you realize you need shoes, and you decide to shop for them. Do you go to a grocery store or an auto parts shop? No. You go to places where they sell shoes—shoe stores, sporting goods stores, department stores with shoe depart-

BENCH NOTES: LOOK FOR HARD EVIDENCE

SUMMARY

Research begins with a question. To discover the answer to the question, begin with information as close to "hard evidence" as you can find. Be unwilling to accept the "evaluations" of others. As much as possible use the work of other people to find hard evidence, but then do your own translation, interpretation, comparison, application, analysis, synthesis, and evaluation. In other words, do your own thinking by systematically carrying your evidence through the taxonomy of information levels.

ESTIMATED WORK TIME

This chapter provides you a rest from specific research tasks, so spend the time mastering the concepts in this chapter. Time invested now on theory will come back to you doubled later.

KEY TERMS

Delineate: To make clear distinctions between one level and another. Thus, "to delineate evidence levels" means to make a clear distinction between evidence on one level and evidence on another level.

Relevance: Connection or relationship. In order to be valid, research information needs to have "relevance," a clear relationship to the question.

Taxonomy: An annotated list. Thus a "taxonomy of information" is a list of information levels with definitions, explanations and examples. See the sample above.

Cognition: A technical term for the process of thinking.

___

ments. This is analogous to Paula deciding that she might find information about track performance times from the conference records office or from a track coach. It's simple. You look for information where you know you are most likely to find it. But be alert; you might be surprised some day to find a special on shoes in the supermarket.

Identify Kinds of Information

First look at your outline and make a list of the kinds of information you will need for each criterion. At this stage you do not need to identify specific sources. You simply want to establish general categories of information you might be able to use. To illustrate, let's look at Paula's outline. The first criterion-based question in her outline is, "Are my skills and aptitudes good enough to make the team and compete on the intercollegiate level, or are they more suitable for recreational running only?" What kind of information will she need to answer that question?

Paula decided that she needed to review her own performance records. She remembered a few of her best (and worst) times, but she had not put together a complete record of her performances. She also decided that she would need a comprehensive account of the times recorded by other sprinters in the conference in which her university competes.

For the second criterion in her outline, "health," Paula thought she should thoroughly examine her own health history, and she wanted to read as much as she could about sports medicine. She wanted to know what happens to the physical condition and health of athletes, especially women sprinters, after they discontinue competition. She wondered whether the health records of recreational runners were significantly different than those of competitive runners.

Under the criterion of, "time," she listed a need for specific information about her daily schedule—her time requirements for classes and studying, for her part-time job, and for her social and other recreational activities. She thought it would be important to know exactly how much time (in addition to the time she now spends running and working-out) it would take to train for and to compete in intercollegiate track. She wanted to know how other women athletes handled the time factor, and especially how they managed their school work.

When she got to the fourth criterion, "psychological, emotional, and mental satisfaction," she had more difficulty. After some thought, she decided that it would be helpful to know with some precision how she feels before, during, and after a race, and whether it made a dramatic difference whether she won or lost. She also thought it would be interesting to see how other competitive runners feel, and whether psychological problems are more common among competitive runners than they are among recreational runners. She wondered whether there were a way to test a person for competitive drive. To answer these questions, she decided to seek information about the psychology of sports competition.

For her final criterion, "social life," she wanted information on how close team members usually become, and on the effects, if any, that following a training regime might have on her social options. And she wondered if there might be information somewhere to help her see if her social status on campus would change if she made the varsity track team.

After identifying the *kind of information* she needed (stage one), Paula was ready to list *types of sources* which might provide it for her (stage two). When she had identified the types of sources she needed, she was ready to begin her search for *specific sources* (stage three). Below is Paula's outline keyed for the first two stages.

Paula's Outline

(Keyed for Information Needs and Possible Sources)

Thesis Question: Should I try out for the varsity track team in the spring or should I continue to run only for recreation?

I. Introduction

    A. Why is this question important to me?

    B. What are my "givens"?

    C. Which "criteria" are important to me?

II. Are my skills and aptitudes in track good enough to make the team and compete on the intercollegiate level, or are they more suitable for recreational running only?

    A. What are the record, average, and minimal performance levels needed to compete in our university's conference?

        1. Information needed—performance times for other sprinters in the conference.

        2. Possible sources:

            a. Conference records office.

            b. College track coach's records.

            c. Media accounts of races.

    B. What were my best, average, and worst performances in high school?

        1. Information needed—my high school performance times.

        2. Possible sources:

            a. High school track statistician.

            b. High school coach's records.

            c. Media accounts of races.

    C. Is there any reason to think I might improve?

        1. Information needed—average chronological performance curves for women sprinters; physical characteristics associated with success in sprinting; analysis of my techniques.

        2. Possible sources:

            a. Books about women sprinters.

            b. Periodical articles about women sprinters.

            c. Advice of expert in sprinting technique.

            d. Advice of prospective track coach.

Paula continued this process through all of her criteria. Once you identify *possible sources* under each information needed, you are ready to identify *specific sources*. For example, once Paula decided that her research would be advanced by an appointment with a sports medicine specialist, she identified a specific physician and made an appointment. Once she decided that books about running would help her, she began a library search for such books.

Key Your Outline for Library Resources

Taking the next step with Paula's outline, we can identify *specific sources* which probably are available in the library. Following this example, add possible specific sources to your own outline of questions and "information needed."

A. What are the record, average, and minimal performance levels needed to compete in our university's conference?

   1. Information needed—performance times for other sprinters in the conference.

   2. Possible sources:

      a. *Conference records.*

      b. College track coach's records.

      c. *Media account.*

B. What were my best, average, and worst performances in high school?

   1. Information needed—my high school performance times.

   2. Possible sources:

      a. High school track statistician.

      b. High school coach's records.

      c. *Media accounts.*

C. Is there any reason to think I might improve?

   1. Information needed—average chronological performance curves for women sprinters; physical characteristics associated with success in sprinting; analysis of my technique.

   2. Possible sources:

      a. *Books about women sprinters.*

      b. *Periodical articles about sprinters.*

      c. Advice of college sprinting coach.

With your outline keyed to library resources, you are ready to begin your library search. As you search, collect a list of all the possible specific sources you think might in some way help you answer your questions. For each, write down enough information to find the source without having to look it up again.

A search for information almost never progresses in a straight line. The process is recursive. Your path will often bend back again to search tools and resources you have used before. You might begin with background reading to help you choose a few start-up terms and topics related to your question. If you already have a subject heading or two in mind, you might begin with an *index-base search.* Once you have a few sources to work from, you will be adding sources by *referral.* Expect to move back and forth from indexes to sources which provide referrals to topics, titles, or people which you will locate by using the indexes again.

To begin a search, you need to know a few things about the library tools—what resources to use for background reading, and what indexes are available in your library and how to use them. The next section will help you become more familiar with your library's resources, and it will demonstrate an *index-based search.*

A *referral-based search* begins with a reference from another source—a footnote, an entry in a bibliography, or a suggestion from someone you interview. Once you have the reference—sometimes only a last name or a couple words from a title—you can go back to the indexes to help you find it. In an index search, you usually begin with a subject heading; in a referral based search, you often have more specific information to begin with.

BENCH NOTES: PREPARE TO SEARCH

SUMMARY

Before you begin collecting information, you need to identify systematically what kind of information you need and what types of sources might supply it for you. For each general category of source you have listed, you will create a list of possible specific sources.

By using your preliminary outline as the basis for your working bibliography you will find it easier to keep track of what you have done and what you still have to do.

Begin your working bibliography with an index-based search.

For your working bibliography, you will not be carefully evaluating your sources. That will come later. In this section and the next, you will be listing as many potential sources as possible.

ESTIMATED TIME NEEDED

You will need at least two hours to key your outline for specific information needs.

PRACTICE AND APPLICATION

Imagine that you have been assigned to determine whether or not your college or university should plan for more or fewer applications and enrollments ten years from now. Among other factors, you are considering the number of children now entering second and third grade, and whether they are more or less likely to want a college education than the current generation of college-age people. As an alternative, you might want to estimate the numbers of people above typical college-age who will be applying.

Begin a partial outline of the information you would need, and identify the probable sources of that information. Prepare a list of subjects you would use in an index-based search, including both specific and general topics.

BENCH NOTES *continued*

KEY TERMS

Kinds of information: The general categories of information a researcher needs. For example, Paula needed information about the short- and long-term health effects of competitive sprinting.

Type of Source: General category of source materials—book, magazine, interview. . . .

Specific Source: A specific magazine article, a specific book, an interview with a specific person. . . .

Working Bibliography: A list of all the sources which, from index citations, appear to have potential for specific information needs. As you examine these sources you will add others by referral, and some you will cut.

Index-based Search: A search for sources which primarily makes use of library indexes, especially those organized by subject.

Referral-based Search A search for information which follows up referrals from authoritative sources already located—bibliographies, notes, and works cited.

Citation: Information about a specific source usually including author, title, publisher, date, and location.

USE THE LIBRARY

Each time I visit an unfamiliar library, I remember a school picnic many years ago. I was responsible for my five-year-old brother. When mealtime came, I took him over to the long tables loaded with delicious food. At this rural school, every dish had been carefully prepared with the cook's pride and reputation on the line. As a hungry, nine-year old, I took care of my appetite first and my brother second. I quickly loaded my plate six inches high, sat in the grass, and started eating. When I began to see the bottom of my plate, I remembered my brother. I found him standing near the food tables sobbing, his face a mess of snot and dirt. "What's the matter?" I asked impatiently, my eyes on the desert table.

"I can't decide what to eat first," he blubbered.

I remember that story in libraries because they too offer so much. I can't decide what to look at first. What's more, like the five-year old at the potluck, I sometimes don't know the procedures—what comes first. That's why I need a strategy, and suggest you follow one too. Plan several steps in advance, write your plans down, and take one step at a time.

In addition to the library, you have access to other resources. Most of the information you need to answer your questions will come from three sources: printed and other media sources available in libraries, people, and your own structured observations.

Identify which of your information needs might be satisfied by the resources of the library.

If you followed the recommendations of the last section, you have gone through your entire outline and circled or highlighted all of the sources you think you can find in the library. Now, when you go there, you will be able to make a much more directed search for the specific information you need. You will spend much less time wandering around confused and overwhelmed by the mountains of information.

To answer her question, "Can I expect to improve?" Paula listed books and magazines as probable sources. She began her search in the library by looking for information which would tell her which body type and musculature correlates best with success among women sprinters. She looked for information which would tell her the approximate age at which women sprinters peak. She also looked for information which might describe how to test her own physique against the ideal sprinter's model. After she found what she needed on those topics, she continued on to her other criteria.

In some cases, information available in the library may also be available somewhere else in a more complete or reliable form. Go to the most complete sources first, and verify what you find by checking it in other sources. Paula was able to get her performance times from the official "Meet Results" sheets, but she also verified those results by local newspaper accounts.

Becoming Acquainted with the Library

On her first visit to the library for this project, Paula and her classmates were met and provided assistance by a member of the library staff. Those of us who teach composition at Paula's school have been lucky. The library staff here helps us teach composition students how to make full and efficient use of library resources. They have helped us prepare practice activities to orient our students to specific resources and they will provide guided tours if we request them. But most of all, they are patient and helpful to the most ignorant of us when we ask dumb questions. Thanks to our library staff and considerable practice, Paula learned how to use the tools she needed to find what she wanted.

Perhaps at this stage in your project, your teacher will provide you with a special orientation to your university library, possibly with the help of the library staff. If not, plan to invest more time on your own.

Develop an Overview

Libraries are my favorite places. If I had to go to one place and stay there the rest of my life, I would ask for a library without hesitation. As long as my eyes held out, I could read for the next hundred years at least—books, magazines, newspapers, microfiche, microfilm, pamphlets, brochures, catalogs, maps, reference books of all kinds. If I got tired of reading, I could look at films, videotapes, slides, maps, atlases, computer programs. If my eyes failed me, I could listen to tapes, records, CDs. I could learn to read braille and browse in the braille collection.

I know you have been told many times that libraries are the storehouses of our civilization, the heart of our democracy, the foundation of education at every level—all true. But I also want you to see that libraries are delightful, fun, and most of all, important to you personally. The resources available to you in libraries can help you answer your questions and solve your problems.

Many college and university libraries are a little intimidating when you first try to use them. Paula told me that her high school library had twelve books about track and field. The university library here has about two hundred and, really, that's not many. In high school, she used only the *Reader's Guide to Periodical Literature* to look for information in magazines. For her paper included in this text, she consulted nine different indexes to periodical literature. The more resources you have in a library, the more difficult it becomes to find the specific source you have in mind. The more complex the collection, the more critical becomes your ability to use indexes.

Even if your teacher or the library staff provide an orientation to your library, you may want to get a head start by exploring it on your own.

Like most complex situations, you can master the library if you approach it systematically. First get an overview so you have the big picture. Then take one manageable section at a time.

For your overview, I recommend that you go to the first big desk or counter you find inside the front door and ask for a "Library Handbook." It may not be called that, but "Library Handbook" will be close enough. Almost every college or university library has one. They may not have it at the first place you ask, but they will probably be able to tell you where you can get one. It may even cost you money. If so, don't hesitate—pay it!

Getting to know a specific library is a little like becoming familiar with complex mechanical or electronic equipment. Different brands or models of the same equipment class all have essentially the same features, but how you get them to work for you is different on each. Your own learning style comes into play here. If you were to get a new VCR or personal computer would you sit down and read the instruction manual from cover to cover before you plugged it in? Or would you plug it in right away and start pushing buttons until something happened, consulting the manual only if sparks flew or smoke came out?

If you style leans toward hands-on experience first, take your handbook and wade right in. Get your list of "source needs" out and see what you can find. I do recommend, however, that you do not wait until sparks fly before you consult your handbook. Try something simple and somewhat familiar first—consult an encyclopedia (you may be surprised to find that your library has forty or more sets). As soon as you have trouble, get help either from your handbook or from a librarian. Both are there to help you find what you need as efficiently as possible. Your teacher may also schedule times when he or she will be available to help you in the library.

On the other hand, if you like to read the manual from cover to cover before you plug in, take your "Library Handbook" and read it through. Many have maps included so that you can locate familiar resources which may, in this building, be in a very different location from the one you expect. I find it very comforting to examine the map of an unfamiliar place I plan to visit. Then when I actually get there, I feel almost comfortable. If you know where the magazine indexes are kept before you enter the library, you can walk in and go directly to them as if you knew exactly what to do.

The Craft and the Process

Sometimes librarians and teachers give the impression that finding information in a library is a straightforward, entirely systematic kind of business. When we are honest, we admit that, like writing, it is a process full of circles, steps backward and forward, including moments of both frustration and luck. You can prepare for the work by becoming familiar with the library tools, but an actual search requires craftmanship which usually develops only through practice and experience. When you have trouble in the library, ask a librarian to help you. They are masters of the research craft, and they know how to use all of the tools.

Like writing, the craft of library research goes better if you understand it as a process with reciprocal stages. Good researchers interact with information in the same way a sculptor interacts with wood or clay. The materials work on you as you work with them. Once you have identified your information needs, you find general information which leads you to specific information, which in turn, usually provides you with additional general information.

The diagram on page 57 provides a visual schema for the recursive process, including some of the tools which help us move back and forth.

What Can You Find in the Library?

As you can see from the diagram, libraries have a variety of materials. Although the most important continue to be books and periodicals (magazines, journals, newspapers), the other resources become increasingly important each year. The central library on your campus may have a million books or more (more doesn't necessarily mean better; some small collections, carefully selected and maintained, may be better than ones twice the size).

Notice on your diagram that, in addition to general works like an encyclopedia, an index is the starting point for finding what you need in most resources. You will need to become familiar with the *indexing systems*.

The major collections in most libraries are indexed in one comprehensive system, traditionally, the card catalog. In the last several years, many libraries have converted to a computerized index of their major collections. The index to the major collections, whether on cards or in a data base, can help you find individual books, series, media materials, reference books, even other indexes—in short, anything with a cover (or box) of its own.

In addition to the index of major collections, every library has many other indexes which will help you find materials which share a cover with other titles. For example, several magazine articles appear together in one issue, and several issues of the magazine make up one volume of the publication. A hundred titles might share one cover. The primary ("comprehensive") index of the library will not list each individual title. To find those materials, you have to use one of the specialized indexes to periodical literature.

LIBRARY RESEARCH STRATEGY

Begin with Outline of Information Needed to Answer Questions

Background Reading (Reference Area)
General Encyclopedias
Specialized Encyclopedias
Guides, Handbooks
Library of Congress
Subject Heading Guides
Biographical References
Other References

Specialized Indexes
Periodical Indexes
Periodical Holding
Indexes to Government Publications
Newspaper Indexes
Review Digests
ERIC, Facts on File, NEWSBANK, Others

Comprehensive Index
(Online or Card Catalog)
Subject
Author
Title

Additional Online Keys

Bound Periodicals and Microform Files
Interlibrary Loan
Microfilm
Microfiche

Government Publications
United States
State
Local

Books in Stacks
Books
Authors' Names
Bibliographies
Notes
Subject references

Audiovisual Materials
Films
Tapes
Slides
Videotapes
Software
Posters
Compact Discs
Other

Useful Specific Information

New Questions

Referrals

Subject Headings

Other Referrals

Referrals

Call Numbers

Subjects, Authors, Titles

Additional Subjects, Authors, Titles

Subjects,

Call Numbers

Indexing Systems—Card Catalog

"How can I find books about artificial intelligence?" I heard the eight or nine-year-old boy ask Mrs. Anderson in the local public library. I listened in because I wanted to see how she would handle his question. The boy seemed small, and by the way he gazed around the room, I got the impression this was his first visit to a library of this size. But his question suggested maturity. Would she simply take him directly to the books, or would she take him to the card catalog. She looked at him for a moment, probably considering the question herself, and then, smiling at him, she led him to the card files in the center of the room. In a short time, she had helped the boy make a profound transition. She had given him one key to the mystery of library order. He no longer had to scan the shelves for the books he wanted; he could use the card catalog.

The three big wooden stacks of card files—*Subject, Author, Title*—provide the most familiar icon of the library—the card catalog. The sheer mass and bulk of the cases, the tactile satisfaction of fingering through the cards, the concreteness of the cards themselves—all these add to their appeal for us. By the time you get to college, you have long ago learned about the Dewey Decimal or the Library of Congress systems. For those who might have forgotten, however, there will be a review later in this chapter. Though the card catalog may have an aesthetic advantage, on-line data base indexes are more efficient tools for finding sources in a complex library.

To begin a subject search with the Card Catalog, find the files marked, "Subject." The cards are arranged alphabetically with sub-headings and frequent suggestions to "see also . . . ." Look through the cards for subjects relating to your information needs. Remember to work from general to specific terms, to look for synonyms, and to build a list of terms which relate to your topic.

For example, if I were trying to decide where in the United States I should move my family, I might begin a "subject" search with something like, Cities—United States." In a short time, I might come up with "Quality of Life" which would yield me this card:

Quality of Life.

REFERENCE

    307.764   Boyer, Rick.

    P69r   Places rated almanac: your guide to finding the
                    best places to live in America / Richard
    CIRCULATING   Boyer & David Savageau. — New York :
    COPY HAS   Prentice Hall, 1989
    SAME   421 p.
    NUMBER   ISBN 0–13–677006–1 : $16.95

Now that I have one citation, I have the name of an author who might have written more on the topic. I can go to the "Author" file. This time the card provides me additional subjects I can explore:

```
REFERENCE        Boyer, Rick.
307.764              Places rated almanac: your guide to finding
P69r                 the best places to live in America / Richard
                     Boyer & David Savageau. — New York : Prentice
                     Hall, 1989.
CIRCULATING              421 p.
COPY HAS                   ISBN 0-13-677006-1 : $16.95
SAME NUMBER
                 1. Quality of life—United States—Statistics.
                 2. Social indicators—United States.
                 3. Metropolitan areas—United States—Statistics.
                 I. Savageau, David.  II. Title.  III. Title:The best
                    places to live in America.
```

Or, if I know the title of the book, but nothing else, I can go to the "Title" file and find the same information:

```
                        Places rated almanac
REFERENCE

307.764          Boyer, Rick.

P69r                 Places rated almanac: your guide to
                 finding the best places to live in America /

CIRCULATING      Richard Boyer & David Savageau. —
COPY                 New York : Prentice Hall, 1989. 421 p.
HAS SAME
NUMBER
                     ISBN 0-13-0677006-1 : $16.95
```

Indexing Systems: On-line data base

Until a few years ago, libraries used a card catalog indexing system to help patrons find *citations* (the title and other publication information) for the books and other materials they needed. Many libraries now have changed over to (or are in the process of changing over to) an "On-line" data-base system. The two systems are essentially the same—the card catalog is a mechanical card system, and the on-line system is a computer system to which you gain access by use of a terminal. Both allow you to find the location (unknown) of a book (or other material) by using clues (known). Card catalog systems use three basic categories: Author, Title, and Subject.

The data base and the electronic circuitry of an on-line system permit you to search for citations with much more flexibility. In addition to the three basic indexes of Author, Title and Subject, most on-line systems provide you with many additional *menu driven* search tools which permit you to *widen* or *narrow* the search with ease once you become familiar with the system. On-line systems vary slightly from library to library. The university library where I teach uses the LS/2000, designed and supported by OCLC to meet the unique needs of specific libraries. So even if your library has a LS/2000 system, it might be slightly different from the one described below. The general principles are the same, however.

A *menu* is a list of options which appears on your computer terminal screen. For example, our LS/2000 system opens with this main menu:

PUBLIC CATALOG   Searching: EC

    Enter the NUMBER of search you wish to perform

        1—By AUTHOR (PERSONAL NAME)
        2—By SUBJECT (LIBRARY OF CONGRESS HEADING)
        3—By SUBJECT (PERSON AS SUBJECT)
        4—By TITLE
        5—For OTHER Searches

            OR

    Enter a KEY WORD to see possible matches

CHOICE:

    Enter a REF number to see the title list; or /ES to restart.

If you enter number five—"by other"—on your terminal keyboard, the screen gives you a second menu:

PUBLIC CATALOG   Searching: EC

    Enter the NUMBER of the search you wish to perform

        1—by AUTHOR (ORGANIZATION/CONFERENCE NAME)
        2—by AUTHOR/TITLE (4,4)
        3—by LANGUAGE
        4—by MATERIAL TYPE
        5—by RESERVE COLLECTION (FACULTY NAME)
        6—by RESERVE COLLECTION (FACULTY/COURSE)
        7—by RESERVE COLLECTION (DEPT/COURSE)
        8—by SUBJECT (ORGANIZATION/CONFERENCE)
        9—by SUBJECT (UNIFORM TITLE)
      10—by TYPE: FICTION, BIOGRAPHY OR AUTOBIOG.
      11—by CALL NUMBER
      12—by PUBLISHER

13—by SERIES
14—by DATE OF PUBLICATION
15—by MUSIC PUBLISHER NUMBER
16—by OCLC NUMBER
17—by SERIAL TITLE
18—by SPECIAL COLLECTIONS (RELATED RECORDS)
19—by SUDOCS NUMBER
20—by UNIFORM TITLE
(MORE)

CHOICE:

Enter a number from one to twenty-seven, and your terminal will display a set of instructions on what to enter next.

You can begin a search on an on-line system with any one of a dozen or more bits of information (''knowns'') which would be useless if you had only the card catalog. Some of the menu items your on-line system shows you, however, will include options (such as the OCLC Number of Control Number) not likely to be of much use to you unless you are a library science specialist. But if you are looking for films of videotapes only, for example, you can concentrate your search by selecting #4—''material type.'' If you are looking for recent material only, you can specify items published since 1980 (or whatever date you choose) by selecting #13—Date of Publication. Do not be intimidated by the richness of the options available through the on-line system. Think of them as limitless opportunities for future growth in your power to find information. *You do not need to understand every corner of the system to make it work for you.*

If your library has an on-line system, consult your ''Library Handbook'' to see how to use it. If you get confused, ask a librarian to help. The central library of the university where I work changed over to an on-line system four years ago, and I am still sometimes confused. But the library staff patiently helps me, and I learn some new amazing strategy every time I use it. Spend a couple half-hour sessions practicing with the system. Unless you kick in the terminal's screen, you won't hurt the system by a little experimentation on it. And certainly the system can not hurt you. *If you have a questions, ask for help.* You'll learn much more about both card catalogs and on-line systems by using them to search for information you need.

Index-based Search Begins with Subject

At the beginning of extensive projects, most researchers conduct a *Survey of the literature* on the basic questions important to their research. Such surveys are almost always *Index-based searches*. In an index-based search, you use the several index systems of the library to find every possible source related to your questions.

Most of the time you will begin a research project with a subject search. At first, you will not be acquainted with the authors who write on your topic, and you will not know any of the relevant titles, but you will know what general subjects you want to explore. Using your outline as a key to your information needs, make a list of subjects you'd like to search. You can supplement the list by doing some preliminary backround reading and by using such library tools as index thesauri.

If you are using a card catalog, go the "subject" index and start looking. If you are using an on-line system, select "subject" off of the main menu. In some cases, you might prefer to begin with a "key word."

In general, you can begin your search with the most familiar word you know for the subject you want to search. As you begin to find materials, you will add synonyms, more specific terms, and more general terms. You will develop a vocabulary of compound terms, Library of Congress Subject Headings, and "key" words, all of which will help you ferret out hidden sources during your Index Based search. You will save yourself time by listing these terms together in a safe and handy place. They will be your personal "key word" collection.

When you begin a subject search—no matter what subject indexing system you use—keep in mind four important principles:

1. the search process is recursive

2. work back and forth between general and specific terms

3. try synonyms; and

4. add additional terms as you go along.

After you become familiar with specific sources, look at their notes and works consulted. Follow their advice by looking up the specific sources they recommend. In other words, from each source you use, seek referrals for additional sources. You will add to your index-based search by using a *referral-based search*. When you follow up a referral, you will have additional information to help you find the material—title, author, publication date and place. Those sources you collect through referral will be easy to locate.

As much as possible become familiar with the system you are using. Most have supplementary tools which help you find the terms likely to yield the best results in their system—*ERIC Thesaurus*, Key Word Indexes, Library of Congress Subject Headings, uniform titles. Such tools will speed up your search.

Using the LS/2000 system, Paula could press a "print" key, and a nearby printer would provide her a hard copy of whatever appeared on the on-line terminal screen. That made it easier for her to compile her working bibliography and it helped me prepare this chapter. I ask my students to hand in with their final papers the print-outs of the subject searches they do during the index-based stage of their research. By combining Paula's print-outs with her research log entries, I am able to provide you here a fairly complete example of how Paula performed her index-based subject search.

Work Between General and Specific Terms

After start-up on the on-line system, Paula initiated a *subject* search and entered the subject heading, "Running." The system turned up 94 titles under the Library of Congress Heading, "running," so the screen asked her if she wanted to "Narrow the Search," "View citations sequentially," or "Start new search."

SUBJECT (LIBRARY OF CONGRESS HEADING): RUNNING

REF	TITLES	SUBJECT (LIBRARY OF CONGRESS HEADING)
R1	94	Running
R2*	52	— (General Works)
R3	5	—Accidents and injuries
R4	1	— Accidents and injuries — Prevention
R5	3	— Addresses, essays, lectures
R6	1	— Africa
R7	4	— Fiction
R8	4	— Juvenile literature
R9	6	— Periodicals
R10	6	— Physiological aspects
(MORE)		

CHOICE: R

To see title, enter REF#. To see related references enter REF#*.

PUBLIC CATALOG   Searching: EC
SUBJECT (LIBRARY OF CONGRESS HEADING): RUNNING   FOUND: 94

Your search has identified many citations. What would you like to do next?

1. Narrow search
2. View citations sequentially
3. Start new search

Paula decided to narrow the search, and the system offered several possible ways to do that.

PUBLIC CATALOG   Searching: EC
SUBJECT (LIBRARY OF CONGRESS HEADING): RUNNING   FOUND: 94
    Enter the NUMBER of the limitation search you wish to perform

1 — Limit by PUBLICATION YEAR
2 — Limit by LANGUAGE
3 — Limit by MATERIAL TYPE
4 — Limit by SUBJECT (LIBRARY OF CONGRESS HEADING)
5 — Limit by TITLE
6 — Limit by Other Searches

OR

Enter a KEY WORD to see possible limiting matches

CHOICE:

Paula chose to narrow by publication date, asking only for those citations published since 1985:

SHOW TITLES PUBLISHED FROM: 1985

THROUGH: 1988

Enter the last year to be included in the search; or /ES to restart.

Now the system gave her nineteen sources:

PUBLIC CATALOG	Searching: EC
SUBJECT (LIBRARY OF CONGRESS HEADING): RUNNING	FOUND: 94
PUBLICATION YEAR: 1985–1988	FOUND: 19

SUBJECT (LIBRARY OF CONGRESS HEADING): RUNNING	FOUND: 19

REF	DATE	TITLES	AUTHOR
R1	1988	Running for lifelong fitness :	Girandola, Robert N.,
R2	1988	The winning edge /	Johnson, Brooks,
R3	1988	Cyberkinetics :	Czarnecki, Gregory
R4	1987	The total runner :	Lynch, Jerry
R5	1987	Runner's world.	Runner's world (Emmaus, Pa. : 19
R6	1987	Runner's world	Runner's world (Emmaus, Pa. : 19
R7	1987	Runner's world	Runner's world (Emmaus, Pa. : 19
R8	1987	Ultramarathons :	Aaseng, Nathan.
R9	1987	The self-coached runner II:	Lawrence, Allan.
R10	1986	World class :	Waitz, Grete,
R11	1986	Inside running :	Costill, David L.
R12	1985	Biomechanics of running shoes /	
R13	1985	Running your best :	Daws, Ron.
R14	1985	The injured runner's training ha	Glover, Bob.
R15	1985	Running for fitness, for sport,	Henderson, Joe,
R16	1985	Focus on middle-distance running	Humphreys, John H. L.
R17	1985	Running without fear :	Cooper, Kenneth H.
R18	1985	Rodale's runner's world	
R19	1985	Complete guide to running /	
(END)			

CHOICE: R
        Enter a REF number to see details of a title; or /ES to restart

PUBLIC CATALOG   Searching: EC

Glover, Bob.
  The injured runner's training handbook : the coach's and doctor's guide
for preventing, running through, and coming back from injury /Bob Glover and
Murray Weisenfeld.
New York, N.Y., U.S.A : Penguin Books,1985.
  xv, 208 p. ; 20 cm.
  A Penguin handbook

Includes bibliographies and index.

Running — Training.
Running — Accidents and injuries.
Weisenfeld, Murray F.

    Press RETURN to continue:

The citation on the screen provides the author's name (and the co-author's name),
the complete title of the work, and publication information. This citation also
provides us with additional words (called traces)—"running-Training," "Running-
Accidents and injuries"—to use if we want to enlarge our search. (At that stage of
her research, however, Paula had not yet learned to follow up such leads.)
    The LS/2000 System describes where the work can be found in the library
(Eau Claire Stacks), the Library of Congress call number (GV1061.5 G545) and the
"status" of the book—whether or not it is available or checked-out, and if it is
checked-out, when it is due back.

PUBLIC CATALOG   Searching: EC

Glover, Bob.
  The injured runner's training handbook : the coach's and doctor's guide
for preventing, running through, and coming back from injury /Bob Glover and
Murray Weisenfeld.
New York, N.Y., U.S.A. : Penguin Books, 1985.
  xv, 208 p. ; 20 cm.

LOCATION   CALL#/VOL/NO/COPY   STATUS

EC/STKS   GV1061.5 .G545 1985   Date due 05/18/90

Paula's Log, Entry #13

I spent the last two hours in the library. I found a few books under "Running," but after I found them in the stacks, I could see they were useless. All the books about women and running are about long distance running. After all that time I came away empty.

According to her research log, Paula stopped her search at that point and went to the stacks to see if she could find the three most promising books on the list. She found all three, but after skimming them, she concluded that they would not help her. All three were about running longer distances. She concluded that "there's nothing in the library to help me," and she gave up for the night.

The next time Paula worked in the library, she enlisted the help of Eugene Engeldinger who was head of the Bibliography and Reference Department at the time. I watched while he coached her. You might be relieved to know that even master librarians like Mr. Engeldinger go through false starts and periods of frustration. As he puts it, "Any good researcher has to work around dead-ends and through moments of frustration."

He reminded Paula to work recursively among general and specific terms, and he explained that the LS/2000 has a "nearest match" feature which provides the "closest match" if no exact match exist in the data base for the entered work. He also suggested *truncating*, typing in only the first part of a word. The system will then provide all the variations available for endings.

Paula decided to try a more specific term than "running," so she tried "sprinting."

She looked over the list of citations under "sprinting," and called up the first citation. "The citation will include a list of related terms which might help us," Mr. Engeldinger suggested.

PUBLIC CATALOG   Searching: EC

Brauman, Ken, 1946—
   The American method of sprinting and relay racing / by Ken Brauman, Ken Taylor ; drawing by Ms. Bambi Bryan.
Ames, Iowa : Championship Books, 1981.
   64 p. : ill. ; 23 cm.

   Bibliography: p. 64.

   Sprinting
   Relay racing.
   Track-athletics coaching.
   Taylor, Ken.

LOCATION	CALL#/VOL/NO/COPY	STATUS
EC/STKS	GV1069.B73 A5	Available
EC/STKS	GV1069.B73 A5	Available

(END) Press RETURN to continue or /ES to start a new search:

Among the four additional terms provided with the Brauman citation, Eugene noticed, "Track-athletics coaching."

He suggested to Paula that she ask the LS/2000 to show what it could find for "Track," in some ways a term more specific than running, and in some ways more general. With Gene's help, Paula called upon a menu through which she could check for additional terms recognized as Library of Congress Headings. Among other promising terms she found, "Track-Athletics for women," (thirty-three titles), and "Sports for Women" (sixty-six titles).

By calling up the titles under both headings, she could see that several appeared on both lists. Using the "Sports for Women" heading, she narrowed the search by date of publication to the last eight years. The list of sixty-six titles was reduced to seventeen.

PUBLIC CATALOG   Searching: EC
SUBJECT (LIBRARY OF CONGRESS HEADING): SPORTS FOR WOMEN FOUND: 66
PUBLICATION YEAR: 1980–1988   FOUND: 17

SUBJECT (LIBRARY OF CONGRESS HEADING): SPORTS FOR WOMEN
FOUND: 17

REF	DATE	TITLES	AUTHOR
R1	1988	Playing the game :	McCrone, Kathleen, E.,
R2	1984	The woman runner :	Averbuch, Gloria,
R3	1984	The woman runner's training diar	Edwards, Sally,
R4	1984	Women's sports and fitness.	
R5	1983	A history of physical education	Lee, Mabel,
R6	1983	The outdoor woman's guide to spo	Maughan, Jackie Johnson,
R7	1983	The sporting woman /	Boutilier, Mary A.,
R8	1983	The wonder of motion :	Price, La Ferne Ellis.
R9	1983	Tea sports for girls and women	Mushier, Carole L.
R10	1983	Women, philosophy, and sport :	
R11	1982	Her story in sport :	
R12	1982	NAGWS guide:	National Association for Girls &
R13	1982	Challenging the men :	Dyer, K. F.
R14	1981	Women's hurdling :	Brooks, Chris
R15	1981	The complete guide to women's co	Stanek, Carolyn.
R16	1980	Women in sport :	Remley, Mary L.
R17	1980	Rules for coeducational activiti	
(END)			

CHOICE: R
Enter a REF number to see details of a title; or /ES to restart.

Paula typed in Ref #2 and got this citation: Searching: EC

Averbuch, Gloria, 1951—
    The woman runner : free to be the complete athlete / Gloria Averbuch.
New York : Cornerstone Library, c1984,
    x, 213 p., [8] p. of plates : ill. ; 24 cm.

    Includes index.
    Bibliography: p. 202–207.

    Sports for women.
    Running.

By working from general to specific, and specific to general in her choice of terms, and by using resources like the list of Library of Congress Headings, Paula had discovered fifteen to twenty potentially usable sources in the same amount of time it had taken her to find three the night before. By examining and adopting the working habits of a professional librarian, Paula was able to increase the speed and thoroughness of her index based search. So can you.

Paula's Log, Entry #15

   Another long session in the library. Better luck this time. Maybe it wasn't luck, exactly. I am becoming better acquainted with the On-line system, and I'm catching on how to use synonyms and work from a specific subject heading to a general heading and back again. For me there are still many unlocked mysteries, however. Next session in the library I'm going to look for magazines. Even some of the periodical indexes are on computer programs now. The reference librarian who helped me tonight suggested I use ERIC and Psychological Abstracts. That's my plan for next time.

Specialized Indexes

In addition to the primary index for major collections, every library has specialized indexes for materials which do not have their own box or cover—magazine and newspaper articles, reports, abstracts, conference papers, reviews. These indexes are extremely important to researchers because they often provide access to more recent materials, and materials with more hard evidence.

Every high school library in the United States has a *Reader's Guide to Periodical Literature*, and I'm confident that all of you have used it. Your experience with the *Reader's Guide* will transfer well to the other periodical indexes. The *Reader's Guide* provides an index only to articles in popular and general purpose magazines, so it will not help you find materials in scholarly or specialized journals. For your research most of you will need the more specialized indexes. The library

Paula used has fifty-four, including *Art Index, Biological and Agricultural Index, Business Periodicals Index, Education Index, Music Index, Psychological Abstracts, Social Sciences Index, Humanities Index,* and many more. Look for these indexes in the Reference Department near the *Readers Guide.*

By the time Paula began searching for magazine articles, she was more comfortable in the library, and her search bore fruit more quickly. On the advice of a librarian, and with a little help as well, Paula tried an ERIC search. ERIC (Educational Resources Information Center) is a clearing house for information and resources related to education—periodical articles, speeches, conference proceedings. . . . Its index is available either in printed form or as a data base. Paula used a computer and the ERIC "Silver Platter" CD-ROM data-base index for her search.

First she looked in the *Thesaurus of ERIC Descriptors*, a list of terms on which the index is based, and to which the data base will respond when asked by a "Silver Platter" user. She looked in the *Thesaurus* under "Athletics," and she found sixty-two sub-headings, including "Women's Athletics."

The "Silver Platter" system, like the LS/2000 system, has the capability of limiting a search by cross referencing additional terms. For example, Paula first typed on the screen the term, "Women," and the computer told her that in the ERIC collection there were several thousand items with "women" (or a variation) in the title. If she had begun by typing in "Athletics" (or a variation), the system would have found a similar number—thousands. By typing in "Women," and then "Athletics," however, the system looked for titles which included both words (or variations). This process of cross referencing (also called "Boolean Logic") uncovered nine useful citations. Here are three of the nine:

SilverPlatter v1.4   ERIC (1/83 - 3/88)

1 OF 9

AN: EJ351671
AU: Burke, -N. -Peggy
TI: Nutrition for Women Athletes. Commonly Asked Questions.
PY: 1987
JN: Journal-of-Physical-Education,-Recreation-&-Dance; v58 n3 p41-45,50-51 Mar 1987
AV: UMI

2 of 9

AN: EJ340684
AU: Potere, -Carol
TI: Women in Sports: The Price of Participation.
PY: 1986
JN: Physician-and-Sportsmedicine: v14 n6 p149–50,153 Jun 1986
AV: UMI

3 of 9

AN: EJ331738
AU: Evans,-Gaynelle
TI: More Colleges Counsel Women Athletes on Pregnancy.
PY: 1986
JN: Chronicle-of-Higher-Education: v32 n3 p37–38 March 19 1986

At first, such citations might seem difficult to read because they rely on abbreviations and codes. A citation from ERIC begins with AN—the ERIC number. AU = author. TI = Title. PY = Publication Year. JN = Journal. AV = Where available. NT = Notes (about length, and so on). You will find library indexes full of codes and abbreviations. You don't need to memorize them. Somewhere near the front of every index you will find the abbreviations and codes explained.

The index to Psychological Literature is also on a "Silver Platter" system. On this index, Paula first limited her search to the most recent five years, and she entered "Women," and then "Running." The system turned up twenty magazine article titles, two of which she eventually used in her paper.

Paula's Log, Entry #16

    I worked with ERIC tonight, and I must say I got along with him pretty well. I wasted a half hour reading the instructions for the "Silver Platter" system, but once I got started things went well. A couple weeks ago, I thought "Boolean" was something you used to make broth.

Hard Copy Indexes

In addition to the data-base indexes, Paula used the traditional printed indexes to periodical literature. One of the most productive indexes for her was the *Physical Education Index*, one of the specialized indexes housed near the *Reader's Guide*. First she looked in the paper-bound index of the most recent articles, and under "Women," she found a subheading "Sports." There were six entries, none of them promising for her information needs. Then she looked under "Track and Field," subheading "Sprint Running." She found four titles, one promising.

Paula had found promising titles in her search of the limited, most recent index, so she moved back in time to the index for the the most recent complete year—a bound volume. Here she found thirty-seven titles, several promising. In fact, three of the titles from this list turned out to be quite useful to her.

Again, these citations might need a little decoding. For example, examine one of the citations Paula used:

> How to Predict Sprint Potential. P. Siris, et al. *Mod Ath & Coach* 24:13–15
> Oc '86

Since the *Physical Education Index* is a subject index, the first item in the citation is the title of the article. Next come the author "P. Siris, et al." The "et al." means there were at least two other authors. The title of the periodical in which the articles appears is the *Modern Athlete and Coach*. The number "24" is the volume number, and "13–15" are the page numbers. "Oc" stands for October, and " '86" is 1986. If you ever get confused, check the abbreviation tables in the front of the index.

TRACK AND FIELD (cont.)

Organizing For Effective Instruction In Track And Field. David Turkington. *CAHPER J* 53:14-19 Ja/Fe '87

Plan For Equalizing Track Competition. Peter Brookes and Rory Cooper. *Sports 'n Spokes* 13:13-14 Se/Oc '87

Reading Your Runners: Before And After Their Race. Jack Hazen. *Sch Coach* 56:48-49, 68 Ap '87

Throw And Push (Part 1). Wolfgang Soll. *Int J PE* 24:Supplement 2-8 (2) '87

Visual Evaluation Techniques Of Movement. Phil Lundin. *T Tech* 98:3116-3117, 3136 Winter '87

Pole Vault

The Contemporary Take Off. J. Nikolov. *T Tech* 98:3124-3125 Winter '87

Perfecting Pole Vaulting Technique. Maurice Houvion. *T & F Q Rev* 85:34-47 Winter '85

Pole Vault. Don Hood. *Tex Coach* 32:44-45 Oc '87

Pole Vaulting Technique. Vitaly Petrov. *T & F Q Rev* 85:29-33 Winter '85

Selecting And Training The Jr. High And High School Pole Vaulter. James Fountain. *Tex Coach* 31:36-37 Mr '87

Should Women Compete In The Hammer, Triple Jump And Pole Vault? Jackie Daley. *Carnegie Res Papers* 1:32-37 De '85

Sports Performance Series: The Pole Vault. Dick Railsback. *NSCA J* 9:5-8, 78 Ap/My '87

Women's Pole Vault And Triple Jump. David Johnson. *Ath Coach* 20:24-27 De '86

Relays

Coaching The Sprint Relays. Roberta Wideman. *W Coach Clinic* 10:14-16 No '86

LSU Women's 4 x 100 Relay Exchange. Ralph E. Steben. *Sch Coach* 56:21-23, 113-115 Ja '87

Meter Relay: 4 X 100 Racing. Jim Santos. *T & F Q Rev* 86:10-12 Winter '86

Relay Techniques Personnel And Placement. George Makela. *T & F Q Rev* 86:12-13 Winter '86

The Sprint Relay Non Visual, Non Verbal Blind Relay Pass. Lee Calhoun. *T & F Q Rev* 86:7-9 Winter '86

Shot Put

Current Trends In Shot Put Training. George Dunn. *T Tech* 98:3118-3123 Winter '87

Developing High School Shot Putters. Anthony Naclerio. *T & F Q Rev* 86:4-5 Spring '86

The Effects Of Depth Jumps And Height Jumps Combined With Weight Training On Vertical Jump And Shot Put - A Research On Power Training (Abstract). Yuh-Jen Pen. *ICHPER ASIAN J PE* 10:15 Ap '87

Elite Coaches' Survey. Vern Gambetta. *T Tech* 100:3179-3184 Summer '87

Exercise Technique: The Push Press - An Alternative To The Bench Press. Pat O'Shea. *NSCA J* 8:28-31 Oc/No '86

The Glide Shot Put Style. Tom Pagani. *T & F Q Rev* 86:13-15 Spring '86

Power Development: New Concepts In Power For The Shot Put. Stanley Lampert. *NSCA J* 8:36-39 De/Ja '87

The Rotation Shot Put Style. Ivan-John Psiakis. *T & F Q Rev* 87:55-56 Spring '87

Rotational Shot Putting. Dick Booth. *T & F Q Rev* 86:17 Spring '86

Rotational Shot...Slowly Gaining Ground. Max Jones. *Ath Coach* 20:24-25 Mr '86

TRACK AND FIELD (cont.)

The Shot Put And Discus (Second Year Of Training). N. Ivanov. *Soviet Sports Rev* 22:28-31 Mr '87

The Shot Put And Discus (Second Year Of Training). N. Ivanov. *Soviet Sports Rev* 22:98-101 Je '87

The Shot Put. Ted McLaughlin and Michael Carter. *T & F Q Rev* 86:6-12 Spring '86

The Spin Shot Put Style. Tom Pagani. *T & F Q Rev* 86:15-17 Spring '86

The Value Of Different Weighted Shots In The Practice And Teaching Of Shot Putters. Ralph Uebel. *T & F Q Rev* 86:18-21 Spring '86

Variations In Shot Put Methods And Their Application. Bill Larsen. *Mod Ath & Coach* 25:33-36 Ap '87

Why Can't A Woman Be More Like A Man? Max Jones. *Ath Coach* 20:10-15 De '86

Sprint Running

The Aim Of Training - The Competitive Model (Sprint). B. Tabachnik and V. Mekhrikadze. *Soviet Sports Rev* 21:184-186 De '86

The Aim Of Training...The Competitive Model (Sprint). B. Tabachnik and V. Mekhrikadze. *Soviet Sports Rev* 21:105-108 Se '86

Alcohol And Its Effects On Sprint And Middle Distance Running. L. McNaughton and D. Preece. *BR J Sports Med* 20:56-59 Je '86

Altitude And Wind Effects On Long Jump Performance With Particular Reference To The World Record Established By Bob Beamon. A. J. Ward-Smith. *J Sport Sci* 4:89-99 Autumn '86

Application Of Principles Of Metabolic Control To The Problem Of Metabolic Limitations In Sprinting, Middle Distance, And Marathon Running. E. A. Newsholme. *Int J Sports Med* 7:66-70 Je '86 Supplement

Basic Running Form. S. A. Embling. *Mod Ath & Coach* 24:16-18 Oc '86

Breakdown Of High Energy Phosphate Compounds And Lactate Accumulation During Short Supramaximal Exercise. J. Hirvonen, et al. *EUR J Appl Physiol* 56:253-259 Mr '87

Classifications Of Energy Systems For Sprint Training. Gary Winckler and Vern Gambetta. *T Tech* 100:3193-3195 Summer '87

Comparative Electromyography Of The Lower Extremity In Jogging, Running, And Sprinting. Roger A. Mann, et al. *AM J Sports Med* 14:501-510 No/De '86

Comparison Of Cerebral Palsied And Healthy Sprinters. Carol Pope and Jerry Wilkerson. *Proceedings: ISBS* 3 & 4:233-238 '87

Contemporary Sprint Technique. E. Ozolin. *Soviet Sports Rev* 21:109-114 Se '86

Contemporary Sprint Technique. E. Ozolin. *Soviet Sports Rev* 21:190-195 De '86

Direct Competition Preparation For Elite Sprinters. Adam Zajac. *T Tech* 98:3114-3115 Winter '87

The Effect Of Athletic Clothing Aerodynamics Upon Running Speed. Chester R. Kyle and Vincent J. Caiozzo. *Med & Sci Sport* 18:509-515 Oc '86

Effect Of Three Spike Configurations On The Ground Reaction Forces In Sprint Starts. Hashim Kilani and Marlene J. Adrian. *Proceedings: ISBS* 3 & 4:225-232 '87

Effects Of Wind And Altitude On The Times Of 100 Meter Sprint Races. Jesus Depena and Michael E. Feltner. *Int J Sport Bio* 3:6-39 Fe '87

Four Hundred Meter Dash Training. Wayne E. Norton. *T & F Q Rev* 86:5-7 Winter '86

How To Predict Sprint Potential. P. Siris, et al. *Mod Ath & Coach* 24:13-15 Oc '86

From Ronald F. Kirby, ed. *Physical Education Index*, Volume 10, 1987, p. 481.

Locating Materials: Periodicals

Once you have a promising index listing, you still have to locate the actual source. For magazines, check the "Periodical Holdings List" (usually a computer print-out stored in the periodicals area as well as in reference) to see if your library has the magazine you need or not. Libraries with on-line systems often do not have a "Holdings List" because they have entered the holdings into the comprehensive index. If so, look for the title of the magazine in the comprehensive index. Once you verify that your library has the magazines for the year your article was printed, you can go to the periodical shelves and to the magazine and the article. If you have trouble locating magazines for which you have titles and dates, ask for help.

Locating Materials: Books

Once you have the call number for a work you need, you might want to consult your library handbook. It probably will have a map in it which labels the areas of the stacks where works with specific call numbers are shelved. The library also will have signs all over describing where works with a range of call numbers can be found. If you have trouble, ask a librarian to help. This Card Catalog "Title Card" for *Places Related* uses the Dewey Decimal system:

Places rated almanac

REFERENCE
307.764   Boyer, Rick.
P69r   Places rated almanac : your guide to finding the
                          best places to live in America / Richard Boyer &
                          David Savageau. — New York : Prentice Hall,
CIRCULATING   1989. 421 p.
COPY
HAS SAME
NUMBER   ISBN 0–13–0677006–1 : $16.95

The "Reference" note above the call number means that the book is shelved in the Reference Area of the library. Reference books must be used in the library only—they do not "circulate." But under the call number, another note tells us that there is also a circulating copy in the general stacks.

The Dewey Decimal number for this book is 307.764 P69r. The Dewey Decimal system begins with large categories organized by "hundreds," and then smaller divisions in the classification system indicated by the "tens," the "ones," and beyond, to the third digit after the decimal. Although it's not necessary to remember which subjects correspond to which numbers, you might want to look over the major categories.

Dewey Decimal System: Major Categories:

000   General Works

100   Philosophy and Related Disciplines

200   Religion

300   Social Science

400   Language

500   Pure Science

600   Applied Science

700   Arts

800   Literature

900   General Geography, History, Travel, and Collected Biography

Two classes of books in the Dewey Decimal system begin with a letter rather than a number:

B   Individual Biographies

F   Fiction

With a Dewey Decimal number of 307.764, the *Places Rated Almanac* will be housed in the Social Sciences collection.

The other major system used in American libraries is the Library of Congress system. In this system, the call number begins with a letter on the first line to indicate the general category, and then a number beneath to show the specific subdivision. Here are the general categories for the Library of Congress system, and the locations in the library where LuAnn, Paula, and Elizabeth did their research:

Library of Congress: Major Categories

Third Floor

A   General Works

B   Philosophy, Psychology, and Religion

C   History (Auxiliary Sciences)

D   History and Topography Except the Americas

DA   Great Britain

DK   Russia

Library of Congress: Major Categories (cont'd)

Third Floor

E History—The Americas (General) and U.S. (General)

F History—The U.S. Local and the Americas Except U.S. Geography, Anthropology, and Folklore

G Geography, Anthropology, and Folklore

GV Physical Education

H Social Sciences

HB Economics, Business

HD Economic History

HE Transportation and Communication

HF Commerce

Fourth Floor

HM Sociology

J Political Science

K Law

L Education

M Music

N Fine Arts

P Language and Literature

PQ Romance Literature

PR English Literature

Fifth Floor

PS American Literature

Q Science

QK Biology

R Medicine and Nursing

S Agriculture and Forestry

T Technology and Engineering

Z Bibliography—Books and Libraries

Your library will have a directory like the one above posted in several locations. If you have a call number, you can go directly to the specific book. If you want to browse, go the general sections identified on the directory.

As in the Dewey Decimal system, the call numbers in the Library on Congress systems extend beyond the basic categories to subdivisions. Thus the LC call number for *Places Rated Almanac* is

$$HN$$
$$60$$
$$.68$$

The "H" places the work in the "Social Sciences" general category, and the other letters and numbers establish its more specific place.

Check the map in your handbook and/or go to the stacks and look at the signs on the shelves. You should have little trouble finding the book. If you don't find it, ask for help.

Other Library Resources

In addition to books and magazines, your library has government documents, media materials, computer software, teaching materials, maps, charts, microfiche, microfilm, photographs, pamphlets, telephone books, . . . much much more than I could tell you about in this short chapter. Many of these resources are important both as general starting points and as sources of specific information. Getting to know a library is a life-time job. As you become more familiar and comfortable with the standard resources, begin to explore some of the corners. Look at the rare books. Ask to see a rare manuscript. Read through 19th-century census material or newspaper on microfilm. Become an explorer in the charted but often unexplored spaces of information.

BENCH NOTES: USE THE LIBRARY

SUMMARY

On your campus, you will find one of the most astounding collections of information ever brought together in the history of the earth—your school library. At the beginning of the school year, I introduced our campus to a new graduate student who had just arrived from Poland. When we got to the library, she said, "This is why I wanted to come to the United States—the knowledge of the world opens to me here."

But many libraries have so much in them you might not know where or how to start. Don't be shy. Walk in. Get acquainted. Ask for a library handbook, look around, try out the machines, ask questions, poke in the corners.

When you have a specific project, key your research questions to the kinds of sources you will need to answer them. If it looks like some of your information needs will be satisfied in the library, initiate an index-based search. The index for the major collections will either be a card catalog system or an on-line system. Your ticket into either will be the subjects about which you need information. Begin with one word, but as you go, add others—synonyms, more specific terms, more general terms, combinations of words, general words with subheadings.

BENCH NOTES *continued*

Once you have found a few sources, see if they provide notes, works cited, or bibliographical information. If they do, you can initiate a referral based search to augment your index search. Remember that the search is recursive rather than linear.

If you are looking for magazine articles, abstracts, reviews, or other sources which are shorter than book length, you will need to use one of the dozen or more specialized indexes. Some are available on-line, and others are in printed form. Again, work your subject heading into a collection of synonyms and other related terms.

The library has much more in it than books and magazines. Look around and see what you can find.

ESTIMATED TIME NEEDED

Beginning with this stage, your research project will require significant time commitments. You *must* invest the time as you need it for each stage of your project. You will not be able to bunch together several stages into one week of vacation or all night work sessions. Do not procrastinate. You will need between six and eight hours to become familiar with the library and perform an index-based search for resources. Invest that time now.

PRACTICE AND APPLICATION

Using the partial outline of information needs you prepared at the end of Chapter Seven, spend fifteen or twenty minutes in the library beginning an index-based search. Try both the general and specific words you listed. As you search, see if you can add other words.

Another suggestion: See how many different heading you can find for an index-based search which begins with the topic, "Research."

KEY TERMS

Index: Any classification system designed to help users gain quick access to specific material or information from among much.

Indexing System: Specific classification system, for example, the Dewey Decimal System.

Comprehensive Index: The library's main index—the card catalog or on-line data base—with entries for every item in the library.

Specialized Index: An index to materials in only specific sources, generally related to a specialized of information—periodical indexes, government document indexes . . . .

Card Catalog: A comprehensive index with library holdings entered on note cards cross referenced by Subject, Title, and Author. Until recently, the standard comprehensive index for libraries.

BENCH NOTES *continued*

On-Line Data Base: A computerized comprehensive index stored on a data base with access gained by patron operated terminals.

Dewey Decimal System: One of the standard classification systems for comprehensive indexes, it is used to organize, store, and retrieve library materials. The other standard system is the *Library of Congress*.

Call Number: An index code number assigned to each item in the library. Essential to the organization, storage, and retrieval of materials.

CD ROM: An abbreviation for "Compact Disc, Read Only Memory." Used for data-based specialized indexes.

Boolean Logic: A strategy of logic which permits users of data-base indexes to narrow a search. If one begins with a broad term ("Athletes," for example) the data base will find hundreds of sources. On a system with a Boolean "and" feature, one can add additional terms to Athletes ("College" and "Women," for example), and the system will supply only items in which all of the terms appear.

Periodical: Any publication which is issued on a schedule of regular intervals—newpapers, magazines, journals . . . .

Recursive: A term used to describe a process which regularly returns to early stages on the way to full development.

TALK TO PEOPLE

The stored resources of the library provide us access to information from the entire world, from the most recent to the most ancient. Yet most people consider the library only the second most important resource for learning on a college campus. What is the first? The people—the faculty, support staff, and the other students.

After you have conducted your library search, begin looking for *people* who might know something about your topic. People offer one clear advantage over library sources. You can ask them questions and they will usually try to answer you. The author of a book or magazine article on a given topic knows much more than he or she included in the published work. If you have access only to printed sources, and what you need to know lies outside of the scope of the article or book, you will remain uninformed. Obviously, most of what people "know" never reaches the printed page. You can gain access to these unrecorded sources by asking questions.

Although print and other media sources are more available than ever before, as students, you still depend on asking questions, speaking, listening, and demonstration for most of your formal learning—one generation passing important information on to the next in much the same manner as the oral tradition has been passed on throughout the centuries.

In contrast to printed resources, the personal interview has a key limitation. You may read something written by Socrates two thousand years ago on the opposite side of the globe, but if you want to talk with someone, he or she must be available at a single specific time and place. Although present-day telecommunications extends the range somewhat, you are still limited by time and space from talking with most people.

Who?

When you select the people you want to talk with, apply the same criteria as you use when you select printed sources. You want the sources to be reliable, and you want their information to be valid. Like printed sources, interview sources can provide direct hard evidence, or they can provide references to additional sources so that you can enlarge your referral-based search. They might also open up for you an entirely new line of thought by pointing in a direction you had not thought to look. During her interview with the university women's track coach, Paula found all three.

Early in her research, Paula realized she'd need to talk with the university track coach. After Joe, her friend from a rival high school, told the coach about Paula, the coach sent her a note inviting her to stop in the Track and Field office for a conversation. According to her "Research Log," Paula was nervous about this visit for several reasons. She was apprehensive that, in mentioning her to the coach, Joe might have exaggerated her skills as a sprinter. She didn't want to come across to the coach as someone who expected to be courted to go out for track. Paula knew that success in high school track was a considerable distance form success in varsity intercollegiate track. She also had anxieties about the coach's possible reaction to her. On one hand, she worried that the coach would not be at all interested in her. On the other, she worried that the coach would be too interested and put pressure on her to go out before Paula could make up her own mind in her own way. In order to cope with her anxieties, she prepared carefully for the meeting.

Paula' Log, Entry #18

Coach Slater made me feel very comfortable during our interview. It was more like reminiscing with an old teammate than talking with a coach. I wonder if that's the way it always is in college sports. I told her about my running experiences, and she told me about some of hers. She has had stress fracture injuries too. I plan to meet with her for my research at least once more. She encouraged me to bring the videotape of the 100-meter race at Sectional last year. I wonder how Otto is doing (Otto is the guy who took the videotape—my "man" at the time).

Plan the Interview

For an interview it is even more important to review your information needs ahead of time. Printed resources wait passively and patiently for you. You may take hours, or even days, to extract the information you need form an article. Living people, however, will not sit patiently while you stumble around trying to decide what it is you want to know from them. Some folks who might have provided you valuable information are likely to send you away empty if you come to see them unprepared.

Consult your outline of information needs. For example, under her question, "Will I have enough time for track?" Paula needed to know specifically when training began, how many hours per day, and how many days per week they trained. She needed to know when the meets were, where they took place, and how much travel time was involved. She wondered if the track team met during the spring recess form classes.

Ask for Hard Evidence

When Paula told her friend, Joe, that she was worried she might not have enough time for track, Joe responded by saying, "Sure you will. In fact, being in track will help you in school. It'll help you organize your time better."

Joe's assertions may be true, or they may not be true. We are not able to tell because he did not provide hard evidence of any kind. If Paula had officially interviewed him, she would have asked him to provide more specific hard evidence: What are the grade point averages of track team members? How does that compare with non-members? What are the grade point averages of track members during the fall semester when they are not competing in meets? How do their grades in the fall compare with their spring semester grades when the track season is in full swing? When Paula went to see the track coach, she asked her if specific academic records for track team members were available.

Below is a sample of the questions Paula prepared for her interview. Under each general question, she prepared questions which she hoped would elicit specific hard evidence:

Reminders. Verify appointment. Arrive on time. Dress appropriately. Introduce myself and explain the purpose of my visit. Describe briefly my past experiences in track. Remember to piggy-back.

Questions.

1. Can you describe the track season for me—when does it begin and end? How much time will it take? How many meets? How often does the team work out together? How long are the workouts? Do team members also work out independently? What happens if I miss a workout because of other obligations? Do we meet during spring break?

2. Will I be able to contribute? Am I good enough? Where can I find the performance records of the women against whom I would be competing? Is there a way for me to predict whether or not I have peaked? Can I expect to improve?

3. What are my chances of getting injured again? Are there sources of injury statistics for sprinters? What resources does the university have for the prevention and treatment of athletic injuries? Where can I find information about the long-term health affects of participation in track during college?

Once she had her questions ready, Paula called the coach and made an appointment to see her in her office. She then sent the coach a copy of the general questions she wanted to cover in the interview. That made it possible for the coach to have her secretary collect printed information (for example, the practice schedule from the year before) and have it ready for the interview.

It was not difficult for Paula to shape her information needs into questions for the coach. Because she came ready with specific questions, Paula relieved the coach of the burden of carrying the interview, and she impressed the coach with her thoroughness and "eyes wide open" approach to the decision. She also got the specific information she needed. In addition, the coach provided her with suggestion for several other sources, and she offered to examine a videotape of Paula sprinting one hundred meters to see if there might be specific techniques which, with work and careful coaching, could be improved.

Paula also derived an unexpected side-benefit from the interview. The coach let Paula know that whether or not she went out for track, Paula had earned the coach's respect. The coach reassured Paula that track was an extracurricular activity, and that whatever decision she made, it would be absolutely respected.

Clearly interviews are more helpful when you come prepared. One word of warning, however—don't treat your prepared questions as if they were a script which must be rigidly followed. Remain flexible. Notice that Paula prefaced her list of interview questions with reminders to herself, including, "Remember to piggyback." We had talked in her class about how inexperienced interviewers sometimes charge through their questions, often ignoring the flow of the interview. Remember, an interview is *interactive*. There are two of you. Be ready to follow up an interesting response with a new question, or perhaps the person you are interviewing will open up an entirely new area of inquiry, one you had not considered. Welcome surprise and be prepared to follow through. Let your natural curiosity flower.

Follow Through

Unlike printed sources, human resources often become interested in your project. If you do a good job in your interview, they will want to know what you decide. As soon as possible after the interview, send the people you have interviewed a short thank you note. When your research is completed and your paper written, send them another with a sentence or two telling them what you decided. Such gestures are simple courtesy, but they almost always pay unexpected dividends.

Protection of Human Subjects in Research

In addition to courteous treatment, the people you interview are also entitled to certain protections under law. The U.S. Department of Health and Human Services regulations (45 CFR Part 46, "Protection of Human Subjects") establish guidelines which protect people who are the subjects of research. These regulations were first used to protect the subjects of research with experimental drugs and medical procedures. Later, other people placed at risk by research of any kind were added. According to the current guidelines, a "human subject at risk" includes any person who might be hurt by the research—economically, legally, physically, psychologically, or socially.

The person you interview generally will be at no risk. You will simply use them as a source of information about your research question. If you do not ask the people you interview to reveal anything about themselves which might get them in trouble, you do not need to worry. Just remember that anything you write down might be read by someone who has power over the person you are interviewing.

Each college and university (and often departments within the institution) has a review board which establishes the specific guidelines for its institution. The kind of research you are doing this semester is probably exempt from these regulations. At those schools were student research is not exempt, your teacher or the English Department Chair will file a single "Certification of Course" for all of you.

Even though you are not officially responsible for compliance this time, knowledge of the guidelines to protect human subjects has become an essential ingredient in the skills needed to do research. Be alert to the need for protection of human subjects when you begin course work in your major field of concentration. In one of the basic courses in your major, you will no doubt be introduced to the specific procedures required for research in your field.

In general, the procedures require you to ask each person you interview to sign an "informed consent form." The consent form should:

1. Explain the purpose of the research.
2. Invite the subject to participate.
3. Explain to the subject why he or she was chosen to participate.
4. Describe for the subject what you expect him or her to do.
5. Provide an estimate of how much of the subject's time you will need.
6. Assure the subjects that participation is voluntary.
7. Describe any risks to the subject.
8. Describe any possible benefits to the subject.
9. Ask the subject to identify anything they would like kept confidential.
10. Assure the subject that everything he or she wants to be confidential will be kept confidential.
11. Provide the subject with a procedure to follow if he or she wants to discontinue participation, ask questions about the research, or complain.
12. Provide the subject a place to sign.

A typical consent form looks like this:

CERTIFICATION OF INFORMED CONSENT

This is to certify that I have freely consented to participate in a research project about _____
being conducted by

_____..

The purpose of this research project has been adequately explained to me. I further declare that I understand this explanation as well as what will be expected of me by virtue of my participation in the research project. The investigator explained to me how I was selected for participation. I understand that my participation is entirely voluntary and that I may withdraw at any time.

If I have any complaints about my involvement in this study, I understand that I may call or write the

Chair-person of the Institutional Review Board
Name of Institution
Address
Telephone Number

I understand that all complaints will be kept in strictest confidence. In addition, I understand that if I have any questions about the purposes and procedures used in this research project, I may call or write

Name, Principal Investigator
Address
Telephone Number

Signature: _____
Date:_____

Release Forms

I want to introduce you to one more kind of form—the "release." When, as part of your research, you take photographs of any kind, or if you record interviews, performances, or speeches, you may need to have the subject sign a form which permits you to use the photo or tape in specified ways.

Because different media and different uses require different forms, I'll simply encourage you to be aware of the general principle. If your research requires the photographing and/or recording of subjects, seek the help of an expert. He or she can give you advice and provide you with a sample form.

BENCH NOTES: TALK TO PEOPLE

SUMMARY

As soon as possible, identify people who have information you need to answer your research question. Request an interview and plan for it by preparing specific questions which will elicit hard evidence. Remember the human being behind the information; be prompt, courteous, and well prepared. Try to keep the interview on track, but respect the reciprocal nature of a personal interview. Pick up leads the interviewee might give you and ask questions which follow up the cues he or she provides you.

Be aware of and follow any applicable regulations which protect human subjects in research.

Send the person you interviewed a thank you note and the results of your research.

ESTIMATED TIME NEEDED

Some of you will depend much more on interview sources than others. On the average, however, you will need between two and four hours for each of the people you want to interview; this counts arranging the interviews, preparing the questions, and conducting the interview itself.

PRACTICE AND APPLICATION

Identify one person on campus who has information you would benefit from knowing. Perhaps you need to know more specifically what the requirements are for your major or minor. Maybe you would benefit form an interview with someone in the student financial aid office. Perhaps someone in the placement office could give you some ideas about how you can get a job if you graduate with an English (or psychology, music, or art) major. Maybe you simply need additional help understanding your math assignment.

After you have identified the person schedule an interview with him or her. Prepare carefully, and then, conduct the interview.

KEY TERMS

Interactive: In interviews, the process of listening carefully to the people you interview, of following up leads they provide, and of becoming an alert, active participant.

Human Subject: Anyone you interview from whom you elicit personal information about traditionally confidential areas.

Informed Consent: A procedure used by interviewers (and other researchers) to make certain that ''human subjects'' know the risks they face by participating in the research projects.

Release: Procedure and/or form for securing permission to use material provided during an interview, concert, or speech, especially if it is audio or video recorded.

STRUCTURING OBSERVATIONS—EMPIRICAL RESEARCH

With a few guidelines and a little practice you can gather up your own hard evidence using the most basic and useful research resource of all—careful direct observation with your own senses. Sometimes it is called *empirical research*. For other kinds of writing before your research paper, you have been using your senses. You have recorded descriptions, narratives, and other kinds of discourse generated out of personal experiences. Your teachers may have set up "structured experiences" for pre-writing exercises—peeling an orange, eating an apple, popping popcorn, examining a stone or other artifacts.

Now take it a step farther. Design the experiment, the controlled observation yourself. In most scientific experiments, the scientist examining the natural world sets up a set of controlled events and sits back to watch and see what happens. Often the scientist uses special instruments to help record with more acuity the events which take place—microscopes, oscilloscopes, scales, spectroscopes, and so on. But the most important instruments of all are the investigator's eyes and ears.

Other scientists, especially social scientists, place more emphasis on observation without intervention, but the approaches are closely related. As a social scientist, you might, for example, observe how many people eat and/or drink in the library where eating and drinking are prohibited by signs every fifty feet. In that situation, the researcher simply observes and records—describes.

If, however, he or she changed the signs—added warnings about consequences, made them a different color or larger—then the observation would become more like the controlled experiment of the laboratory scientist.

Direct Observation

Direct observation of a carefully structured kind will often provide you valuable hard evidence. For example, one of my students, Pete, wanted to ask the question: "Should I continue to live in Towers Dormitory next year or should I move to 611 Water Street with John and Fred?" What kind of research should he do? Certainly, he found relevant material in the library, and he got additional information by talking with people. But most importantly, for this topic, he designed a series of structured observations to collect hard evidence.

He listed "study environment" as one of his criteria. As sub-headings he included "noise levels" and "interruptions" during his peak study times—7:00 to 11:00 at night. As a resident of Towers, he was in a good position to do his observations there. He wanted a "controlled" observation rather than random impressions, so he designed a log (a chart) on which he recorded interruptions of various kinds—phone ringing, someone at the door, comments by roommate or visitors, and so on. He also logged the length of each interruption. He maintained this log over a one-week period so that, by using interpretation, he could calculate the average length and duration of interruptions for a typical weekday study period. Then he arranged to study at 611 Water Street (he knew the current residents) for three nights during two one-week periods and one more on a different day the next.

His data from 611 Water Street was not as complete nor as meaningful as from Towers, but he considered it an adequate sampling. In both situations, he concealed the recording of his observations from those he observed.

In addition to logging interruptions, he set up a decibel meter (which he borrowed from the physics library) to generate a continuous graph of the noise levels during the study session he had designated as "experimental." Using the physics lab computer (although he could have performed these interpretations without the help of the machine, he was able to do it more quickly and accurately on the computer), he used the graphs to record peaks, lows, and average decibel levels for both environments.

As he studied, he recorded in his log any especially irritating or disturbing noises so that he could assess the quality of the noises as well as the quantity. For example, at the 611 site, he mentioned as especially irritating and distracting the frequent hacking coughs from the elderly upstairs neighbors, and at the Towers dormitory site, his roommate talking baby-talk to his girlfriend on the telephone.

When Pete had finished his controlled observations, he had solid hard evidence on which to base his analysis, his interpretations, and his comparisons. He reached a subconclusion on this criterion using evidence based on solid research, but it was research of his own design.

Each controlled observation requires a different design and preparation, but all of them must meet certain criteria to be useful in your research paper. You want the results to be *valid*, so you need to be sure you are describing what you say you are describing. You want your results to be *reliable*, so you need to set up your observations so that any other reasonable observer looking at the same situation would see the same things you are seeing.

Pete wanted to find out what the study environment would be like at 611 Water Street, and he wanted to compare it with what he would probably have if he lived in the dormitory again. Obviously, he had to take his observations during his usual study times. If he took his readings from 3:00 A.M. until 7:00 A.M., or during a vacation, the results would be invalid as a test of study conditions during Pete's preferred study times.

Pete was very careful to design his log so that his record of interruptions and their durations would be reliable. If he were carrying on a more sophisticated observation, he might have arranged for a second observer to be present and run a parallel record as a check against his own. If he had, anything turning up on one log but not on the other would probably be eliminated. When Paula measured her vertical leap on the Sargant, she took along a witness to record and verify her results. That's reliability.

Notice that it would be very difficult for Pete to establish reliability for his "qualitative" observations—the hacking cough, the baby-talk. Pete knew, without any other verification, that he could recognize what kinds of noises irritated him more than others. He was not trying to find out what noises irritated people in general, or even a class of people, students, for example. He was trying to find out what environment would be least irritating to *him*. Thus, he could treat his "irritating" noise observation as if it were a survey of only one (but critically important) person. Pete tells himself, ''On a scale of one to ten (ten as worst), note any noises you hear in the next four hours which rank eight or above.'' Someone else would probably have a different list. But an observer watching Pete, perhaps with assistance from sophisticate electronic sensing devices, would probably come up with the same list Pete put down. If he had gone to such lengths, he could have established reliability.

While some studies might be invalidated by a single ''unreliable'' component, fortunately for Pete, his was not. On the ''irritating noises'' criterion, Pete found his two options approximately equal, and thus of little impact on his final decision. In addition, he knew that the specific conditions he observed this year would not exist next year when he would actually be living in one place or the other. The noises he logged were simply representative noises, and thus his observations would not be *entirely* valid anyway. As a conscientious researcher, he could not give such observations important weight in his findings.

The ''cough'' and the ''baby-talk'' did show him, however, that many variables which affect the quality of life in one place of residence over another change in unpredictable ways. He realized that, in the jargon of social scientists, his research was predictive, but not a prediction. It gave an estimate of the study conditions that might be present in either location, but did not provide any certainty.

Paula's Log, Entry # 30

My roommate Jane came with me to the P.E. building to help me with my Sargant test. I had to do some "empirical research." They have a board set up there with little rubber pegs at graduated heights. I could have done it alone, but I wanted a witness to make the test more valid. I was going to to go over early to warm up and have Jane meet me, but she said she was nervous about walking into the Phys Ed complex by herself. That really got me. Even though she's tiny (her nickname is "Squirt"), Jane seems like such a confident person. I suppose I'd be intimidated walking into the music building alone, too (She's a music major). It made be realize how much at home I feel in gymnasiums. I've started writing the "Am I good enough?" section.

Polls, Surveys, Questionnaires

Whenever researchers want to discover how a group of people feels or thinks about a subject, they can systematically collect and observe their responses by using polls, surveys, or questionnaires.

Although the creation of such research instruments can become very complex, you will need to learn only a few basic principles for your purposes. Those of you who eventually major in the social sciences will learn much more about these research devices.

As with other kinds of empirical research, you need to make sure you observe what you think you are observing. You need to seek hard evidence, and you need to interpret the evidence accurately.

As you learn more about polls, surveys, and questionnaires, you will discover that the procedures for insuring validity and reliability can be as elaborate and difficult to design as setting up a complex experiment in a chemistry laboratory. If you find this kind of work intriguing, you might want to take additional courses in statistics, or in one of the social sciences where advanced research techniques are taught.

As with the people you interview, those who respond to your poll, questionnaire or survey should be extended both courtesy and the protections required by the U.S. Department of Health and Human Services.

Resist Inferences

For polls as with other kinds of research, try to secure as much hard evidence as possible. Try to avoid depending on inference.

A few years ago an editor for a university newspaper wrote an editorial calling for all dormitories on her campus to be coed. For her article, she wanted an informal poll of women living in women-only dormitories. She stood in the main lobby of Elizabeth Roth Hall (an all women dorm) late on Monday afternoon and asked the first twenty women who came in the door to answer some questions. Nineteen out of the twenty women she asked thought that Roth Hall should become coed.

When the editorial appeared in the paper under the headline, "ROTH WOMEN DEMAND CHANGE TO COED," the receptionist at the Roth Hall front desk who had been on duty on that Monday wrote a letter to the editor. She pointed out that many woman from Morris Hall (a coed dorm) next door went to Roth Hall for an aerobics class on Monday afternoons. "More than half of the women coming in the door during the time the editor conducted her poll were residents of Morris, not Roth."

The writer of the editorial thought she was polling Roth Hall women, but she had not made sure. She could easily have made her first question, "Do you live in Roth Hall?"

Postpone Making a Generalization

For many years, I taught a course for international students who had never been to the United States before coming here to school. The course was supposed to be an introduction to American culture. As one of the assignments for the class, I required that the students keep a journal of observations about the U.S. natives they saw around them. Although I encouraged them to make their observations as specific as possible, they enjoyed making generalizations: "Americans take showers in the morning, never at night." "American people ignore their parents." "American people are always happy."

After the first two weeks, I collected the journals and made a list of the generalizations they had made in them. Then I assigned each student one generalization and asked him or her to carry on an empirical examination of the generalization. For example, one person might observe the students in his or her dormitory to note the number who showered at night, the number who showered in the morning (or other time of day), and the number who appeared to shower not at all. If he or she wanted to know if typical out-of-school adults showered at different times than typical students, he or she would also poll selected adults. In this way, I encouraged them to recognize complexity and base their generalizations (if they could not resist making them) on more solid empirical evidence.

Like these international students, I find myself often rushing to generalization, especially when I am confronted with an abundance of new information. Generalizations provide comfort, a sense of solid understanding when everything seems overwhelming. I often need to make a conscious effort to resist generalizing from insufficient information.

To get through our daily business, all of us necessarily make a thousand inferences every day. When you engage in research, however, you will need to wait until you have gathered as much hard evidence as possible. Be patient.

BENCH NOTES: EMPIRICAL RESEARCH

SUMMARY

In the box of tools available for your research, you have library materials and personal interviews. Now add direct observation—empirical research. Plan your observations so that you can control as many of the variables as possible. To insure validity, make sure that you observe what you think you are observing. If you doubt your results, replicate the observation. If you get the same results the second time, probably your research is reliable.

ESTIMATED TIME NEEDED

If you build into your research an average amount of empirical observation, you will need approximately three to five hours to plan your observations, carry them out, and note the results.

PRACTICE AND APPLICATION

Select a generalization you believe to be true but have never tested empirically, and devise a way to test it by direct observation. For example, perhaps you have always believed that highway X was the shortest and quickest route from point A to point B. Perhaps highway Y is shorter. Test it. Using a stopwatch and watching your odometer carefully, drive route X one day and route Y the next. I am confident that you will find dozens of such generalizations you could test by empirical observation.

BENCH NOTES *continued*

KEY TERMS

Empirical: Direct observation through one's senses.

Empirical Method: A strategy for collecting information by direct observation. Includes isolating and controlling selected variables, and directly observing results, often with the help of specialized instruments.

Valid: Having direct relevance to the outcome of a research question. Evidence may be "invalid" if it does not deal directly with the issues under investigation.

Reliable: Producing the same results when observed again. Evidence may be "unreliable" if the results are not consistently the same.

Inference: Reaching a judgment from incomplete information.

CHAPTER FOUR

COLLECTING, SORTING, AND USING BORROWED INFORMATION

SELECT AND EVALUATE SOURCES

TAKING NOTES

DOCUMENT YOUR SOURCES OF BORROWED MATERIAL

SELECT AND EVALUATE SOURCES

If you have done your work, you will now have a long list of possible sources of information—printed, human, and empirical. You won't be able to use them all, nor will you want to, so you need to select those which are most *valid* and *reliable*.

The valid sources are those which can provide hard evidence specifically relevant to the questions you want answered. When we look for validity, we look for current information, for information carefully gathered, for information directly related to the questions (not some shirt-tail relative), and we look for information not distorted by fallacious thinking.

Confirm the validity of the information you use by showing in the text of your paper how it relates to your specific questions. For example, if you were choosing a place to live, and one of your key criterion were access to a school of veterinary science, you would look for information about veterinary schools, not other kinds of schools. In *Places Rated Almanac,* Boyer and Savageau establish their rankings of educational quality by adding up scores for every kind of school available in the metro area—public and private elementary schools, trade schools, two-year colleges, four-year colleges, and universities (184). They do not mention whether or not there is a veterinary school. Thus their ratings are invalid for your information needs.

Reliable sources are those you (and your readers) trust. You trust reliable sources because the authors have established reputations of careful observation and clear thinking. You trust them because they, and their publishers, do not seem either moved by (or prone to use) the distracting practices of propaganda and faulty logic.

You will be able to eliminate some of the many sources in your working bibliography very quickly. For example, if your research question involves technology—something like, "What kind of personal computer should I buy?" you will need current information. Anything even more than one or two years old will be obsolete for this kind of topic and, therefore, invalid. Any question which deals with economic issues must also be current. For example, if your question were, "How should I invest the $16,000 my grandmother left me?", you would eliminate immediately most sources more than a year old.

Eliminate also the sources which, from their titles and/or annotations, appear to deal primarily with issues outside of the information you need. Paula, for example, cut most of the sources which dealt exclusively with men's track and field competition. She did, however, retain some which promised information about both men and women. She also eliminated several sources which seemed dedicated primarily to long-distance runners rather than to sprinters. Always keep your questions in mind, and ask yourself, "How likely is it that this source will help me answer my questions?" Remember that an invalid source does more harm than good. An invalid source gives us the illusion that we are getting closer to the answers we need; an obsolete or misplaced source may actually lead us off the track. If no genuinely valid sources are available, it's better to acknowledge it and to do what you can with what you have.

Usually, it is possible to eliminate a number of sources because either the author or the publication clearly lack reliability. Tabloids and digests generally do not pass the test of reliability. If you are serious about finding out the truth on any issue, probably you would eliminate *The National Inquirer* and other similar publications from your bibliography. Although one might occasionally find carefully collected and scrupulously handled information in such a periodical, more often what one reads there is simply not reliable. Probably you should cut from your list anything published in a digest. A digest, by definition, provides condensations and summaries rather than fully developed texts. Such sources seldom lead us to hard evidence levels. Periodicals which primarily provide reviews of complex studies for popular audiences (*Psychology Today*, for example) also need to be used with caution. If possible, go to the original study itself. While such publications perform important functions, they usually are not reliable enough to use as a source of information for research purposes. Make it your business to discover the reliability of the books and periodicals you use.

You might find other sources on your list which should be eliminated because the author lacks reliability, either because he or she is not qualified to write on the topic, or because his or her bias on the topic is well established and often stated. One frequently finds, for example, articles written by celebrities who write on areas entirely remote from their own expertise. Shirley McLain is an expert actress, but in matters of the occult, she is essentially amateur and, therefore, unreliable. Former (often fired) Presidentialaides ought not to be entirely trusted about how they perceive the operations of government.

If you are careful, however, you will be able to use information provided by otherwise unreliable sources. The key is to insist on hard evidence. For example, if you are looking for information to answer the question, "Should I buy a Kawasaki or a Harley Davidson motorcycle?" you definitely ought to include dealers for both manufacturers on your list of sources. Of course, you know that the Kawasaki or the Harley salesperson will have a strong bias toward the machines he or she sells, and a powerful self-interest in having you buy one. However, the dealers do have access to important hard evidence, and if you ask the right questions, they will provide it to you. Naturally, they will be more than eager to jump to evaluation level ("Kawasaki handles much better than the Harley," "Harley's craftsmanship is much better than the imports"), but if you insist that they stick with hard, verifiable evidence, they can help you. For example, they can give you a specific price for a specific model. They can give you information about warranties, and specific service requirements. They can even give you—if you insist—specific performance information: engine sizes, gas mileage, and so on. Be sure to do your own interpretation and analysis, however. Use your sources; don't let them use you.

BENCH NOTES: SELECT AND EVALUATE SOURCES

SUMMARY

As much as possible, work with sources which provide hard evidence. Be suspicious of those which rely on propaganda or some other device to direct attention away from the evidence. Analyze the stance of each source and eliminate those which have reputations for bias, error, or slanted selectivity. Try to use sources which established a reputation for reliability.

ESTIMATED TIME NEEDED

You will need between two to four hours to sort through your sources, selecting those which are valid and reliable, and rejecting those which are not.

PRACTICE AND APPLICATION

Buy or borrow three periodicals which range, in your judgment, from wildly unreliable and invalid to very reliable and accurate. Examine them carefully and describe what specific clues you would use to rank each of the three on a continuum from most reliable to worthless.

TAKING NOTES

Now begins one of the most difficult stages in your research project—selecting and recording the specific information you need from within your sources. At this stage, some people have trouble keeping in the main channel. As they begin to find information, the lure of some sweet and interesting tributary leads them off into a maze of sloughs and backwaters. Others have trouble because they have begun to see the answer to their central question emerging from their research, and they don't see the point of going on. Some student researchers unintentionally practice plagiarism. All of these hazards have the potential of leading to disaster. Help is available, however.

By performing first an index-based search and then following up referrals, you have by now collected and sorted dozens of sources. When you have decided which ones seem more likely to be valid and reliable, you are ready to collect information from them for your research. To insure that your records are accurate, easy to use, and complete, you will need a system for taking notes and/or filing information.

The strength of your conclusions rests firmly on the validity and the accuracy of the information you use. If you have been keeping up, you have by now assured yourself of the validity of your sources, and now you will learn accuracy—how to move information from your sources into your own paper without bending, breaking, or mutilating it.

Gather and Survey

Whatever system you use, the first step for printed resources will be the same. As you follow up the "probable" citations on your working bibliography, *gather* magazines articles and/or books to look at more carefully. (If your library has closed stacks, or if you are working with rare materials, or in some cases, microfiche or microfilm, you might not be able to collect a "stack." Instead, you might prefer to work one source through all of the steps at once.) *Survey each source,* estimating the reliability of its author, the validity of its information, and its relevance to your research. If it passes those tests on the first quick read through, set it aside for a more careful read-through and note taking later.

Prepare an Annotation Worksheet

Whether you are reading from the library's copy or a copy you make for yourself, the next step will be to *read each printed source carefully.* If you have your own copy, you might want to have a pen, pencil, or highlighter ready to mark passages of special importance. If you are working with a copy not your own, be prepared to take notes, either on note cards or in a notebook.

During this read-through, I encourage you to look for information potentially valuable to your topic, but also for information of the kind you need to answer the questions on the *Annotation Worksheet* below. This worksheet will help you to assess the validity and reliability of the sources, and to be accurate and complete when you use borrowed information. Not every question on the worksheet needs a full answer for every source you use. It is intended simply as a checklist of information valuable to know about each of your sources. For some minor sources, some questions you will leave blank, and others you will answer with a word or two. For your major sources, however, you will want more full answers.

Annotation Worksheet

For each of the sources you wish to consult and/or cite, prepare one of these Annotation Worksheets. In addition to providing a record of essential bibliographical detail, this sheet will help you remember the context for any information you cite and help you judge its validity and reliability. In addition, this worksheet will help you prepare the annotation required for every cited or consulted source.

1. Record below a complete citation (using the MLA forms) as it will appear on your works cited or works consulted page.

2. Write a sentence or two about the author. What is his/her occupation, position, education, experience? In your judgment, is the author qualified and reliable?

3. As far as you can tell, what was the author's purpose for writing the article, doing the research, offering the interview?

4. To what audience is the work addressed? (Is it intended for the general public, for scholars, policymakers, teachers, . . .?)

5. Does the author have a bias? What is it? Does he/she make assumptions? What are they? How were you able to tell?

6. What methodology did the author use to collect information? (Direct observation, interviews, polls, laboratory experiments, other?)

7. What conclusions did the author reach?

8. Does the evidence support the conclusions? Why or why not?

9. To what degree does this source agree with others you have used? Disagree?

10. Has the author provided you with any supplementary resources— additional sources, charts, maps, photographs, recordings, . . .?

This worksheet is adapted from "Preparing An Annotation," created by Eugene Engeldinger, Reference Department, Wm. D. McIntyre Library, University of Wisconsin—Eau Claire, August, 1988.

Although I strongly recommend a form like the Annotation Worksheet, you may sometimes want to take a shortcut. If you skip the worksheet process completely, be very careful to make a *bibliography card* as a substitute. Enter on a note card all of the bibliographical information you need to cite the source in your text and to enter the source on your works cited page.

Once you have a secure record of the bibliographical information, you need only an abbreviated form for your notes.

Note-Taking Systems

Note Cards. Traditionally, English teachers recommend a *note card* system— 3″ × 5″ or 4″ × 6″ note cards, one "idea" per card. That's the system I was taught in college, and the system I also tried to teach for many years. When I worked on my own research projects, however, I somehow never could make the note-card approach work for me. Each time I started a new project, I'd go to the bookstore and dutifully buy two hundred cards, resolving to use a carefully organized card system this time. Once into my work, feeling guilty and inadequate, I'd fall back on my own old chaotic and wasteful systems—copy machines and note books.

In recent years, other folks have confessed that they couldn't make the cards work for them either, and other approaches have become more acceptable. Please understand, however, that the note-card system does work well for many people, and you may be one of them. By examining how people actually work as they go about their research, we have been able to understand a variety of ways to get the job done. Most of you will create a hybrid system of your own incorporating some elements of the card, the notebook, and the copy machine systems. Whatever system you use, you will want it to be *accurate, easy to use,* and *complete.*

Copy Machines. Many researchers prefer to copy the articles and the segments of books they intend to use in their research. Most libraries have conveniently located and inexpensive copy machines. The main library at my university has ten machines in the periodicals area alone. One copy costs a nickel. Usually I can get two pages of a journal article on one copy page, so a ten-page article costs me a quarter. For a dollar, I can copy four articles; for ten bucks I can copy forty articles. I consider that a tremendous bargain. Most libraries also have machines which copy microfilm and microfiche. I find it much more convenient and more accurate to have copies, especially of the printed materials I might want to cite.

Two words of caution:

1. If you copy chapters of books or periodical articles, be sure that somewhere on the copy you have the author, title, volume number, date, and page numbers.
2. If you copy several articles and/or book chapters, create a filing system for yourself.

If you have made a copy of a short article (up to twenty pages), not much reason remains to take notes on note cards. You will be able to refer directly to the complete source. For books, however, especially if you do not want to write in them, or if the material you need is widely spread throughout the work, note cards may be the most efficient form. I'll illustrate with an example later in the chapter.

Work for Precision

Whatever system you use, the goal will be precision. When you borrow information, you want to present accurately the information as it appeared in the original sources, and you want to give the author or authors appropriate credit. Sloppiness at this stage will bubble up onto the surface of your finished project.

For example, in other papers you have written, did you ever make up a page number for one of your citations? Did you ever make up an entire citation? If that happened to you, perhaps you forgot to write down the source or the page number when you took your notes. Then when you wanted to use the information in your paper, you had to make up a citation because you had no idea what was the true source. Maybe your teacher required you to have three books, five articles, and one government document. You were short one article, so you made one up. I hope you will never again make up a page number or a citation.

Whether you use note cards, photocopies, or a notebook, every detail of the borrowing process requires attention to accuracy.

Paula's Log, Entry # 30

The copy machine in the library ate up my entire copy budget tonight. I was trying to copy this article on "Menstrual Irregularity and Stress Fractures in Collegiate Female Distance Runners," and I couldn't get the copies to come out right. Then the machine ran out of toner. Fifty cents down the chute. And then, when I read the article more carefully, I realized it didn't have any information I could use. Maybe I should have read it more carefully before I lost all those nickels. I filled out a "claim" report so maybe I'll get thirty cents back some day next month.

Extracting Borrowed Information

There are three basic ways you might choose to package the material you borrow from printed sources: direct quotations, paraphrase, and summary. Each has its uses.

Using a Summary of Borrowed Information. From the beginning of this text, I have been encouraging you to borrow evidence as close to the "hard evidence" level as possible. In most cases, a summary, by definition, provides general level (translation, interpretation, and, in some cases, synthesis) information of some kind, and little, if any, hard evidence. Usually, then, you will be using summary information from other sources only when you tie it with either direct quotations or paraphrases.

You might want to provide a summary which *describes the context* of the hard evidence you want to present. For example, on page twelve of Paula's paper she provides us some summary information about Dr. John Albright's work with the "Big Ten Injury Surveillance Survey." That helps her readers understand the context and estimate the validity of the specific information which comes after that.

For this kind of summary, the information stored on the Annotation Worksheet will help.

In her paper, LuAnn provides first a summary describing the context of a study she cites, and follows it up with specific hard evidence:

> *Who Needs Nurses,* by Curron, Minnick and Moss reports statistics from a December 1986 survey conducted by the Organization of Nurse Executives. The results of the survey showed . . . . (9)

You might want to borrow a summary to *confirm a conclusion* you have uncovered through other, hard evidence-based means. For example, Paula has learned from both her own direct experience, and from evidence provided by Dr. Wimmer, that stress fractures usually occur when runners suddenly add to their already rigorous training. She provides this summary provided as a direct quote from Dr. Wimmer:

> Runners, especially women, develop stress fractures when they suddenly go from a reasonable training program to an excessive one, and then top it off with competition. (17)

Although she considered Dr. Wimmer reliable, on this point he did not provide her "hard evidence," so she looked for other sources to confirm or refute his assertion.

She found a summary statement from an article about stress fractures by two other orthopedists who arrived at the same conclusion:

> Patients who have stress fractures almost always have a history of high-intensity training, and they frequently have abruptly increased their training regimen in the recent past. (17)

Unless you have more than one summary statement by authoritative sources, your research will be stronger if you have provided at least some confirmation based on hard evidence.

Using a Direct Quotation or a Paraphrase from Borrowed Information. Practice in the use of paraphrase is central to learning in every area of education. When you paraphrase, you demonstrate that you have been able to internalize—make your own—the concepts or information presented in classes or in books. Every essay exam, to some degree, is an exercise in paraphrasing. In class discussions, teachers often ask their students to restate, in their own words, the materials presented in a recent lesson. In recent years, through the encouragement of the "Writing Across the Curriculum" movement, more teachers in every subject area are asking their students to keep a learning journal for their classes. A typical entry in these journals might be a paraphrase or a summary of the important concepts presented in the most recent class. Such practice in paraphrasing helps you learn by revealing what you still do not understand clearly and what you have mastered.

In such paraphrase practices, you truly depend on your own words because the words of the original source are not in front of you. In order to write an accurate paraphrase, you must have "mastered" the material.

Placed on a taxonomy of critical thinking skills, however, paraphrasing performs primarily a "translation" function—only one of the several cognitive levels. When you become genuine practitioners of research, you need to function on every level.

Ironically, because the paraphrase lies at the center of education, frequently it is abused, especially in "research" papers. Beginning perhaps in the fourth grade, students are asked to write "reports" on topics about which, before they begin their "research," they are almost completely ignorant. For example, a teacher might ask students to write a report about Sardinia. Most often the students know nothing about Sardinia and so go to the library to look in the encyclopedia or perhaps find a book. During this process, students learn to use reference tools, how to locate books in the library, how to use indexes. They may also learn something about Sardinia.

At this stage, problems with paraphrasing emerge, however. The teacher will want the students to show that they have learned to use the library resources and to share what they have learned about Sardinia. But it is difficult for students to go from knowing almost nothing about a topic to presenting a written report on it? The device most often used is a paraphrased report. Unless the student is provided guidance in this process, however, the paraphrase will almost always be technical plagiarism. The student will not be able to sufficiently master that large amount of information quickly enough to write a genuine paraphrase. A genuine paraphrase can only be prepared if the writer could close the book, not look back at it, and then relying only on his or her mastery of the material, write the paraphrase.

After many years of practicing paraphrase tactics which are actually technical plagiarism, what will those students do when they are asked to write a "research" paper in high school or college? Many will continue to copy their sources word for word, or some combination of the sources' words and their own. Their teachers, if they notice, will be upset and mark the paper "plagiarized" and give it a failing grade.

Plagiarism—Technical and Intentional

"Plagiarism" is a broad term which we use to describe everything from intentionally using a purchased or borrowed paper and submitting it as one's own, to producing a sloppy paraphrase as part of an otherwise careful paper.

I believe most students have no doubt about what constitutes "intentional" plagiarism: stealing a test, presenting a complete paper written by someone else as one's own, copying answers. That kind of deliberate attempt to pass someone else's work off as one's own is clearly unethical and morally wrong.

Students who practice technical plagiarism, on the other hand, usually have only a vague notion that they might be doing something against the rules of academic honesty. Solving the problem, then, does not involve moral reform. It simply means learning what technical plagiarism is and how to avoid it.

What can you do to avoid technical plagiarism? First, you need to make the transition from "report" writing to "research." That's the central purpose of this textbook. You need to borrow information on a "hard evidence" level from your sources so that you can do your own thinking.

Learn to Recognize Plagiarism. In order to avoid technical plagiarism, make certain you can tell a legitimate paraphrase from one which could be labeled "plagiarism." Consider the following example which appeared in a *Psychology Today* article, "City Stress Index: 25 Best; 25 Worst," by Robert Levine (Nov. 1988, 54):

> As *Time* magazine pointed out three years ago: "Whether the subject is the beefiest burger or the biggest corporation, Americans have a penchant for making lists of the best and worst, then arguing about the results. . . . No rankings have inspired more disagreement than those about home sweet home."

Levine introduces his source in the text and uses a direct quotation, so he has left no room for a challenge of plagiarism. If he had chosen to paraphrase instead of quote, however, he would need to translate the notions expressed in the quotation into his own words. A *good paraphrase* might look like this:

> A 1985 *Time* magazine review of *Places Rated,* observed that Americans like to rank everything from food to businesses, and that they are usually ready to fight if their own home towns did not rank as high as they thought they should.

Again, in this sample, the author introduces his source in the text. (If the article had included a Works Cited, you could have found the full citation. In that case, he would also have provided a page number.) In that way, the borrower marks the passage as a paraphrase. Beyond that, he has taken the information from the original and translated it into his own words and sentence order. This is a legitimate paraphrase.

Now let's look at three examples of technical plagiarism, ranked from "bad to worst." A *bad paraphrase* might look like this:

> *Time* magazine mentions that Americans rank everything from burgers to

corporations. They create rankings and then argue about the results. They argue most about how their home sweet home ranks.

Although this paraphrase introduces the source, it is still a "bad" paraphrase because it is too close to the original. The words come too close too often to the ones in the original—"burger" and "burgers," "corporation" and "corporations," "arguing" and "argue." It repeats key phrases—"home sweet home." And the points in the paraphrase are ordered in exactly the same way as the original. This is an example of technical plagiarism. But because he introduces his sources, it is quite mild.

This next one is *worse:*

Americans like to rank everything from food to businesses, and they are usually ready to fight if their own home towns did not rank as high as they think they should.

In this case, the author has provided a genuine paraphrase. The word choice and sentence order are his own. But he does not introduce his source and he does not provide a citation. We have no way of knowing that this is borrowed material. This is a serious case of technical plagiarism. *Please remember that anytime you use information you were not aware of before beginning your research, you must provide documentation. Introduce the source in the text and provide a citation.*

The most serious form of plagiarized paraphrasing comes when you combine the offenses of the "bad" and "worse" examples above.

Then you get *worst:*

Americans have a penchant for ranking everything from the beefiest burger to the biggest corporation, and then disputing the results. They especially like to argue if the rankings are about home sweet home.

This example is blatant plagiarism. When English teachers find something like this, we have a difficult time believing that it is not intentional. The source is not introduced. There is no citation marker. The words and sentence order follow the original almost exactly.

Read for Understanding

Even in genuine research, of course, you will continue to do a certain amount of "reporting." When you do, you must try to master the information so that your paraphrases can truly be your own words. In fact, I recommend that *anytime you paraphrase, have no book open, no magazine article in front of you, nor anything but the resources of your own memory* and understanding of the borrowed information available to you. In that way, your paraphrase will always be legitimate.

Do Not Rely Too Much on Paraphrase

Whenever possible, provide a quotation instead of a paraphrase. If you find yourself filling your paper with paraphrase (or quotations), you probably have not chosen a topic which permits you to do enough of your own thinking.

In some cases, a paraphrase is clearly needed. I recommend a paraphrase when the original source uses unreadable jargon. For example, during her reading, Paula came across this passage at the beginning of an article entitled, "The Maximum Speed of Female High School Runners":

> The purposes of this study were to develop a cinematographic technique to obtain selected parameters over an entire 100-m run to evaluate selected characteristics of the maximum speed phase (MSP) and the final phase (FP). (John Chow, *International Journal of Sport Biomechanics* 3 (1987):110–27)

By the time Paula had read the article, she understood what the jargon meant, and she was prepared to paraphrase. She didn't cite information from the article in her paper, but if she had, she might want to paraphrase this passage into something like this:

> Using high-speed cameras, Mr. Chow developed a technique to determine the point in a 100-meter sprint when the runner reaches her fastest speed (MSP), and he compared that point with her speed at the end of the sprint. (110)

I also recommend a paraphrase when the language of the original source distracts from the significance of the information. For example, I think it's distracting to quote a source which uses nonstandard usage. When you want to capture the linguistic character of the source, of course, you should quote directly. If your informant seems otherwise authoritative but uses nonstandard English, probably you should either use an indirect quotation or a paraphrase.

Whenever you work with borrowed information try to borrow mostly information as close to the hard evidence level as possible. That way you will be able to do your own thinking, and you'll be less likely to have problems with technical plagiarism. As you take notes and write your paper, always show clearly what you have borrowed. If you do, you will have no difficulty.

Keep in the Main Channel While Taking Notes

Many folks who do research face serious hazards to their successful navigation through the world's abundant resources in the library. Sometimes you will get distracted by information somewhat related, but not directly relevant, to your information needs. These distractions are like side channels and tributaries on a trip down a river.

Paula's Log, Entry #23

   I spent the entire work-time today reading in the <u>Coaches Guide to Sport</u>
<u>Psychology</u>. I knew I was going way off from my "information needs," but I
couldn't stop myself. The chapter on "Managing Psychic Energy" would help
me in school as well as track. If I do go out for track, I'm going to read more
in this book. I think it would help me perform better and be less upset when
I don't win. Maybe I should be a coach someday.

   As you look for information, you inevitably come across fascinating articles,
reports, or books which simply seem to demand that you stop everything else and
attend to them. "Read Me Now!" they say, and sometimes you will. If the
information turns out to be interesting, and it often is, you are likely to want to use it
somehow in your paper. You may even change your research questions somewhat
to fit more easily the information you have rather than the questions you want
answered. When that happens, you have strayed off the main course.

   During her research, Paula uncovered many articles (like the one by John
Chow above) which examined sprinting techniques. As a sprinter and a curious
thinker, Paula strayed away from her primary information needs to read such
articles as, "A Kinematic Analysis of World Class Sprinters" and "Neuromuscular
and Anaerobic Performances of Sprinters at Maximal and Supermaximal Speed."
Instead of surveying Rainer Martens' book, *A Coaches Guide to Sport Psychology,*
for the segments relevant to her questions, she read all 180 double-column pages. In
short, she discovered a world of information fascinating to her which she had not
known existed before.

   Wonderful! But don't forget your central purpose—find the answer to your
questions.

   When you are tempted to stray too far from the center of your question,
remember this old parable:

Looking for the Key

One evening, close to midnight, a man walked home through a gentle snow
fall. When he arrived there, he reached in his pocket to pull out his house key,
but his hands were cold and instead of pulling out only the key, he dumped the
entire contents of his pocket into the soft new snow on his sidewalk. He
picked up a few of the things he could see there in the dark by his door—his
gloves, his wallet—but his key he didn't find. He continued looking, but,
without noticing, he was slowly moving his search toward the street.

Finally he was down on his hands and knees earnestly searching under the street light and another man came along. "Here, let me help," the man said. "What have you lost?"

"The key to my house," the searcher answered, and so the two of them began to search together in the snow under the street light. After about twenty minutes, the second man was beginning to get cold, and so he stopped looking.

"We have looked over every inch here. Are you certain this is where you dropped it?"

The other man looked up, scratched his head, and said, "No, this is not where I dropped it at all. I dropped it over there by my front door."

"You idiot," the second man shouted at him. "If you dropped the key over there by the doorway, why are you looking for it here under the street light?"

"Why, I don't know," the man replied, "I guess because the light is better over here."

Sometimes, as researchers, all of us are tempted to change our search because more information seems to be available on a related topic ("the light is better").

What Do You Do To Keep On Track?

Most people travelling the upper Mississippi in a boat take a map to keep track of its many channels and sloughs, especially if they are new to the area. If you feel you might stray from your central questions, go back to your outline of information needs. By reviewing your questions and by reigning in your curiosity a little, you should be able to keep on track.

Paula's Log, Entry #25

Another work session spent reading AROUND BUT NOT ON my topic. I can't believe how many articles in the last few years have been published about women athletes. There are so many I want to read, but I know they won't provide me exactly the information I need for my paper. I've got to control my curiosity a little more. I'm going to go home this weekend and go to see Dr. Wimmer, the orthopedist who treated my stress fracture. My appointment is on Friday afternoon, so I've got to skip Biology lab to get there on time.

The Notes. Using your outline of information needs as your map, read each of your sources carefully and note any passages or information you might want to cite in your paper. If you are working with a photocopy of an article or a book chapter, I suggest you simply mark the passages on the copy with a box, a highlighter, or underline in ink. If you do not own the copy, you'll need to copy the passages you want to save either into a notebook or onto notecards.

Notebooks permit you to keep everything from one source together in one place. Note cards permit you to move segments of information around at will. It's an issue of format, of packaging, not principle. The question is, What kind of vehicle—in this situation—works best for you?

Note Cards. Many scholars prefer the traditional tool for taking notes—note cards. Some use them for every kind of note taking, and others save them for special applications where copy machines are irrelevant and notebooks not flexible enough.

When you want small bits of information from many different, places, note cards are very efficient. For example, if you are examining your university's publications for sexist language, you would probably use note cards. Note cards work well because they permit you to extract the examples from context and then classify them later. To illustrate, let's say you are looking for occupational or position titles followed by personal pronouns, either plural, masculine, feminine, both, or neuter. In one source, you find, "Go see your *advisor* before classes begin and ask *him* to help you. . . ." In another, you find, "If you will be absent from class because of illness, call the *nurse* on duty in the University Health Service and tell *her* your symptoms so that she can notify the *doctor. He* will call you if. . . ."

When you collect samples on note cards, you can later put all the examples of one type together in one stack. All the examples of a position title followed by a masculine-only pronoun would be in one stack—"advisor—him," "doctor—he." In another stack, you could conveniently put all of the feminine-only examples— "nurse—she." A photocopier would not help you on this project; a notebook might work if you had your categories established ahead of time and you did your classifying as you collected samples. I think you would find it clumsy, however. The note cards enable you to change classifications or add subclasses.

Another example: Let's say you are looking for food images in five selected short stories by Kate Chopin. You are working on this topic because you learned in another literature class that Kate Chopin used many food images in her novel, *The Awakening,* but you had never heard whether she also used food images in her short stories. You also don't know what the significance of the images will be even if you find them. In other words, you want to identify and collect the images first, and then see if patterns emerge. In an application like that, note cards will work well.

In one section of her paper, LuAnn faced a similar situation. She wanted to find out whether job announcements for nurses specified BSN or RN requirements. As her basic source she selected the classified ads section of recent issues of the *American Journal of Nursing.* She used note cards to extract the information she needed. The sample cards are on page 106.

In cases where your information comes in small units and where you need to

AJN (Aug. 1987) 1110

Hillsdale, MI

Acute Care
RN required (BSN not mentioned)
"Competitive" salaries

AJN (Aug. 1987) 1110

Coos Bay, OR

Acute Care
RN required, BSN preferred
"Competitive" salaries

AJN (Aug. 1987) 1110

Klamonth Falls, OR

Acute Care
BSN Required
"Excellent" salaries and benefits

arrange and rearrange these units, note cards have a clear advantage, especially if the full context is secondary. In cases, however, where you need to describe a complex study or provide significant background information, note cards do not work as well as a marked-up copy of the original or a notebook description.

BENCH NOTES: TAKE NOTES

SUMMARY

Once you have found information which helps you answer your research questions, you need a strategy for transferring it from the source where you found it into your own research paper. You want the strategy to be as accurate as possible, but you also want it to be easy to use and leak-proof. Many people still prefer the traditional note-card system, but others have added the copy machine and notebooks to their tools for taking notes.

Whatever strategy you use, remember that you are responsible for conveying an accurate sense of the context from which you borrowed information as well as an accurate paraphrase or quotation. Attend to details like page numbers and dates. To help you meet these obligations, I recommend that you prepare an Annotation Worksheet for every source you use.

As you go about collecting information, keep an eye on your research outline so that you don't stray too far from the main channel.

ESTIMATED TIME NEEDS

If everything goes smoothly for you, and you work quickly without distractions or frustrating confusion, you might be able to collect all of the information you need in ten hours. More likely, it will take you at least twenty. Plan for twenty-five.

KEY TERMS

Survey: Quick read-through to estimate an item's value to your research project.

Annotation: Information which you provide about a citation—its contents and its value to your project. Annotations may be as short as two sentences or as full as several paragraphs.

Bibliography Card: A note card on which you record a single citation along with its call number or other guide to the item's location. Useful in the initial stages of research to help you locate and sort your sources, and later, to help you provide documentation.

Note-card System: Traditional strategy for recording, sorting and arranging borrowed information. Employs 4" × 6" or 5" × 8" note cards, one for each segment of information you want to record from your sources.

Copy Machine System: Alternative or supplement to note-card system. Employs library copy machines to duplicate complete sources or parts of sources.

BENCH NOTES *continued*

Borrowed Information: Any words, information or concepts we borrow from other sources. If you were not familiar with the information before you located it, it is borrowed information, and you have an obligation to give credit to its source.

Summary: A general description of borrowed information, especially useful to provide a context for more specific paraphrased or quoted information. Must be documented.

Paraphrase: Translating into your own language information you have borrowed. Must be documented.

Direct Quotation: Word for word presentation of borrowed information. Must be documented.

Plagiarism Technical: Out of sloppiness or ignorance, presenting borrowed information is a poorly paraphrased form, or without complete appropriate documentation. A lapse of skill and/or effort, but probably not moral judgment.

Plagiarism Intentional: Intentionally presenting borrowed materials as your own. An ethical and moral violation of Western intellectual traditions.

DOCUMENT YOUR SOURCES
OF BORROWED INFORMATION

Riding up the elevator last week I overheard this conversation:

"Jack was interviewed by Cray Computers. I hear he's gonna get the job."

"Yeah? Where'd you hear that?"

"His name is on the interview board under "Cray" in the Placement Office."

"Did you see it?"

"No, but my cousin Sharon told me she saw it."

"So? That's just an interview. Who says he's gonna get the job?"

And so on. One hears such conversations often. One person makes a statement, and the other person wants to know, "Where'd you hear that? "Who says?" or "Where'd you get that information?" In our culture, we routinely insist on knowing from where information comes, and so we demand attribution. We want to examine the source of the evidence as well as the evidence itself.

When you do research, you go beyond unstructured personal experience for information. You search the library. You set up experiments, you conduct polls, you survey, you consult other people with access to information you need. Whenever you draw on information outside of your own storehouse of memories, you have an obligation to show your audience where you found it. But the value of citing sources goes beyond obligation. By showing your readers where you got your evidence, you share with them an opportunity to judge whether or not the evidence is valid and/or reliable.

Select a Style Manual

Over the last thirty years, the procedures for citing sources in printed materials have changed. When I was in school we were using *op cit* and *Ibid,* which seem almost like fossils now when one sees them in a text. In addition, the conventions and the forms for documenting sources of information vary from discipline to discipline. The sample papers in this text use the forms recommended by the Modern Language Association in 1984 and published in *The MLA Handbook for Writers of Research Papers.* Most U.S. college and university English departments prefer the MLA style.

Other scholarly and professional groups also have designed their own styles for documentation. These groups publish the styles they prefer in "style manuals." There are a dozen or more "styles," but, in addition to MLA, the most commonly used are the APA style (developed by the American Psychological Association), the Chicago style (developed by the University of Chicago Press):

> American Psychological Association. *Publication Manual of the American Psychological Association.* 3rd ed. Washington: American Psychological Association, 1983.

> *Chicago Manual of Style.* 13th ed. Chicago: University of Chicago Press, 1982.

You might also encounter one of the following:

> Council of Biology Editors. Style Manual Committee. *CBE Style Manual: A Guide for Authors, Editors, and Publishers in the Biological Sciences.* 5th ed. Bethesda: Council of Biology Editors, 1983.

> American Chemical Society. *Handbook for Authors of Papers in American Chemical Society Publications.* Washington: American Chemical Society, 1978.

> American Mathematical Society. *A Manual for Authors of Mathematical Papers.* 7th ed. Providence: American Mathematical Society, 1980.

> American Institute of Physics. Publications Board. *Style Manual for Guidance in the Preparation of Papers.* 3rd ed. New York: American Inst. of Physics, 1978.

If you'd like to see a complete list of style manuals, consult

Howell, John Bruce. *Style Manuals of the English-Speaking World*. Phoenix: Oryx, 1983.

All of these style guides will help you document your sources. Like the MLA style guide, the other style guides will provide you information about how to format information in the text, how to arrange the materials on the page, and much other useful information about presenting your written work in a form most likely to receive approval by your audience. When you decide on your major field of concentration, it's a good idea to become familiar with the style manual preferred in that field.

Introduce Borrowed Materials

Whenever you want to bring in borrowed information, introduce the source and make clear where the borrowed information ends. In other words, put a frame around the borrowed materials so that your readers can see where it begins and where it ends. Look at LuAnn's paper for samples. Each time she uses information from outside her personal experience, she makes certain her audience understands exactly where it comes from. For example, on page four of her paper, second paragraph, she describes the process she used to gather information:

> To begin, I went to the classified ads of a national nurses magazine to get an overview.

Then she introduces her specific sources in the text:

> In the May, 1987, *American Journal of Nursing,* ''Classified Ads,'' . . . .

> The August 1987, *American Journal of Nursing,* ''Classified Ads,'' . . . .

> ''Chicago Story,'' an article by Catherine Ballman, reports that . . . .

Notice that LuAnn does not stop with her first introduction. She continues to *remind us in each new sentence* until she comes to the end of the borrowed information:

> In Ballman's interview. . . .

> Ballman comments that. . . .

> Ballman's article includes. . . .

Following LuAnn's example, put a frame around your borrowed information. Introduce each source in the text, and continue to remind your readers in *each new sentence* that the information continues to come from the source you introduced. In the MLA style, you also frame the end of the borrowed material by inserting a parenthetical citation. That way there's never any confusion about where the borrowed information ends and your own thinking begins.

Pages four and five of LuAnn's paper provide an example of another kind of introduction which sometimes confuses the beginning researcher—the source within a source. The source cited by LuAnn—Catherine Ballman—also cites sources of her own: Janet Moore, Patricia Baker, and Marjie Townsend. Once you commit yourself to full introductions, the process becomes rather straight-forward (although sometimes a little awkward):

> In Ballman's interview with Janet Moore, R.N., Associate Vice President at Rush Presbyterian, Moore states that. . . .

> Ballman's article includes an interview with Patricia Baker, Director of Personnel at Humona Hospital, Hoffman Estates, who states. . . .

> Ballman reports that, during an interview, Marjie Townsend, R.N. recruiter for Mercy Hospital, told her. . . .

LuAnn not only introduces her sources; she also tells us something about their qualifications to provide the information she cites. Thus, we, as her readers, are able to assess reliability and validity for ourselves.

As you draft your paper, you may feel that all those introductions are intrusive, redundant, and boring. In fact, the introductions are a basic part of your evidence. They help your readers see the complete chain of your evidence from borrowed hard evidence to your own higher level thinking about the evidence. When you reintroduce your source each new sentence, you reassure your audience that you have been scrupulous about making a clear distinction between what you borrowed and what you contributed yourself. Finally, almost always, precision and full detail are more interesting than pointless ambiguity.

Parenthetical Notes

In the new MLA style, complete introductions in the text supplemented by brief parenthetical citations are preferred over either endnotes or footnotes (though both are still used for explanatory notes). Very often, as you introduce your sources, you will provide enough information so that your reader will be able to locate them among the works listed on your works cited page which comes at the end of the text. In that case, all you need in your parenthetical note will be the page number.

Examine these samples from LuAnn's paper:

> Carol Mishler, in her article, "Adult Perceptions of the Benefits of a College Degree," reports on a survey of adult graduates of the University of Wisconsin System, three to five years after graduation (224).

Mishler concludes with the statement, "Although the adults received their degrees later in life than their younger counterparts, it seems clear that most benefitted greatly from the college experience and the possession of a bachelor's degree. Thus benefits appeared in both their work lives and personal lives" (227).

In the first example, LuAnn introduces her source and provides a summary description of the article she's using. Because she has provided the name of the author and the name of the article, her readers will have no trouble finding the full citation in LuAnn's works cited page. From there they will be able to go efficiently to the specific issue of *Research in Higher Education* where the original article appeared.

Since the article is sixteen pages long, LuAnn's readers might still have to page through the article to find the exact page with the specific reference. To save her readers that inconvenience, LuAnn has provided the page number in parentheses inserted into the text. Note how it is punctuated:

. . . after graduation (224).

The parentheses fit between the last word of LuAnn's summary and the final period.

In the second example, LuAnn uses a direct quotation. To introduce her source here, she uses only the last name of the author because her readers already know the name of the article. Nothing more is needed except, again, the specific page numbers which LuAnn provides in parentheses. Note again the punctuation. The end quotation marks follow the last words of the quoted material. Then come the parentheses with the page number inside, and finally, the period. The MLA committee which recommend this configuration decided on it only after six years of debate; it is a compromise.

Whenever you use borrowed information, you have three responsibilities. First, almost always, you will *introduce the source in the text*. After you have introduced your source and presented the information, *provide (in parentheses) page numbers and additional identifying information* which the reader needs to find the source easily in your works cited page. Following the text of your paper, *provide works cited or works consulted* pages, preferably fully annotated.

Prepare Works Cited and Works Consulted Pages

The new MLA documentation style recommends a works cited page which includes a full citation for each source cited in the text. With this documentation style, you need neither footnotes nor endnotes, nor a separate bibliography. The MLA Committee on Documentation Styles wanted to simplify the documentation process as much as possible. They suggested that one list which included complete publication information for each cited source would be enough. If the researcher also wants to include information about consulted (but not cited) sources, the committee recommends that the list be called a works consulted page. Some provide two lists, one for works cited, and a second one called Additional Works Consulted.

By now you have learned how to introduce your sources in the text, and how to show your audience quickly and clearly what you borrowed and what you contributed yourself. You learned to provide sufficient information about the source in the text so that your audience can assess the reliability and validity of the evidence. By introducing your source in the text, you also make it possible for your audience to find a full citation in your works cited or bibliography page.

Now you need to make sure that the full citation is complete and consistent with the citation style you are using so that your readers can decode it. Some of them may want to use your works cited page as a referral to their own research.

Citations for Your Works Cited and/or Consulted Page

A citation in a footnote, endnote, works cited page, or bibliography includes four categories of information in this order:

1. Name of person or persons primarily responsible for preparing the publication.
2. Title and format (book, magazine, pamphlet) of the publication.
3. When, where, and by whom it was published.
4. Specific location in the source, usually by page number.

Author. The first part of your citation will be the author—the author(s), editor, compiler, organization, or agency responsible for preparing the text of the source.

An MLA style citation with a single author looks like this:

Martens, Rainer. *Coaches Guide to Sport Psychology.* Champaign, IL: Human Kinetics Publishers, Inc., 1987.

In a bibliography or works cited/consulted page, the family name comes first, followed by a comma, then the first name, middle name or initial, and a period. If two authors have prepared the source, it looks like this:

Barrow, Gary and Subrata Saha. "Menstrual Irregularity and Stress Fractures in Collegiate Female Distance Runners." *American Journal of Sports Medicine* 16 (1988): 209–16.

The names will be in alphabetical order unless the authors have agreed to have one of them be the "lead" author. The family name of the first person will appear first, followed by a comma, and then his or her given name and middle name or initial (optional). The conjunction "and" connects the first and second names. The second name will have the given name first and the family name last.

When there are more than two authors it will look like this:

Gill, Diane L., David A. Dzewaltowski, and Thomas Deeter. "The Relationship of Competitiveness and Achievement Orientation to Participation in Sport and Nonsport Activities." *Journal of Sport and Exercise Psychology* 16 (1988): 139–50.

Sometimes an organization or agency will be listed as the author:

American Psychological Association. *Publication Manual of the American Psychological Association.* 3rd ed. Washington: American Psychological Association, 1983.

If the person primarily responsible for the publication did not actually write most of the material, she or he may be identified as the editor, or compiler:

Caplan, Frank., ed. *The Parenting Advisor.* Garden City, NY: Anchor Press-Doubleday, 1977.

When the original work is translated by someone other than the author, the translator's name is added after the title:

Rolvaag, Ole Edvart. *Giants in the Earth.* **Trans. Lincoln Colcord.** New York: Harper & Row, 1927.

If you interview someone, you treat the person interviewed as the author:

Satchel, Barbara. Personal interview. 15 Oct. 1988.

Newspaper stories and magazine articles often do not identify the author. In such cases, go directly to the title of the article:

"Boston University to Shut down Its School of Nursing." *American Journal of Nursing* 87.8 (1987): 1095.

Some handbooks, pamphlets, and other materials published by organizations also do not provide an author or editor:

Chicago Manual of Style. 13th ed. Chicago: University of Chicago Press, 1982.

Titles. The title information in your citations will sometimes be one complete work—a book, a pamphlet, a play, a film. In such cases you need only worry about the overall title. Often, however, you will be citing a work—a periodical article, a speech, a poem, an introduction—which is part of a collection of works. In such cases, you have to provide both the specific title of the segment you used, and the title of the larger collection in which the segment is housed.

Unless no author is provided, the title appears second (after "author") in your citation. If the title is two-part—a shorter work included in a collection, for example—the smallest comes first:

> Barrow, Gary and Subrata Saha. **"Menstrual Irregularity and Stress Frac-tures in Collegiate Female Distance Runners."** *American Journal of Sports Medicine* 16 (1988): 209–16.

Notice in these examples that the smaller unit (the title of the article) appears in quotation marks, and that the title of the larger unit (the periodical or book) is underlined. The title of less-than-book-length materials will almost always appear in quotation marks—short stories, poems, one-act plays, book chapters. The title of larger units—books, periodicals, feature length films or plays—are underlined. If you prefer, you may also put the titles of larger units into italics:

> Glover, Bob and Murray Weisenfeld. *The Injured Runner's Training Hand-book*. New York: Penguin Books, 1985.

Publisher. Most citations also include the date, place, and name of the pub-lisher. *The Injured Runner's Training Handbook,* for example, was published by *Penguin Books,* in New York City, New York, in 1985. If the location of the city of publication is well known (New York City, for example), the name of the state is left off. For lesser known cities (Garden City, New York, for example), the abbreviated name is also provided.

The specific city of publication is not included in periodical citations, nor is the name of the publisher. The name of the periodical often is same as the publisher, however.

Page Numbers. Citations for complete works such as books, do not include page references. The citation suggests that the entire work was consulted. Also, in the MLA style, page numbers are provided in the parenthetical citations.

For sections of books, periodical articles, and other segments, the works consulted citations will include page numbers:

> Barrow, Gary and Subrata Saha. "Menstrual Irregularity and Stress Fractures in Collegiate Female Distance Runners." *American Journal of Sports Medicine* 16 (1988): **209–16**.

In this sample, the article by Barrow and Saha takes up only seven pages (209–216) of the total *American Journal of Sports Medicine*. The numbers which follow the periodical name tell us exactly where in the larger work we can find the specific article. The *American Journal of Sports Medicine* is published with page numbers that continue from one issue to the next until the entire *volume* is complete. The number "16" is the volume number, and the number in parentheses is the year the volume was published. If the page numbers start over with each issue within the volume, an issue number will follow the volume number.

Most specialized scholarly periodicals are *journals.* Periodicals published for a more general audience are called *magazines.* Magazines usually begin the page numbering over again with each individual issue. Thus the citation for a magazine is slightly different. Instead of a volume and issue number, the specific date is provided:

> "America's Best Colleges: What's Behind the Rankings." *U.S. News & World Report* 16 Oct. 1989: 58+.

If the article runs on continuous pages, the page numbers would be listed as in "209–16." If the article begins on one page and continues somewhere else in the periodical, page numbers are shown as above; the article begins on page 58 but continues elsewhere in the periodical.

Provide Annotations. On both works cited and works consulted pages, provide complete bibliographical detail. In many cases, you will also want to provide your readers with an *annotation.* In some situations you will provide a quick one or two sentence summary of the source. In others, you will want to provide a paragraph or more. Highlighted below are some samples from LuAnn's works cited page:

> "ANA's Change in Nursing Education." *Nursing Success* Mar. 1986: 27. **The news item stated that North Dakota is the first state to require nursing education to be at the Baccalaureate level after Jan. 1, 1987.**

> Ballman, Catherine. "The Chicago Story." *American Journal of Nursing* 87.10 (1987): 1338–46. **The article contained information on the trend toward preferring B.S.N.'s, advantages of B.S.N.'s and salary differences.**

> Blaney, Doris. "An Historical Review of Positions in Baccalaureate Education in Nursing as Basic Preparation for Professional Nursing Practice 1960–1984." *American Journal of Nursing* 86.5 (1986): 182–85. **This article gave me insight on the beginning of the B.S.N. Proposal by the American Nurses Association—where it is now and why the association favors it.**

Here are some others from Paula's paper:

Alfred, Richard H. and John A. Bergfeld. "Diagnosis and Management of Stress Fractures of the Foot." *Physician and Sportsmedicine* Aug. 1987: 83–89. **A technical description of the causes and treatments of stress fractures among athletes, including the specific type I suffered last spring.**

Barrow, Gary and Subrata Saha. "Menstrual Irregularity and Stress Fractures in Collegiate Female Distance Runners." *American Journal of Sports Medicine* 16 (1988): 209–16. **A complex analysis of women distance runners who suffer both menstrual irregularity and stress fractures. They conclude that most such women also suffer from eating disorders and thus inadequate diet.**

Gill, Diane L., David A. Dzewaltowski, and Thomas Deeter. "The Relationship of Competitiveness and Achievement Orientation to Participation in Sport and Nonsport Activities." *Journal of Sport and Exercise Psychology* 16 (1988): 139–50. **A report on the field testing of the Sports Orientation Questionnaire (SOQ) which was developed by Diane Gill, one of the authors. They conclude that the instrument is valid and reliable, especially on the "general competitiveness" scale.**

When you first identified the sources you were going to use for your research, you prepared an Annotation Worksheet for each. These worksheets will provide you everything you need for your works cited and works consulted pages. Look at the samples above, and "Works" pages for the sample papers. I have checked their citations, and as far as I can tell, they are consistent with the new MLA guidelines. If you are using a source unlike any they have used, check the new *MLA Handbook for Writers of Research Papers*.

Paula's Log, Entry # 41

I've checked over my IBM's and my citations. I blush when I remember the last "term paper" I wrote. The topic was "Witches in Puritan New England." I must have copied at least half of it from one book. Well, I did change a few words here and there. I sprinkled in footnotes, but I made up page numbers because I forgot to write any down. I even completely made up a couple sources. Please don't tell my high school teacher. I'm sure he explained how to document sources, but I must not have been listening. Can they take back my diploma?

BENCH NOTES: DOCUMENTATION

SUMMARY

The American academic tradition emphatically insists that any writer who borrows information, concepts, specific words or images has an obligation to acknowledge their original source.

In recent years, the conventions which govern documentation have moved toward more directness and simplicity. It is no longer enough to have a discrete little footnote number in the text where the materials appear. The contemporary code, especially in the humanities and social sciences, calls for the writer to introduce the source directly in the text. In addition, if the introduction leaves out information a reader needs to find the source on the works cited page, the writer must provide it in parentheses as soon after the information as possible.

As the final element, writers provide a list of all the sources they cited in the text. In many cases they also list the most important sources they consulted but did not cite. Thoughtful and thorough writers go one step more. They provide annotations for each of the sources they used.

In the final chapter of this text you will find a ''Quick Guide to Documentation'' in both MLA and APA format.

ESTIMATED TIME NEEDED

If you have been following the process, most of the work for this section will have been done in the ''Taking Notes'' section. For this unit you will only need to check the forms and perhaps work on the smoothness of your introductions. Laying out and typing the works cited and works consulted pages will be the most time consuming processes. Estimated time—two to three hours.

PRACTICE AND APPLICATION

Try translating your introductions, parenthetical notes and works cited page into APA style (See ''Quick Guide to Documentation APA Style'' near the end of the text).

KEY TERMS

MLA Style: The forms of documentation and manuscript preparation recommended by the Modern Language Association.

APA Style: The forms of documentation and manuscript preparation recommended by the American Psychological Association.

Chicago Style: The forms and documentation and manuscript preparation recommended by the University of Chicago Press.

Document Sources: The process of introducing and identifying the sources of borrowed information. The specific forms differ slightly from style to style.

Cite Your Sources: Same as ''Document Your Sources.''

BENCH NOTES *continued*

Introduce Sources in the Text. Introducing the name of the author and/or the title of the work directly in the text of the paper immediately before paraphrasing, summarizing, or quoting.

Parenthetical Citation: Publication information enclosed by parenthesis included in the text to help the reader find the source on the works cited page.

Works Cited: In the MLA style, a list of citations provided at the conclusion of the paper. Includes only those sources specifically cited in the text.

Works Consulted: In the MLA style, a list of citations provided at the conclusion of the paper. Includes the works which were cited in the text and, in addition, other works which were consulted.

CHAPTER FIVE

WRITING IT ALL DOWN

DRAFTING

REVISION

REACH CONCLUSIONS

WRITE THE LEAD

EDIT AND POLISH

DRAFTING

When you reach this chapter, the real fun begins. You have been working on bits and pieces—refining your question, identifying the givens, choosing your criteria, shaping your outline into questions, defining your information needs, searching for information, collecting information. Now all those steps come into focus in the paper itself. Those of you who invested much care and thoroughness in the early stages now get your reward—your paper will snap together and lift like a well-made tent. If you have left out or skimmed over some of the steps, you'll find the process more difficult. During this chapter we will work with the main body of your paper. The "givens" and "criteria" sections you have already completed, and the lead and conclusions we will save for later.

Work with the Questions in Your Outline

During the initial stages of the drafting process, you can treat each question separately. Look at the major questions in your outline and choose the one which you feel most confident about answering. Answer that question and its subordinate questions as clearly and completely as you can. Then go on to another major question, working through your outline until all of the questions are answered. As you go, define terms, explain your methodology, begin with hard evidence, work through the evidence levels, and all along the way, show us your work.

Describe Your Methodology

If you can, describe the procedures you used to answer your question. Did you design an experiment, conduct a poll, interview people? Did you depend primarily on library sources? Why? Show your reader how you have shaped your question and how you have collected the information.

Work Through the Evidence Levels

At this stage in your project, you probably know the answers to your questions. You have been working with the evidence, and you know where it leads. Because you have become an expert on your topic, you might assume that everything so clear to you must also be clear to your readers.

Remember, however, that most readers will come to your paper quite ignorant of most of the information you now know intimately. Please be patient with your readers. Teach them. Show them your hard evidence, and then show them how you took that evidence, followed a rational system, and moved it through the taxonomy of evidence levels to evaluation. This might be a good time to review the ''Levels of Information'' taxonomy in Chapter Three.

An Example

In the following passage from LuAnn's paper, she begins to answer the question: ''What are the differences between a B.S.N. and a three-year diploma in the marketplace?'' After introducing the question, she describes her methodology:

> To begin, I went to the classified ads of a national nurses' magazine to get a broad picture.

Then she shows us what she found:

> In the May 1987 *American Journal of Nursing* classified ads, there were twenty-two nationwide job announcements. Of these, eleven stated that only an R.N. license was required and supplied no job description. Two required a B.S.N. and specified the jobs as a psychiatric nurse and a clinical coordinator. Nine faculty positions required a masters degree (744–45). The August 1987 issue of the same journal contained twenty-five employment announcements. Thirteen required an R.N. license, four called for a B.S.N. and eight called for a masters degree. There were no specific salaries quoted for any of these positions (1109–10).

Before writing this paragraph, she had scanned the ads, *analyzed* them for relevant information, selected *(interpreted)* those she wanted, and entered each on a note card *(translated)*. She then sorted the cards according to those which specified a R.N. and those which specified a B.S.N. *(interpretation and comparison)*.

In the paragraph which follows, LuAnn provides a short summary (additional *interpretation*), and she specifically *compares* the jobs available to B.S.N.s to those available to those with R.N.s. She reaches a judgment *(evaluation)*.

The classified ads I examined show that some advertised positions specifically require a B.S.N. While twenty-four positions were open for R.N.s, six additional were available for B.S.N.s. Since I already qualify for the R.N. positions, it's clear that I could increase by twenty-five percent the number of positions open to me by earning the B.S.N.

Because LuAnn shows her hard evidence, and then leads her readers through the steps she took to arrive at her judgment, she earns their trust. When she writes that "I could increase by 25% the number of positions open to me," most readers will believe her because she has demonstrated how she arrived at that judgment.

Borrow Judgments If You Must

In spite of your best efforts, you will not always be able to find direct hard evidence. But even when you must borrow the judgements of others, delineate the evidence level as much as possible. For example, in the next passage from LuAnn's paper, she uses a library source, which in turn, has been based on interviews carried out by the author:

> "Chicago Story," an article by Catherine Ballman, reports that Rush Presbyterian/St. Lukes Medical Center in Chicago is one of the first hospitals to require a B.S.N. for employment. In Ballman's interview with Janet Moore, R.N., Associate Vice President at Rush Presbyterian, Moore states that "The policy for requiring B.S.N.s has felt the cold glare of publicity and heated skepticism from nursing and hospital administration who said it wouldn't work." Moore concludes, however, that the experiment has been successful (1342).
>
> Ballman comments that Rush Presbyterian offers the B.S.N.s flexible hours and both clinical and academic appointments with salaries starting at $22,256 and ranging to $40,179.

Although in the first paragraph, LuAnn borrows "evaluation" level information, she assures its validity by establishing the reliability of the sources. In the second paragraph, the same source provides more specific, "hard evidence" level information.

To verify the judgments of the first source, LuAnn cites another of the Ballman interviews:

> Ballman's article continues with an interview with Patricia Baker, Director of Personnel at Humona Hospital, Hoffman Estates, who states, "degrees are not required, although to move into management we prefer a B.S.N., but it depends on the person" (1342).

LuAnn further checks the findings of Ballman by conducting interviews in her own region:

> I did several phone interviews to identify, locally, the trend toward having a B.S.N. versus a three-year Diploma, and to estimate the salary differences between the two. Sandra Everett, Employment Assistant at Holy Cross Hospital in Clear Water, revealed that B.S.N.s and three-year Diploma R.N.s, working as staff nurses, have the same responsibilities and receive the same salaries. She stated, however, that Holy Cross prefers B.S.N.s for managerial positions. These administrators receive higher salaries than do staff nurses. I asked Ms. Everett if she thought the day would come when Holy Cross Hospital would require a B.S.N. and she replied that "we have no plans to do so, but if other are hospitals required it we would follow suit."
>
> According to Phyllis Homes, Clinical Director at Grace Hospital in Eau Claire, no distinction is made—either in job responsibilities or salary—between a B.S.N. and a three-year Diploma R.N. when hired as a staff nurse. They do, however, prefer B.S.N.s for supervisory positions that are compensated at a higher salary.
>
> Rapid River Valley Nursing Home's Director of Nurses, Helen Neibauer, stated that they have no specific positions for B.S.N.s and concluded with the information that she is a three-year Diploma R.N. and is Director of Nurses. She also revealed that salaries for both B.S.N.s and three-year Diploma R.N.s are identical at her facility.
>
> Jean Willets, Director of Nurses at Signet County Health Care Center, Signet, Wisconsin, stated that "not all my head nurses are B.S.N.s but all my B.S.N.s are head nurses." She also stated that being a head nurse provided the advantages of working only the day shift, plus a higher salary.

Although LuAnn's sources do not provide specific data, she provides enough context so that we can assess the reliability of the sources and the validity of the information. In addition, by contacting several sources, she creates her own data—three out of the four administrators she spoke with expressed that B.S.N.s have advantages in their institutions. All along the way, LuAnn has shown her work.

When she reaches her own answer to the question with which she began this section, her readers are likely to agree:

> In general, both the administrators interviewed by Ballman and the ones I talked with suggest that B.S.N.s have a slight advantage over R.N.s in opportunities for supervisory positions.

Define Terms

Paula begins the body of her paper with the question, "Am I good enough?" Since "good enough" implies a judgment based on comparison, she decided that she needed a working definition for those words. Writers have the privilege of establishing *working definitions* for terms they use in their work. Many do it when they want to use a general term in a more specific way, as Paula does with "good enough."

Show Your Hard Evidence

Paula wanted to find out if she were good enough, so she defined "good enough," and she collected hard evidence—her high school sprinting times, and the sprinting times of the women against whom she would compete. In the first draft of her paper, she had provided only the averages of each. I recommended that she back up a step and include in her paper the actual times.

Show the Intermediate Steps

With the actual times—the hard evidence—directly in front of her readers, she can show them how she interpreted the hard evidence and calculated averages. Using analysis, she determined which times to include in the calculation of the averages, and which times to use in her next step—comparison. Showing your work to your audience helps you establish credibility with them. When they can see the logic behind your progression from hard evidence to evaluation, they will more likely trust you and your conclusions.

When we arrive at her comparisons, we know exactly what is being compared to what, and what the results mean. When she tests the results of her comparison against her definition of "good enough," we are probably ready to accept her evaluation.

Paula's Log, Entry #38

I told Jane about my troubles with section V. She listened and asked me a few questions, and all of a sudden, I saw how I could handle it. As you see from my log, I'm finally making progress again.

The sample passages from Paula's paper below appear in the text after she has defined "good enough" and set out all of the hard evidence she can in answer to her question, "Am I good enough?" Now she is ready to take the hard evidence through the evidence levels, showing us each intermediate step. She describes her methodology, and sets out the results of her analysis and comparison:

Since I am interested in knowing how I would do against the competition in our conference, I compared my times with those from the conference meet finals. My average time in the 100 last year was 12.96. The average time in the conference finals was 13.15. If I were able to run as well as I have (or improve), I would probably be better than average in the 100.

She continues the analysis to another level:

Unless I improved tremendously, however, I could not expect to compete at the nationals. The last place runner at the NAIA nations ran the 100 in 12.01, nine-tenths of a second better than my best time. Over a short distance like the 100, nine-tenths of a second is light years.

   To my surprise, it appears that I could be more competitive in the 200. The average time in the 200 at the conference meet finals was 26.68. My average time last year in high school was 25.87, eight tenths of a second faster than the conference average. In 1988, at least, I think that I could have won the 200 meter dash at the conference meet. And although I couldn't yet compete at the nationals, I was surprised to see that the difference between my best time (25.12) and the last place finisher at the nationals (25.03) might be closed with maturity and practice.

Although Paula had entered the times she refers to in table form earlier, she does not depend on her readers to do the analysis for her. Show the intermediate steps so that your readers can see easily the connection between your hard evidence and your evaluation level conclusions.

Reminders

After you finish one section of your outline continue to the next. Remember that this is an early *draft*, and at this stage you need not concentrate on polishing your text. Your work plan includes time for revision later.

   I hope you remember the "Exhortations" in Chapter One. If not, please re-read them. The first time I used this text in manuscript form, my students suggested that I move the section on procrastination closer to the front of the book. Otherwise, it comes too late, they said. This stage of the process is especially hazardous, however. Many writers have trouble getting down the first draft. They feel so uneasy about how messy it seems. Just remember to think of the first draft as embryonic. It may seem a tangle right now, but if you continue to nourish it, it might grow into something lovely.

BENCH NOTES: DRAFTING

SUMMARY

Draft your paper in sections, one major question at a time. Work through the evidence levels. Begin with hard evidence and show each of the intermediate steps so that your audience can see how you get from hard evidence to the evaluations in your subconclusions. When you finish one section, go on to the next, until the body of your paper is completed.

BENCH NOTES *continued*

ESTIMATED TIME NEEDED

If you have prepared carefully, the actual writing of this first complete draft could take as little as twelve hours—less than an hour per page. Most people require more time, even if they are thoroughly prepared. Eighteen hours should do it.

PRACTICE AND APPLICATION

No supplementary practice will be needed this time. You will get plenty of practice on your own paper.

KEY TERMS:

Draft: The stage in the writing process during which you attempt, for the first time, to move ideas and information in your head onto paper in a form you hope will lead to a final draft.

REVISION

In the rhythms of a long writing project, getting down a first draft brings you to a major pause. You have your garden planted, and now you might want to sit back, look it over and rest. You know that soon enough you'll be watering it, weeding it, and defending it against rabbits, but right now you feel more like you've come to the end of something rather than to the beginning. Enjoy that feeling.

But don't enjoy it too long. Your rough draft is just seeds in the ground, not yet ripe tomatoes and fresh green beans on your table. After a short rest—no more than two or three days—come back to your project and begin to revise. Read it over with a marking pen in your hand and look for places where it would be better with another paragraph or major section. *Enlarge* it. Check each paragraph and see if added detail or a more full explanation would strengthen it, make it more clear, more vivid. *Elaborate.* As you read through it now, you might see that one section or one paragraph might work better in another place. *Rearrange* it. Read your paper through out loud. Does it flow? Do the sentences work? Would a different word here or there work better? *Refine* your work. Finally, you might discover a section, a paragraph, a sentence which does not seem to add anything. *Cut.*

All stages of a writing project engage both our critical and our creative thinking skills. As we compose, we imagine a sentence, rehearse it in our minds, critique it, perhaps revise it, or scrap it altogether and create another. The reciprocation from creation to criticism as we compose occurs so rapidly and so often we seldom notice it. During the revision stages, however, the balance shifts slightly to the critical, at least at first.

As you compose a first draft, you want your creative powers to dominate over the critical. You want to get the draft out. Now with a draft secure before you, you can afford to let the critical side push slightly forward, but not too far forward. Of the five categories of revision (enlarge, elaborate, rearrange, refine, and cut), the first two require primarily the creation of additional writing. The third (refine) requires us to see the weaknesses of a passage and to imagine a new variation. The fourth requires you to imagine a new arrangement. The fifth (cut) is the only one which relies heavily on our critical faculties. Every part of the writing process requires keeping our creative and our critical skills at alert.

As part of the revision process, you might want to work with another reader, or a group of readers. It's possible your instructor will read your paper, or ask you to get the responses of a "writing group" or "writing partner." At this point in your project, fresh eyes can help you a great deal. Please remember, however, that you are the one responsible for this work. Listen carefully to all questions, suggestions, and criticisms, but do not give up ownership.

Enlarge

You might spot places where your research would be strengthened if you added another major section—one more criterion, for example. Or maybe you need only another paragraph in a couple places—another sub-question, for example, or another source to verify a point where you had depended entirely on one.

The authors of the three sample papers in this text all enlarged their papers between the first draft and the final. LuAnn added an entire section by considering the question, "Will the short-term personal sacrifices result in long-term personal gains?" When she began her paper, she had not considered "personal satisfaction" as a criterion because she thought she had to concentrate on "professional" considerations, and also because she thought she would not be able to find any hard evidence on the question.

As she worked through her rough draft, she became more and more aware that "personal satisfaction" was an important ingredient in her decisions. She went back to the library to search for sources of information to answer her new question, and in a short time, found what she needed. After adding this section, she felt much more confident that she had made the right decision.

After she had completed her first draft, Elizabeth Ryan was already distressed by how "big" her project had become. But after looking it over, she still was not satisfied. She had not included her child's special speech needs in her study, and she felt she would not be satisfied until she did. She added the entire section about "speech needs."

Although Paula did not add an entire section, she did add paragraphs. For example, after her interview with Dr. Wimmer, the orthopedist who treated her stress fracture, she wrote the rough draft of that section of the paper without checking Dr. Wimmer's assertions. Later, during an interview with Jackie Slater, the university women's track coach, she learned about the "Big Ten Injury Surveillance Survey." By following up Ms. Slater's referral, she was able to check and verify the information provided her by Dr. Wimmer, and add an additional paragraph to her text.

How much to add (and where) depends primarily on your judgments about what you need to know in order to answer your question, first of all for yourself, and then, for your board of directors. Probably if you sense a gap and feel uneasy about it, you should enlarge your paper.

Elaborate

"Elaboration" is simply another term for the process of providing full paragraph development. Within each paragraph, have you provided adequate detail, sufficient explanation of the detail, enough information to answer the questions your readers might raise?

Consider this paragraph from the "Other Areas of Concern" of Elizabeth's rough draft:

> I was also worried about the provider getting sick. In home-based care, I might have to find alternatives myself. In group care, this is not a problem. The substitute already knows the children.

After re-reading the paragraph, she realized that she needed to provide more detail and more explanation. For example, if the home based provider gets sick, how soon would the parent find out? In the group care situation, who would the substitute be? Why would the substitute already know the children? Keeping these (and other) questions in mind, Elizabeth elaborated the rough draft until the final draft looks like this:

> Another concern I have is what happens when the provider is sick or for some other reason is unable to provide care. I found that with all the home-based day cares, the problem of alternative care was left to the parents to resolve. They all said that they would give me as much notice as possible, but that I needed to find alternative care. I could find out that morning that I needed care for that afternoon. With a State Licensed Group Day Care this is not a problem. By state law they are required to provide a qualified substitute to replace all missing employees. In fact, the group day care I presently use has a person who spends a short amount of time with each group every day so that the children already know her if she is needed to substitute.

With the additional information and explanation, Elizabeth's readers now have a much more complete understanding of topic she deals with in the paragraph: What happens if the provider is unavailable?

As you elaborate, you might feel you are adding too much. Don't worry about it now. You can always cut it later.

Rearrange

Experienced writers expect to discover some of their most important points while they write their first drafts. Some even write a preliminary draft which they call their "discovery" or "exploratory" draft. Certainly new ideas will occur to you as you put down your first draft, and you will enlarge and elaborate your project as the process of writing stimulates new notions. As you write through your first draft, and as you look it over after you complete it, you will be better able to see if the parts fit together as you want them. You may want to rearrange entire sections, or perhaps only a paragraph or two.

Even when your project is in final form, you may see parts which might work better fitted in somewhere else. For example, when Paula wrote her "evaluation" for her own paper, she was still concerned that she should have incorporated the section, "What will track do to my social life?" into the section on "Affiliation." She wrote:

> The trouble is, I wrote the section on "Affiliation" after I wrote the section on "Social Life." I probably should have gone back and put them together. They both seem to deal with the same points.

She may be right. As with other elements in a writing project, however, you have many alternative ways to get the job done. Organizing your paper is like loading a truck with different sized boxes. You can get them to fit in a hundred different ways, some more efficient and some very inefficient. Try to fit your paper together in the most efficient way possible. And don't put the refrigerator on top of the crystal glasses.

Refine

You will want your prose to be a flawless window through which your readers can see your thoughts exactly as you intend. Build your sentences to place emphases exactly where you want them. Choose precisely the right words to show your readers the clarity and precision of your ideas. Balance your general notions with carefully selected specific illustrations. Help your readers get safely from one sentence to the next, and from one paragraph to the next. As you revise, refine.

Most of the prose created by humans and submitted as "final draft," could be further refined if the author had the skills and chose to invest the time. At some point, however, every writer says, "That's close enough." In addition, the English language offers us a variety of ways to express the same notions, many of them equally clear and acceptable. Trust yourself. Invest time and effort: rewrite awkward or misleading sentences, replace ambiguous words with more precise ones, check the consistency of all your sentence elements. Your text will get better.

I hope Elizabeth will forgive me if I use a paragraph from her paper to illustrate. Her original paragraph reads:

> The current belief in education of speech correction is mostly working to increase the number of sounds made and to reinforce them with modeling. Children with speech problems should not be punished for incorrect speech,

nor should they be made to feel ashamed, dumb or inferior to their peers. Adults working with these children must be consistent in the approach they use. Therefore, it is very important that a provider for Jessica be in complete agreement with the form being used to work with her. This provider must frequently model the correct speech patterns that most people take for granted (Barach, 157–59). At this point the issue of age-appropriate activities must be considered on all levels of development, not just in the are of speech. It is therefore very important that activities offered be at the correct age level, not her current speech level.

Let's see if we can refine the first sentence. Her original reads:

The current belief in education of speech correction is mostly working to increase the number of sounds made and to reinforce them with modeling.

When I look at this sentence, I wonder who the "believers" are—speech therapists? Looking further into the paragraph, I see a parenthetical citation. Maybe "Barach" is the one who believes. Yes. Let's make "Carol Barach, author of a guide to parents of children with speech problems," the subject instead of "The current belief." In this sentence, a variation of belief (believe) would make a stronger verb than "is." Now we have, "Carol Barach, author of a guide to parents of children with speech problems, believes. . . ." What does she "believe?" She believes in "working." Fine so far. Let's also change "sounds made" to "the child makes" because I do not like the passive voice there. I want to know who makes the sound. The word "them" might be ambiguous. Let's make it more specific by repeating, "the sounds." Here is our refinement:

Carol Barach, author of a guide to parents of children with speech problems, believes in working to increase the number of sounds the child makes and to reinforce the sounds with modeling.

The second and third sentences seem strong, but if they continue the paraphrase from Barach, each should be reintroduced: "She says . . ." and "She also recommends that. . . ."

By reintroducing Barach, we replace the "it" subject of the fourth sentence which in Elizabeth's version reads:

Therefore, it is very important that a provider for Jessica be in complete agreement with the form being used to work with her.

"Barach" becomes the subject "Barach suggests that. . . ." Now the sentence works well enough until we get to the word, "form." What does it mean? From other context clues, we can guess that it means "with the strategies recommended by Barach (and chosen by the parents)." The revised sentence becomes:

Barach believes that the provider should be in complete agreement with the strategies her parents have chosen for her.

Now the parenthetical citation at the end of sentence six needs only a page number. The frame around the Barach paraphrase closes. I also think Elizabeth should close this paragraph and begin another.

Carol Barach, author of a guide to parents of children with speech problems, believes in working to increase the number of sounds the child makes and to reinforce the sounds with modeling. She believes that children with speech problems should not be punished for incorrect speech, nor should they be made to feel ashamed, dumb or inferior to their peers. Barach also suggests that Adults working with these children should be consistent in the approach they use, and that the daycare provider frequently model correct speech patterns. She believes that the provider should be in complete agreement with the strategies her parents have chosen for her (157–59).

By refining this paragraph we have provided a sharper frame around the paraphrased material from Barach, and we have improved sentence clarity. Probably we could refine the paragraph even more.

Go over each of your paragraphs, sentence by sentence. Refine your project as much as possible. If you invest patience and persistence here, you will help your project glow like a carefully finished piece of fine wood furniture.

Cut

After you have completed the other four steps in your revision process, look over your paper and see if you can cut something. You might find this easier if you call the material you cut, "out-takes," as film editors do. All along as you compose, you write segments which you abandon and never take up again. That is one kind of cut, not so painful. Cutting a polished sentence, however, requires assertiveness. Cutting an entire completed section may seem like amputation. But it isn't. The final form of your project has a life and a shape, but the form of the shape is the one you put on it. If a cut makes the shape more streamlined, more clear, well then, cut.

BENCH NOTES: REVISE

SUMMARY

After your first draft is completed, examine it, and begin your revisions. Enlarge the project by adding new sections or paragraphs. Elaborate by providing more explanation or detail to your paragraphs. Rearrange the parts if the organization makes more sense with a new order. Refine your sentences, your documentation, and your word choices. Cut, if necessary.

BENCH NOTES *continued*

ESTIMATED TIME REQUIRED

Some writers alternate the draft and revision cycles so quickly that they do not see them as two separate stages. Some try to get a complete draft down before they do any revision at all. Do what works for you. In both cases, you can expect to spend about ten to twenty minutes revising for every hour you spend writing. In other words, if you draft for an hour, expect to spend another ten to twenty minutes getting the draft into a polished form.

PRACTICE AND APPLICATION

Select a passage from one of the sample papers and apply to it the principles of revision from this chapter. Most writers find it easier to revise someone else's work than their own. But after a little practice on another writer's work, it's easier to apply the principles to one's own work.

KEY TERMS

Enlarge: During revision, to add entire sections, paragraphs, or other major elements.

Elaborate: During revision, to add detail, explanation, or other elements of development.

Rearrange: During revision, to move large or small segments of writing from one place to another.

Refine: During revision, to reshape sentences, clarify diction, and, in general, do whatever is necessary to improve the quality of the writing.

REACH CONCLUSIONS

Long and complex projects are more manageable when you divide them into workable segments. Your large central question became subquestions based on the criteria they address. These smaller units should have *both* a clear relationship to the whole *and* integrity as independent sections.

Devote Thirty Percent of Your Text to Reminders

An analysis of effective writing reveals that good writers help their audiences by reminding them often where they have been and where they are going. Sentences are tied together by repeated key words, and paragraphs are tied to each other by reminders which show the readers where in the text they have been, where they are now, and where they have yet to go. The "subconclusion" sections of your paper serve those functions.

By reaching a distinct subconclusion for each major section, you permit your readers to come to temporary closure on that section. Then they can file the section as a unit and begin a new section with an uncluttered field of attention. Think of each major section as a file, and of your subconclusion as the folder which holds the file contents together. Your readers open a file, read it through to completion, and then they can put it away for future reference. They can give the new file their undivided attention, but they also know that the file they put away is easily accessible. Each subconclusion is the evaluation level summary for that file.

Although LuAnn did not use a special heading for her subconclusion sections, she clearly uses them to summarize and close up each major section of her paper. For example, one major section of her paper addresses the question, ''What effect will the nursing shortage have on job flexibility and the mandatory B.S.N. Proposal?'' After consulting a dozen sources LuAnn presents her answer to the question:

> The research reveals that there is a serious nursing shortage and with the number of nursing schools, both three-year and B.S.N., declining, the shortage will last for some time. Although the nursing shortage has created vacant positions that institutions may be forced to fill with non-B.S.N.s, it appears that they still prefer B.S.N.s. The nursing shortage may delay the mandatory B.S.N. proposal, but this is not conclusive.

By reaching a clear subconclusion, LuAnn has completed the file on the question she had asked in that section of the paper, and she closes it. Now the way is clear for her to go on to the next question. But the file remains accessible, ready to use when she needs it for her comprehensive conclusion.

Subconclusions Provide the Basis for Conclusion

When you have completed each of the major sections of your paper, bring together all of your subconclusions into a *summary*. Because each subconclusion represents closure on one criterion, you no longer need to reexamine evidence on other levels of the taxonomy of information. When you weigh your subconclusions against their priority as criteria in your question, you will be ready to reach your final conclusion.

Paula's Log, Entry #44

    I just handed in my first complete draft. I finished printing it just before class, and I didn't have time to do my log entry. I meet with the teacher to go over it on Tuesday. Until then, I'm on vacation from that [expletive, expletive] paper. What a relief.

Examine the summary and conclusion sections of each of the sample papers. Notice that the summary in each case is simply a restatement of the subconclusions, a reminder of what had been established in each of the subsections. After the summary review of the subconclusions, reaching the overall conclusion is simply a matter of adding it all up into a clear conclusion.

Remember, however, that your overall conclusion should be a qualified conclusion if that's what the evidence reveals. "Clear" does not always mean "definite."

BENCH NOTES: REACH CONCLUSIONS

SUMMARY

The subconclusions and the final conclusion come directly out of the evidence preceding them. This is your opportunity to examine your paper to make sure all the elements of the paper fit together. Wherever necessary, rewrite so that your readers can see clearly how all of the parts relate to each other and to your central question.

ESTIMATED TIME NEEDED

If you have been keeping up with the earlier work, it should take you only about a half-hour to check your subconclusions and write your final conclusion.

KEY TERMS

Conclusion: The comprehensive, evaluation level decision which culminates the written presentation of the research. The answer to the overall research question.

Subconclusion: Intermediate, evaluation level judgments reached at the end of each major section of the research. The answer to one of the "criterion based" subquestions.

Summary: A recapitulation of all of the subconclusions.

WRITE THE LEAD

"Why have you put the chapter on introductions so close to the end of the book?" my daughter, a college senior, asked me as she glanced over the manuscript and chapter outline. "Shouldn't it be one of the first chapters?" I hope that you have been wondering, too, because I have some answers ready.

Traditionally, the introduction provides the reader a preview of the text, placing what follows in context, introducing the central questions or concepts. For most writers, the ground around the text will be better illuminated after they have completed their research and most of their writing. Understanding of the project's essential unifying elements grows as the writer works through the process. This is especially true in research writing because all good research begins with questions. You didn't know the answer to your question when you began. Now you do. Now you are ready to complete your introduction.

If we define "introduction" more broadly to include all of the parts of the text which provide background information, you have already written most of the introductory material for your paper—the givens and the criteria. In this chapter, however, I'd like to have you concentrate on the opening paragraph or paragraphs (the "lead") where you introduce your readers to the essential drama of your paper.

An effective lead packs a full load of information. It's easy to see why "getting started" is the hardest part if you begin there. In a good introduction, you want to acknowledge your audiences, and place yourself in a clear relationship to them—Who will read this? What is my relationship to him, her, them? In the jargon of composition research this is called "identifying with your discourse communities," or "situating discourse."

Your lead should provide a preview of what's to come, not only of the content, but of possible conflicts, of personalities involved, of the scene of action. In short, you want to generate interest in the dramatic elements of your research. You want your audience to share with you the excitement of discovery, the stimulus of not knowing the answer until you have struggled through the process. Can you get all of that into your lead? Yes, but only now that you have completed the rest of your paper.

Have you been keeping in mind your audiences—everyone who has a special interest in the outcome of your question (family, friends, employers), the other members of class, and your teacher? When you began your paper, you probably knew little more about your question than any of these people. All you had was your question. Now you have become an expert. You have collected and processed evidence, and you can speak with voice of an expert, an authoritative voice.

When Paula began her paper she prefaced every comment about varsity track in college with, "I really don't know much about this, but. . . ." By the time she completed her research, however, she began to speak about her topic with much more authority, citing evidence and sources. Because she gained confidence in her right to assert a position, her audiences responded. Her classmates deferred to her on questions about the health hazards of running. According to Paula's process log, even her grandmother, who had been absolutely against her going out for track, seemed to listen to her with more respect.

Paula's developing confidence in her own voice as an expert permitted her to relate to all three of her audiences in essentially the same way. As her teacher, I became just another reader, interested more in the results of her research than in what grade I'd have to give the project. Now that you are an expert on your question, I hope the same thing happens to you. You have put in hours of work to become informed. Use the authoritative voice you have earned through your research.

The Traditional Inverted Triangle

The textbook I used in 1960 as a college freshman recommended only one form of introduction for academic and research writing—the inverted triangle. When you use the inverted triangle to open your paper, you begin with very general statements about background or context, and then you work toward the narrow end of the triangle by making each sentence more and more specific until you arrive at the last sentence of the introduction—your thesis statement, central idea, or unifying question.

If Paula had used this kind of opening for her paper, it might have looked like this:

> Very likely since the beginning of human history, people have run to escape their enemies and to pursue animals for food. Children seem to be running all of the time, just for fun. The ability to run fast is an important skill in many games, and racing was probably among the first of competitive sports. Competitive running has been shaped into races as long as fifty kilometers or more, and as short as 100 meters. Everyone knows about the thousands who run in the Boston Marathon, but almost every community over 20,000 now sponsors a marathon, a 10K race, or a Tin Man Triathlon. Joggers of both sexes run through every park and up and down every lane in the country. . . . Especially in schools, track for women has progressed dramatically in the last ten years, both in high schools and colleges. I myself ran the 100-meter and 200-meter races in interscholastic competition in high school. Now I am trying to decide if I should try out for track in college.

This exaggerated example illustrates the principle. It is a variation of a sequence my brother and I used to repeat as children lying on the grass on a summer evening looking up at the stars: "The Milky Way Galaxy, the Sun's solar system, the planet Earth, North America, the United States, Wisconsin, Taylor County, the town of Little Black, our farm, our yard right here." In cinema, an opening like this is called an "establishing shot." It opens with a very wide and inclusive field, often at a great distance. Then the camera zooms, booms, or dollies increasingly closer to the heart of the film's action, establishing both the central character(s) and the larger context.

Alternative Leads

Especially in recent years, film makers and writers often prefer to begin in some other way. Instead of the "funnel" or "establishing shot" approach, many writers begin by establishing a dramatic conflict, by introducing characters, by describing the sensory impressions radiating from a specific place, by introducing a seemingly outlandish assertion, or by pointing out any irony. Scholars have begun to use the techniques of fiction and drama to introduce their scholarly adventures. In journalism, the opening paragraph is called the *lead*. In even the most scholarly journals, you will find articles which begin with interest-grabbing leads.

The sample below by Richard Behm appeared in a publication of the National Council of Teachers of English, *English Education*, a publication read mostly by college faculty who teach students preparing to become English teachers. I wanted you to see it because Richard uses several techniques you might want to try:

You Want A Workshop or a Revival Meetin'?

Richard Behm

Southern Wisconsin has never looked more beautiful than this autumn morning. A blue mist clings to the bottomlands and pastures where Holsteins graze. Maple and aspen leaves ripple in waves of gold and red. The sun spills light down the hillsides. As I drive along, I roll down the window; the air is fresh and clean, tinged with the smell of pine, woodsmoke, and hint of ice.

I am driving to a small town to do an in-service on writing, an offer I accepted after two colleagues turned it down. That should have been my first warning signal. The second signal should have come when I spoke to the administrator in charge of the in-service, an earnest-sounding man who reminded me of my great uncle—an intense gravelly voice, staccato sentences, and a tendency to use lots of intensifiers in his speech. When I first spoke to him on the phone and asked what he wanted me to do, he replied "Anything you want." He proceeded to launch into a sermonette on what it was he <u>actually</u> wanted.

"I want a really rousing speech. A real barn burner. Something to get the old adrenalin flowing. A real motivator. Maybe something with some patriotism. And don't forget spelling. Spelling's a real problem with us." As so it went. The decline in morals in today's youth. Hippies (this was in 1982). The failure to teach grammar. The increase in teenage pregnancies. He implied a cause-effect relationship between the last two.

Then and there I should have had the wit to beg off as my colleagues had done before me. He didn't want an in-service; he wanted a tent revival.

(<u>English Education</u>, Vol. 17 No. 1, February 1985, page 39.)

Remember Your "Discourse Community"

Writing for *English Education,* Professor Behm had a clear idea of who his audience would be. By using key words like "in-service," and "colleagues," and familiar phrases like "administrator in charge of in-service," and "tendency to use lots of intensifiers," in the second paragraph, he introduces a context which he knew would be familiar and interesting to his "discourse community." Without specifically addressing them, he has shown his audience that he is one of them.

Look over the list of people you expect to be in your audiences, both primary and secondary. Keep them in mind now, as you write your lead, and throughout the drafting and revision process.

Set the Scene

Professor Behm devotes his first paragraph to "setting a scene." He establishes the scene by calling on the specific sensory impressions he experienced in the place. Notice especially his use of *specific* detail. The animals are not "cows"; they are "holsteins." The plants are not "trees"; they are "Maple and Aspen." His readers see the "blue mist," the "waves of gold and red," and the sun spilling light. We feel the air. We smell "the pine and the woodsmoke."

Paula also sets a scene to open her paper—a track meet, the lane lines, the starting blocks, the people in the crowd, the voice of the starter and then the crack of the pistol. Her readers get an immediate sense of being in a specific place.

If you begin with a specific place, however, you need to select a place which illustrates the tension imbedded in the questions you deal with in the text of your paper. The details of the place you describe become important to us when we realize that a drama is underway. Richard Behm chooses the highway as his place—on his way to an inservice he would like to be a workshop, but which the administrator in charge would like to be a "Revival Meetin'." Paula chooses the track as her place—lining up to start a 100-meter race, or sitting in the bleachers watching.

Think through your question and select a place where the tensions come together, a place where you can not resist thinking about your question, a place where dramatic events relating to your question are likely to happen.

Introduce Dramatic Action

For Richard, the pleasure of the early autumn morning is disturbed by his realization that the road he travels takes him directly to confrontation. He shows us the "warning signals" in the second paragraph. Paula begins with the drama inherent in the final seconds before a race, and she augments the tension by showing us the larger drama going on in the heart and mind of the woman who could be either the runner or the spectator.

Reveal Incongruities

The first sentence of LuAnn's paper introduces an incongruity: "I am forty-five years of age and a college freshman, a difficult but interesting situation to be in after having been employed as a registered nurse for the past twenty-four years." Sometimes this kind of lead is called a "hook," because the incongruity grabs our interest. Like other kinds of dramatic action, the hook establishes conflict. From LuAnn's lead we get an immediate image of the tension experienced by someone old enough to be the mother of most other students in her class. She shows us the stress which results from going from a position of responsibility and authority back to the humbling status of student.

Introduce Characters

Dramatic action often begins with conflict between people. Your audience will respond with more concentrated interest if you make the characters sharp in outline and memorable. In his opening paragraphs, Richard Behm introduces the "administrator in charge of in-service." By using vivid description and dialogue, Professor Behm sets up the conflict between his idea of an in-service and the administrator's ideas. Sometimes this technique is called a *character throw* because you quickly toss the character into the conflict by describing his appearance, his voice, his opinions. Dialogue works especially well for a quick character throw.

Paula's Log, Entry #45

The idea for my lead came to me last night when I went with Jane to see the university production of Fiddler on the Roof. At least six times during the play Jane said, "Oh, it looks like so much fun. Why didn't I try out. I know I would have been a great Hodel." Finally, I had to remind her how many times over the last six weeks she had said she was grateful she wasn't in the play because rehearsals take up so much time. Watching her, I began to wonder how I would feel sitting in the stands during a track meet.

Connect the Lead to the Text

Remember the purpose for the lead. You want to attract readers' attention, but you want their attention to be on the questions you address in your paper. The drama you present, the incongruities you reveal, the characters you throw—whatever you use should "lead" the audience into the central issues in your text.

Create Leads for Subsections

A long paper works in cycles. Within the single large cycle of introduction, body, and conclusion, several smaller cycles rotate, each with its own beginning, development, and conclusion. Though related to the whole, each of these smaller sections will pull more weight if provided with its own lead. The principles are the same: attract the attention of your readers to the questions you address in the section. Present a setting, a drama, a character, an incongruity, but do it on a slightly smaller scale so that you do not steal the show from the center ring.

BENCH NOTES: WRITE THE LEAD

SUMMARY

Many writers save the lead and sometimes their entire introduction for last. By waiting until the rest of their text is almost complete, they insure themselves of knowing more firmly what they want to say in the introduction.

By now you have become an expert on your topic. You speak with an authoritative voice, and your discourse community will respond to your lead with interest and respect.

Help them into your text by providing a lead with drama in it—describe action, throw a character, reveal an incongruity, use dialogue. Give your research a human context.

ESTIMATED TIME NEEDED

Expect to spend about a half hour on pre-writing—jotting down possibilities, searching your memory for a moment or situation which encapsulates the conflict in your question. After that, you will be able to draft your lead in slightly less than an hour.

PRACTICE AND APPLICATIONS

After you complete the first draft of your lead, try three more. If you used dialogue the first time, try a character throw this time. Then try an ironic or incongruent statement, or a dramatic situation.

KEY TERMS

Lead: Opening paragraph or two which draws the audience into the text of the paper by using techniques drawn from narrative writing.

EDIT AND POLISH

On a Wednesday morning, in the small town where I grew up, if you happened to walk anywhere near the newspaper office, you could get your weekly news early. The paper went to press on late Wednesday afternoon in order to be ready first thing Thursday morning, so Frank, the editor, spent Wednesday morning proofreading the final copy. He had an interesting technique. He read the entire paper in a loud, ringing tenor voice—even the advertisements—audible blocks away.

He claimed it was the only way he could stay awake reading all that dull stuff. Since he was the one who had written most of it, people laughed and thought he was making a joke on himself. I'm convinced it was no joke. As the only person in the newspaper staff who worked with copy, he had to write it, revise it, edit it, lay it out, proof it, and then proof it again. No matter how interesting he thought his articles were on first draft, by the fifth reading, I imagine he truly did find it pretty dull stuff.

I suspect you understand Frank's difficulties. You have been working with your paper for several weeks and you probably think of it as "finished." Some sections you may have read over five times or more. From here on, you have to fight boredom and fatigue, but the efforts you make now can have a tremendous effect on the quality of your paper. Adopt, adapt, or create strategies like the one Frank used with his newspaper to keep alert and on task.

These are some of the basics: Schedule enough time, begin when you are well rested, get as much help as possible, work systematically through a checklist, and put it all together in an appropriate package.

Paula's Log, Entry #47

I am so sick of this paper. I don't ever want to see it again.

Arrive Early

If you have been doing each step of your project on schedule, you have already engaged this strategy. If you haven't been keeping up, it's too late to "arrive early" on this paper, but keep this important strategy in mind for future projects. You absolutely must schedule adequate time for proofreading and editing. Your paper is not "finished" until you have carefully checked to see if your work is complete, accurate, and in the appropriate format. Those still writing on the night before the due date have abandoned their opportunities to edit and proofread.

Start Fresh

Schedule at least two days between the time you complete your penultimate draft and the beginning of your proofreading and final edit. During those two days, don't even look at or think about your project. Then you can come back to it with at least slightly renewed, fresh eyes.

Put a fresh ribbon in your typewriter or your printer, and begin your final edit and proofreading session when you are well rested. This stage requires freshness and concentration. It works best if you can complete this step of the process in one session, so schedule a block of time at least two hours long.

Get Help—People

Have someone help you—an equally well-rested, sympathetic, intelligent person, if possible. Ask him or her either to search for specific problems on your checklist, or to read the paper carefully from beginning to end, identifying probable problems.

Keep in mind that this is your paper, however, and that not even the best proofreader is infallible. Do not give up ownership. The final decision about every detail should remain in your hands.

Get Help—Machines

If you have used computer software to prepare your paper, take advantage now of any special features it offers—spell checkers, text analysis, "fault finders." Play with the format, the margins, the headings. Use the machine to help you get your paper just the way you want it. Please remember, however, that the best machines do not substitute for a careful human eye.

Work Systematically

You will be less likely to overlook mistakes if you work systematically through a checklist. When you read your paper now, you no longer need to look at the accuracy of information, the development of the paragraphs, or the coherence of the ideas. Now you need to examine small details. That kind of work is easier if you can isolate a specific kind of detail—page numbers, for example—and concentrate on that kind only. When you have assured yourself that the page numbers are accurate, you can go on to quotation marks. You can develop your own checklist or use one of the several already available. My students use this checklist:

EDITING CHECKLIST

HAVE I INCLUDED ALL OF THE REQUIRED PARTS?

- ☐ Title page?
- ☐ Full sentence outline?
- ☐ Text with division headings?
- ☐ Annotated Works Cited Page and Works Consulted Page?
- ☐ Preliminary Drafts and other working materials?

HAVE I PROVIDED APPROPRIATE DOCUMENTATION?

- ☐ Introduce borrowed material in the text?
- ☐ Parenthetical citations where needed?
- ☐ Quotation marks where needed?
- ☐ Legitimate use of summary and paraphrase?
- ☐ Format of Works pages complete and consistent?

DO ALL OF MY PUNCTUATION MARKS DO WHAT I WANT THEM TO DO?

- ☐ Commas, semi-colons?
- ☐ Dashes, colons, parentheses?
- ☐ Periods, question marks, exclamations?
- ☐ Quotation marks, possessives?
- ☐ Italics, underlinings, bold print?
- ☐ Upper and lower case?

ARE MY SENTENCES CLEAR?

☐ No fragments?
☐ No run-ons?
☐ No misplaced or dangling modifiers?
☐ Parallel elements grammatically parallel?
☐ Pronoun references clear?
☐ All elements in agreement?
☐ Tenses and moods consistent?

ARE MY SENTENCES STRONG?

☐ Primarily active voice?
☐ Verbs show action?
☐ Forms of the verb, "to be," limited?
☐ Variety in the use of subordinators?
☐ Sentences linked to one another by references?
☐ Adjectives and adverbs carefully distributed?
☐ Sentences pass the "Read Aloud" test?

IS THE DICTION PRECISE AND THE USAGE APPROPRIATE?

☐ Exactly right word choice?
☐ Appropriate level of usage?
☐ Standard inflections?
☐ The most specific words possible?
☐ Unnecessary jargon avoided?
☐ Consistent tone?

DOES EVERYTHING FOLLOW THE FORMAT GUIDELINES?

☐ All spelling/typographical errors corrected?
☐ Typewriter or printer ribbon dark enough?
☐ Consistent spacing for text, titles and headings?
☐ Margins at specified width?
☐ Page numbers complete and in order?
☐ All stray marks removed?
☐ Check the spelling of your teacher's name?
☐ Appropriate cover, folder, or fastenings?

Paula's Log, Entry # 48

I am sitting here in the computer lab watching the printer hammer out the final draft of my paper. I'm wondering if I should have spent the money to have it printed on the laser-jet printer (1$ per page). I put a new ribbon in the "near-letter quality" printer and it looks pretty good, but Jane had hers done on a laser-jet and it looks GREAT.

Do Not Over or Under Dress

I once received an essay about the architecture of Notre Dame Cathedral in Paris. The text of the paper did not address the assignment, it was ridiculously sloppy and vapid, and most of it was poorly handled borrowed material. But the cover! The cover was an exquisite ink drawing of a gargoyle. How could I evaluate such a paper?

I had not asked for a cover; I had asked for a title page. I had to ignore the beauty of the cover and give the paper an ''F'' on the basis of the work which had been assigned. The author of the paper thought that he would compensate for the weakness of his paper by putting on a special cover. It didn't work.

Choose a format appropriate to the assignment. A three-dollar cover will not hide a fifty-cent paper. On the other hand, it's silly to extend yourself on a million dollar paper and then leave it naked. I remember especially a paper on Thoreau's journals. The paper was brilliant, exquisitely written, but it had no title page, no page numbers, and the tractor-feed margins had not been removed. That paper deserved better.

Ask your teacher how he or she would like to receive your paper. I ask my students to submit their research papers in a simple pocket folder, the final draft in one side pocket, and earlier drafts and other materials in the other side. The paper stays together, but I can take it out and turn the pages to read it.

On Time

Have your paper ready and deliver it exactly when you have been asked to deliver it. That way your paper will stay together with the others in class as your teacher reads them and records his or her evaluation. If you ask for an extension, remember that you are asking for a privilege others in class have been denied. Unless you have suffered a serious unforeseeable emergency, your paper will be in on time.

BENCH NOTES: EDIT AND POLISH

SUMMARY

Imagine that you have stayed up late to finish your paper by the deadline. You will be handing it in in five minutes and you glance at the title page. The teacher's name is misspelled.

To avoid such a situation (or much worse), schedule your work so that you have at least three days left to edit and polish. Tackle the job when you are fresh and alert. Get someone to read it through for you. Read it aloud to yourself. If you can, use a spell checker and other software designed to help you edit. Work systematically through a checklist.

Dress the paper in an appropriate format and deliver it exactly on time.

BENCH NOTES *continued*

ESTIMATED TIME NEEDED

If you have no major revisions and only a few minor problems, you will be able to complete your editing in less than two hours of concentrated work. If you have major glitches or many little problems to correct, you might need as much as four hours, especially if you have not been using a computer.

PRACTICE AND APPLICATION

Have you found any typographical or spelling errors in this textbook? Have I made mistakes in any of the areas reviewed on the checklist? If you locate any, please send me a note identifying the error and the page where you found it. I'll make the correction for the next edition. Send your suggestions to Tim Hirsch, care of the publisher.

CHAPTER SIX

FOLLOW THROUGH

EVALUATION

OTHER APPLICATIONS

EVALUATION

When English teachers are asked what they like least about teaching composition, they always put "grading papers" at the top of the list. Reading and evaluating student work gobbles an enormous amount of time. Our eyes blur and our brains suffer brown-out. Most painful of all, our psyches become numb from the anxiety generated by having to put grades on your work. Sometimes it's no fun for you either.

Like it or not, however, our schools will continue to require teachers to evaluate student work. Experts in assessment continue to search for better ways to measure student performance in writing, but it is a complex and sometimes mysterious process. For the kind of project you are doing this semester, at least three approaches to evaluation are possible. First, you instructor could wait until your paper is complete and evaluate only the final draft. This kind of assessment evaluates the *finished product*. If your teacher uses this approach, he or she can do it in one of two basic ways—*holistically,* or by the examination of *primary traits*. As an alternative to evaluating your finished product, your teacher can evaluate the way you perform each of the steps in *the process*. Most teachers will use a combination of these approaches.

When teachers choose to base their assessment mostly on an evaluation of your finished product, they often use a holistic approach. As the first step in this approach, the teacher reads quickly through the entire set of papers to identify the best paper, the worst paper, and one somewhere in the middle. These three papers become the *anchor papers*. Then the teacher carefully reads each paper again, judging it against the anchor papers. Those papers which are as good as (or nearly as good as) the "best" paper receive the highest rating. Those similar to the worst receive the lowest ratings. Those somewhere in the middle receive one of three possible "middle" ratings. In each case, the project receives only one overall grade.

In general, the holistic evaluation of finished products by trained evaluators has remarkable reliability. If the papers are evaluated holistically again, even by a different evaluator, there is a high probability that the results will be the same. For that reason, holistic evaluations are used in national, statewide, or school district assessments.

Holistic evaluation has limitations, however, for use in a classroom situation. Holistic evaluation provides no information to students about what they did wrong or right, about what they can do to improve, or about what criteria were used to arrive at the rating attached to their work.

Teachers generally limit the use of holistic evaluation to an occasional assignment or to essay examinations. Most also modify the holistic approach by including marginal or end comments and by using some elements of primary trait scoring.

Primary trait evaluation of writing also uses a finished product. Unlike unmodified holistic scoring, however, primary trait evaluation begins with an established set of characteristics ("traits") the evaluator expects to find in the finished product—a clear central idea, effective paragraphs, conventional usage and syntax—whatever the evaluator wants to emphasize. Using this approach, each "trait" in the finished work is assessed and assigned a "grade." Sometimes important elements are weighted more heavily in the calculation of the composite grade. Sometimes the individual grades for each trait remain discrete and no composite score is determined.

Primary trait evaluation works well in composition classes. By identifying important primary traits, both students and teachers focus attention on the characteristics of good writing. An evaluation based on the examination of primary traits helps students see more clearly any weaknesses in their writing, and thus, they see with more confidence what they have to do to improve their writing.

Teachers who evaluate the *process* do not wait for the completed product. They examine and rate the performance of each student in each step of the process. This approach works especially well when the final product comes only after the successful completion of many complex steps. By evaluating each step in the process, teachers help students see that careful work on each step is the most certain route to a completed product of high quality.

Each teacher works with a unique group of students, a one-of-a-kind teaching situation, and beliefs about evaluation earned through experience and training. Using adaptations and combinations, they will find the assessment tools which work for them. If your teacher uses another evaluation instrument for your paper, you may still use the examples which follow to perform self-assessment. Evaluation Form One is designed to evaluate performance during the research process. Evaluation Form Two is designed to evaluate the primary traits of a completed paper.

Evaluation Form One
Evaluation of Steps in the Research Process

	On Time	Thorough	Resourceful
SELECT QUESTION Due date: _____ Ready by: _____	1 2 3 4 5	1 2 3 4 5	1 2 3 4 5
ESTABLISH GIVENS Due date: _____ Ready by: _____	1 2 3 4 5	1 2 3 4 5	1 2 3 4 5
IDENTIFY CRITERIA Due date: _____ Ready by: _____	1 2 3 4 5	1 2 3 4 5	1 2 3 4 5
DEVELOP AN OUTLINE OF QUESTIONS Due date: _____ Ready by: _____	1 2 3 4 5	1 2 3 4 5	1 2 3 4 5
KEY THE OUTLINE FOR INFORMATION NEEDS Due date: _____ Ready by: _____	1 2 3 4 5	1 2 3 4 5	1 2 3 4 5
IDENTIFY SOURCES—INDEX BASED SEARCH Due date: _____ Ready by: _____	1 2 3 4 5	1 2 3 4 5	1 2 3 4 5
SELECT THE MOST VALID AND RELIABLE SOURCES Due date: _____ Ready by: _____	1 2 3 4 5	1 2 3 4 5	1 2 3 4 5
SUPPLEMENT WITH REFERRALS Due date: _____ Ready by: _____	1 2 3 4 5	1 2 3 4 5	1 2 3 4 5
TAKE NOTES Due date: _____ Ready by: _____	1 2 3 4 5	1 2 3 4 5	1 2 3 4 5
WRITE THE FIRST DRAFT Due date: _____ Ready by: _____	1 2 3 4 5	1 2 3 4 5	1 2 3 4 5
DELINEATE EVIDENCE LEVELS Due date: _____ Ready by: _____	1 2 3 4 5	1 2 3 4 5	1 2 3 4 5
INTRODUCE BORROWED MATERIAL Due date: _____ Ready by: _____	1 2 3 4 5	1 2 3 4 5	1 2 3 4 5
PREPARE WORKS CITED/WORKS CONSULTED Due date: _____ Ready by: _____	1 2 3 4 5	1 2 3 4 5	1 2 3 4 5
REACH CONCLUSIONS Due date: _____ Ready by: _____	1 2 3 4 5	1 2 3 4 5	1 2 3 4 5

Evaluation Form One
Evaluation of Steps in the Research Process

	On Time	Thorough	Resourceful
CREATE A LEAD Due date: _____ Ready by: _____	1 2 3 4 5	1 2 3 4 5	1 2 3 4 5
PROVIDE A COMPLETE ATTRACTIVE PACKAGE Due date: _____ Ready by: _____	1 2 3 4 5	1 2 3 4 5	1 2 3 4 5

Explanation of Numbers on Scale: 1 = failing
2 = inadequate
3 = acceptable
4 = good
5 = excellent

Explanation of Evaluation Criteria

Your work on each of these steps will be evaluated as failing, inadequate, acceptable, good, and excellent, according to the following criteria: On Schedule? Thorough? Resourceful?

The first of these criteria, *on schedule,* is the only one which can not be modified by additional or revision work. If you have the work completed on time, your rating on this criterion will be "excellent." If you have most of it done except for one little fragment, your ranking will be "good." The more you have yet to do, the lower the ranking. If you are uncertain about due dates, check with your teacher or check your class schedule. No excuses of any kind will be considered.

For the remaining criteria, you have an opportunity to improve your ranking. For example, if your rating on thoroughness is inadequate, you may ask for a reassessment when you have done a more thorough job. Each day you go beyond the scheduled date for initial assessment, however, the more rigorous become the assessment standards. For example, if your index-based search is rated "inadequate," and the day after the initial assessment you are ready for a reassessment, your chances for a higher rating are much better than they would be if you took three weeks. In short, remedy any deficiencies as soon as possible.

To score well on *thoroughness,* do everything you possibly can to complete every detail. Anticipate as much as you can what else you might be expected to do. Think of yourself as one of the best students in class, and do everything you think the other "best" students will do in order to be thorough.

To be thorough, take care with details. Be patient and willing to spend extra effort if necessary to make your work outstanding.

The research process requires the use of many resources for each stage of the process. To do well on the criterion of *resourcefulness,* you will be expected to use the available resources with skill and precision. If you do not know how to use a certain tool, you will teach yourself or find someone to teach you. You will be inventive in finding new tools and using old ones in new ways. To be resourceful, you need to "work smart," be clever, use your intelligence. Again, ask yourself what the best students in class will do. If you find it impossible to think of yourself as among them, commit yourself to make up for it by scrambling a little harder.

At any time, if you do not understand why your work was rated as it was, contact your teacher. Do not brood in silence. This evaluation instrument is intended to help you learn the research process, never to punish.

Evaluation Form Two

Name ————————————————————

A. Selection and Clarification of the Question
> Level of significance to self and/or society
> Clarity of the question
> Clarity of the conclusion
> Quality of insights represented in the question

B. Approach to the Question
> Organization of the paper
> Outline
> Delineation of evidence levels
> Clarity of criteria

C. Research
> Thoroughness of the search
> Validity of the sources
> Honesty of transcription
> Balance among sources

D. Quality of the Writing
> Paragraphs (ordered, developed, unified)
> Sentences (coherent, standard syntax, variety)
> Diction (Standard usage, precise)
> Style (general character)

E. Format and Editing
> Title page, outline margins, documentation forms, works cited
> Spelling, typing, punctuation
> Overall appearance
> Assigned sequence (Did you have each step completed on time?)

COMMENTS:

Paula's Log, Entry # 50

Filled out the "Evaluation Sheet" for my paper. I gave it an "A" in every category. Is that wishful thinking, over confidence? In two minutes I hand it in. I feel both pride and relief.

BENCH NOTES: EVALUATIONS

SUMMARY

I enjoy reading my students' work, but I don't like giving it a grade. Like it or not, however, it's my job and I endorse its purposes. I hope you do too.

Teachers of writing can examine and grade only the final product, or they can observe the writing in process and assess progress through the writing stages. If they evaluate the finished product, they may use a holistic approach, or a primary trait approach.

If you understand how your work will be evaluated, you should be able to improve your writing and get a better grade besides.

ESTIMATED TIME REQUIRED

To complete an evaluation of your own paper, you will need approximately one half-hour.

PRACTICE AND APPLICATION

Using Evaluation Form Two, grade one of the three sample papers.

KEY TERMS

Primary Trait: An evaluation strategy during which the evaluator examines specific components of the work and assigns a score for each "trait."

Holistic: An evaluation strategy designed to consider the work as an entity. Generally most valid if the work evaluated is one of a group.

OTHER APPLICATIONS

Congratulations! Once you have arrived at this section, you have completed the research paper assignment for this class, and you are ready to see now what, if anything, all of your hard work has to do with the rest of your life—"the real world" as some folks like to call it. For the class assignment, I encouraged you to follow exactly the steps of the process outlined in this text. Now that you have completed this class exercise, however, I will encourage you to be flexible and creative in your application of the process to other situations. I hope you will remember the essentials—begin with questions, find hard evidence, think the evidence through the levels, give credit to your sources and guidance to your readers—but I also want you to make thorough use of the tools you have developed. I hope you will apply what you have learned to other personal questions, to other academic exercises, to financial questions, to literary questions, to political questions, to business questions, to every dimension of your life. I hope the idea of research becomes a habit of thought for you, and the practice of research a habit of action.

Other Personal Questions

Most of you used the research opportunity provided you by this class to answer a personal question. Please continue. Use the tools you have developed to make your life the best life possible for you. You won't develop every little decision into a full-blown research project, of course.

Some will get fifteen minutes of research in the public library, and others might get three years of intensive searching among hundreds of sources. Judge each question on its importance to you, but research should be the first impulse for any troublesome, unanswered questions.

Other Academic Questions

Most of you will be writing "term" papers or "research" papers for other courses while you are in school. Sometimes the instructor will provide you with very specific assignments and/or guidelines. If his or her requirements preclude use of the process you have learned this semester (or a variation), remember that your first responsibility—and the most certain route to success—is to satisfy the stated requirements of the assignment. In most cases, however, your instructor will give you considerable freedom to define your own project. Remember too, that the research process stretches greatly without snapping.

Let's begin with one specific example (hundreds are possible). Let's imagine that you are in a psychology class—"The Psychology of Early Childhood." The teacher asks you to do a nine-page term paper on any aspect of child care, infant through five-years old. You could do your paper on the question, "Which of the four child-care centers near the university provide the best psychological environment for two-year-old children?"

Note that by restricting the question to four centers, and to two-year olds, we have already limited and shaped the question. Since this is a psychology class, we have also limited the question to the "psychological" environment and will include the physical environment only so far as it affects the psychological. If you feel the question remains too general, we could further restrict the questions by identifying one, two, or three hypothetical children so that we can be more specific in our description of the givens. The criteria for your paper will come directly out of your course materials—What factors are needed for the psychological well being of two year old children? The answer to that question becomes the list of criteria, and the criteria shape the outline of your research and your final paper.

Perhaps the class is, "The Psychology of Aging." Your paper could examine the facilities available for the housing and extended care of stroke victims. Again, you would need to shape and limit the givens, and the criteria would come directly out of class materials. Try making up suitable questions for the classes you are in now, even if you have not been assigned a long paper. I think you will be surprised to find out how easy it is. If you have trouble, ask your instructor to help you apply what you have learned in his or her class to the new academic assignment. In a business class, you might use the strategy you learned this semester to select among marketing strategies, among investments, among locations for the building of a retail store or factory. In computer science, you might use the strategy to select hardware, software, or a system for a specific application. In a political science class you might use the strategy to assess political candidates, specific policies, or political actions. In every case, remember that the strategy you learned this semester is adaptable; the only essential ingredients are that you begin with questions, that you try to answer those questions with hard evidence, and that you do your own thinking.

The approach you learned works well for a variety of questions about literature or language. For example, if you have ever studied the poetry of Emily Dickinson, you probably remember that only six of her poems were published during her lifetime. These six poems were altered by her editors before they appeared in print. Most readers of Dickinson's poetry today prefer her original versions to the edited versions. We often assume that her poetry was "ahead of its time," and that the conventions of her time were inferior to those which came later. You might wonder, however, to what degree the editors' judgments were true reflections of the poetic traditions of the 1860s. If you were curious about it, you could write on the question: "Are the poems which Emily Dickinson presented for publication, or the edited versions which appeared in print, more in tune with the poetic conventions of the 1860s?"

To answer such a question, follow the same procedure as for more personal questions:

a) Begin with a question,

b) establish the givens,

c) identify the relevant criteria, and

d) work through the evidence levels.

Among the givens would be a precise statement of exactly what happened to these six poems. You would show the versions Emily presented for publication, and the versions which eventually appeared in print. Also among the givens would be a description of the poetic conventions of the time.

The criteria grow out of the givens and are shaped into questions. For example, after examining the available critical analyses about 19th-century prosody, you could establish the 1862 conventions for meter, for rhyme, for other poetic devices, for appropriate poetic subject matter. In your outline of questions you would include such questions as: "Do the original or the edited poems best satisfy the 1862 poetic conventions for rhyme?"

In an Introduction to Literature class, your instructor might ask you whether James' "The Jolly Corner" is a better choice for the course anthology than his "The Turn of the Screw." How would you approach a question like that? You establish the givens, articulate the criteria you are going to use, and then look for hard evidence in the text itself (and in secondary sources if your criteria include critical acclaim and/or popularity). Again, the criteria come directly out of class materials—elements of the short story. You will have spent class time considering what kind of action works well in short stories, what kind of characterization, what kind of language, what kind of thematic and symbolic elements. Class discussions and your other experiences with literature will provide you with your criteria.

Try a little more complex question: Using Sarah Orne Jewett's story ''A White Heron'' and Willa Cather's ''Neigbor Rosicky,'' examine the idea of innocence in American Literature. What can you do with that? Again, we begin with questions: What is meant by ''innocence,'' especially in the context of American Literature? What do we know about the authors? What criteria can we establish as evidence of the ''innocence'' theme (a character who is free from evil deeds or intentions, a character who trusts—sometimes too much—a character attracted to ''nature'' and a free, simple social life rather than a sophisticated formal social life)? Once we have established our criteria, we can examine both stories for hard evidence. Specifically what does Sylvia (the central character in Jewett's story) do? What does she say? What does she think? What does Rosicky do? What does he say? What does he think?

Obviously, not all the writing you do will be shaped like the paper you did using the text. But each time you begin a long writing project, please consider the basics: What questions do I want answered? What are the givens? What are the important criteria which must be considered? What is the relevant hard evidence? What steps in the taxonomy of information do I need to take? I guarantee the time you devote to asking such questions will help you no matter what form your final project takes.

Community Decisions

Two years ago, Altoona, Wisconsin, a nearby town of about four thousand people decided to build a new outdoor swimming pool (see ''Practice and Application'' exercises in Chapter Two). The City Council asked the city Director of Parks and Recreation to recommend which of the five properties then available for the pool would be best. One of my students worked as an assistant to the Director, and because he needed a topic for his research paper, he volunteered to prepare the recommendation. He learned that the city planned to use updated plans for a pool they had considered building ten years earlier, so the design of the pool was a ''given.'' The amount of money available for landscaping, parking lot, and other site improvements was also a given. The five possible locations were properties already owned by the city, and no others would be considered.

After he had defined the ''givens,'' he conferred with the Director and the Council ''Pool'' Committee, and he searched the libraries for printed information which would help him establish the criteria he should examine. He decided on ''Safe Access,'' ''Convenient Access,'' ''Proximity to other Related Recreational Facilities,'' ''Parking,'' ''Access to Utilities,'' ''Compatibility with Neighborhood,'' and ''Appearance.'' Although his paper turned out to be three times as long as he needed for our class assignment, he was rewarded by the response of the Director of Parks and Recreation, and by the City Council's decision to follow his recommendation. He confessed to me that whenever he passes the new pool, he thinks to himself, "I was the one who decided where it should be." When he wrote the paper, he was "undecided" about his career; now he plans to be a civil engineer.

Every community (or business, institution, church, organization) needs a systematic way to reach decisions. If you are able to recommend a calm, rational process, one which lays open its logic to scrutiny, you will provide valuable service. Right now in my community, a city of fifty thousand, controversy rages about whether to build a new bridge across the river at point X, Y, or Z. We can't decide what to do with a beautiful but useless old railroad depot which stands where someone wants a parking lot. A group of boosters would like to bring a minor league baseball team to town. All of these problems grow closer to solution when the issues are approached as questions, when we establish what we know and what is unlikely to change, what we think are the important factors (criteria) to take into account as we make the decision. Then we need as much relevant information as close to hard evidence as possible. The solutions will emerge.

BENCH NOTES: OTHER APPLICATIONS

SUMMARY

Although you cannot plan and control every dimension of your life, you now have a strategy for research you can use when you want to. Each time you face a decision, ask yourself, "Will my work or my life be better if I use research to answer this question?" If the answer is, "yes," apply the strategies you have learned.

CHAPTER SEVEN

SAMPLE PAPERS

PAULA WEILER'S PAPER

LUANN FLETCHER'S PAPER

ELIZABETH RYAN'S PAPER

A Runner's Question

A Documented Paper
by
Paula Weiler

Presented to
Tim Hirsch
English Composition 110

on

November 21, 1988

Outline of Contents

THESIS QUESTION: Should I try out for the varsity track team in the Spring or should I continue to run only for recreation?

   I. Introduction

       A. Why is this question important to me?

       B. What are the "givens"?

       C. What "criteria" are important to me?

  II. Are my skills and aptitudes in track good enough to make the team and compete on the intercollegiate level, or are they more suitable for recreational running only?

       A. What are the record, average, and minimal performance levels needed to compete in the conference?

       B. What were my best, average, and worst performances in high school?

       C. Is there any reason to think I might improve?

       D. Subconclusion: Will I be good enough?

 III. How will my health be affected if I run competitively rather than for recreation only?

       A. What are the possible health affects of running for recreation only?

          1. How will it affect my health while I'm doing it?

          2. How will it affect my health later in my life?

       B. What are the possible health affects of running in competition?

          1. How will it affect my health while I'm doing it?

          2. How will it affect my health later in life?

       C. Subconclusion: Which would be best for my health?

  IV. Will I be able to afford the time needed to run competitively?

       A. How much time do I now invest in recreational running and other physical recreation?

       B. How much time will I need to invest in training and competition if make the varsity track team?

       C. Which option leaves me the time I need for other activities, including school work?

       D. Subconclusion: Which will give me the time I need?

V. Will I receive more psychological, emotional, and mental satisfaction from participation in varsity track or from recreational running?

    A. How do I react to the stress of competitive racing?

        1. How do I feel when I win?

        2. How do I feel when I lose?

    B. What are my thoughts and feelings about recreational running?

    C. Subconclusion: Which best satisfies my psychological and emotional needs?

VI. Will competitive running or recreational running help me establish the kind of social life I want to have?

    A. What will the training and competition of varsity track do to my social life?

    B. What can recreational running do for my social life?

    C. Subconclusion: Which will be best for my social life?

VII. Summary: What have I learned?

VIII. Conclusion: What have I decided?

A Runner's Question

Defined by two parallel white lines, the one hundred meters of her lane stretch ahead of her. She shoots a glance down this path and stretches her right leg backward, settling it against the block.

"Runners, to your mark." She puts her hands down on the synthetic track surface, her fingers bridged, eyes focused eight inches in front of the starting line.

"Set." She lifts her weight onto her legs and fingers.

In the third row of bleachers near the finish line sits her doppelganger, watching. Though she is a spectator now, the woman in the stands knows the tension the runners face. She used to race herself, but now she runs only for fun and exercise. Although still in excellent shape, she does not feel finely tuned, indomitable as she once did in the peak of training. On the other hand, she feels ironically more durable, not quite as brittle because she has a little more fat on her bones.

The sound of the starting pistol explodes into her ears.

As the sprinters charge toward her and the finish line, she feels a mild excitement and curiosity. The sprinter with the long legs and red braid flying behind seems to have a slow start, but by the halfway point she has come even with the leaders. She crosses the tape almost ten meters ahead of the next runners.

The winner's teammates greet her with hugs and pats. The coach shakes her hand. The public address system announces her winning times—a new school record. The girl in the stands feels poignant envy as the fans around her clap and cheer for the victorious runner, but before long the next heat is announced and the attention of the crowd shifts.

Which would I rather be—the runner, or the girl in the stands? That's the question I hope to answer through this research project.

The Givens

Since third or fourth grade I knew I could run fast. I found that when we played "kick the can," or "gray wolf," or any other neighborhood

-4-

game I could catch or outrun all the other kids in our gang, including the boys. I didn't think much about it then, but when I won four events in the sixth grade all city track meet, I began to realize that the ability to run fast made me special. I liked that. Whenever I was afraid or embarrassed in school or in a social situation, I used to think of myself running, faster than the teacher, faster than my arch-enemy, Molly, faster than Tom who never paid any attention to me, faster than my parents.

During my high school years, track became even more important to me, but also, more troublesome. I ran cross-country in the fall and did not like it. I didn't enjoy the long tedious runs and I found that other kids could beat me in the longer distances. I found, however, that I loved the spring track season. With the help of the coaches, I discovered that sprinting was my real forté. I began to train hard for the one hundred and two hundred meter dashes. I also ran on the 400- and 800-meter relay teams. Though I loved it, I sometimes came home from a workout so tired I didn't feel like doing anything else. I tried to keep strict training rules during the season, and some of my friends would laugh at me for it. On balance, however, I am sure I would have had no doubts about going out for track in college if I had not had an injury at the end of my senior year.

I had been having a good season, better even than my junior year when I won the conference championship in both the 100- and 200-meter sprints. During my senior year I set conference records in both events and was second at the state meet in the 200 and first in the 100.

The day after my final race at the state meet, I couldn't walk. My foot had been bothering me a little, but now I could tell it was not just a slight sprain but something more serious. I had it X-rayed and discovered I had a stress fracture of the calcaneus in my right foot. At first my doctor thought it would heal if I wore a pad in my shoe, but when that didn't work, I had to wear a walking cast for six weeks. It made my summer miserable, and I thought my racing days were over.

When I got here to college my foot seemed completely healed, and I started working out a little again, just for fitness. I started with aerobics three times a week, and gradually got back in shape. Now I am

-5-

working out in the Nautilus center three times a week and running three (I take Sundays off). I currently spend about one hour and fifteen minutes a day on my work-outs.

One day when it was raining, I ran on the indoor track and I met a guy from another school in my high school conference. He remembered me and asked me if I would be ready for the spring track season. He assumed I would be trying out. When I told him I had not planned to go out, he couldn't believe it. I later found out that he knew the women's track coach quite well, and he told her about me. Since then the coach has contacted me and has been encouraging me to try out. I am considering going out, but before I make the commitment, I want to answer several important questions.

The Criteria

First of all I want to assure myself that I would be good enough to help the team and perhaps even win a few races. When I was in high school, I used to wonder why some of the mediocre runners bothered. They'd work themselves to death during practice, and then during the meet they'd come in maybe fourth or fifth. That's not for me. I don't need to win every time, but I want to be competitive, one of the people in the conference to contend with. I know enough about myself to realize that, if I can't compete on that level, I should spend my time in some other way.

Probably the most important question I want to explore is, "How will my health be affected?" I know that the program of exercise I'm in now feels good to me, but is it best for my body? Would the rigor and fine tuning of preparing for competition (not to mention the race itself) be better for me, or would I be in danger of injuring myself again. I have heard many rumors about the effects of strenuous training on the future health of women athletes. I want to find out if they are true, whether or not ten years from now I might have problems with my knees or not be able to have children because I ran track in college.

Will I be able to afford the time? As it is now, I spend more than an hour every day just on "recreational" training. How much more training time will I need for competition? How much time does the track team spend on the road or waiting for the meet to be over? I am finding that I need to spend much more time here at college studying than I did in high school. I want to do well in my classes and I don't want to commit myself to something which could jeopardize my grades. I also work six to seven hours a week in the university mail room. Will I be able to continue if I go out for track?

The next criterion seems more difficult to research, but it is important to me. I want to find out how participation in track is likely to affect my psychological and emotional health. Right now I feel pretty good about myself. I'm getting above average grades in my courses and I have many good friends. Although I have some bad days when I feel completely alone and forgotten, I feel like I have adjusted as well as most freshmen to dorm life and living away from home. There is no special man in my life right now, but I don't feel a strong need for one because I have men friends and even an occasional flirtation. In general, I like my life the way it is.

Finally, I want to find out if track will reduce my contacts with friends and acquaintances. The track season here at college is almost twice as long as the high school season. That means many days devoted to meets when I might otherwise be having a good time with friends.

When I hear Joe (the guy I met on the track) talking about track meets, I feel myself get excited. I wonder if track would be the way for me to overcome this sense I have here of being forgotten, not very special to anyone ("just a number" as I heard other students often say). While I was in high school track, I enjoyed the realization that I was an important member of the team, and I wonder if that would happen here. I'm not sure much "hard evidence" can be found to research this criterion, but I would rather make my decision with whatever information I can find rather than with none.

Am I Good Enough?

When I first arranged my criteria into an outline form, I had put "health" first because I consider that the most important one. After thinking it over, however, I decided to find out first if I'm good enough to compete or not. If I found out I wasn't, I would give up this topic and choose another.

To answer the question, "Am I good enough?" I planned the following procedures. First I need a definition of "good enough." Then I need to see if my existing performance records, plus my potential for development, are equal to or better than the performance records of the other sprinters in our intercollegiate conference.

"Good Enough" Defined

For some people who participate in athletics, the important element is the opportunity to be with teammates and enjoy the fellowship. The value of participation remains even when they are not successful in competition. Both through my research for this paper (see section five) and through my own direct experience, I have come to see that, for me, winning (or at least coming close) is an essential element. "Good enough," therefore, for this paper means good enough to win an occasional race and come close in the others. If I am going to train and compete, I would like to know that I have a reasonable chance, and that I can contribute to the success of the team.

How Fast Did I Run in High School?

Although I participated in track for three years in junior high and three years in senior high, my twelfth grade performances are the ones most relevant to what I am likely to do in intercollegiate track. Since the 100-meter and 200-meter events were my best ones in high school, and the events in which I am most likely to compete in college, I have decided to concentrate on those two events.

Counting the Regional, Sectional, and State Meets, I participated in fourteen meets. For some meets, I ran more than one heat in the same event, so I ran the 100 meter twenty-two times in competition, and the 200 meter eighteen times. I copied the times below directly from copies of "Meet Report" sheets maintained by Patricia Lammers, my high school track coach. Whenever possible, I verified the times by consulting the Wisconsin Interscholastic Athletic Association Yearbook.

| | | TIMES | |
MEET	HEAT	100 METER	200 METER
Rapids Invitational	First	13.60 (Muddy track)	
	Final	13.42 (Muddy track)	27.88
Wausau West Dual		13.02	25.89
Merrill Invitational	First	12.90 (Wind assisted)	
	Final	12.98 (Wind assisted)	25.60
Rapids Dual		12.98	26.00
Everest Invitational	First	13.00	
	Final	12.98	25.45
Pacelli Dual		12.97	25.95
Lumberjack Invitational	First	12.94	26.11
	Final	13.04	25.86
Waupaca Dual		12.89	25.85
Point Special Invitational	First	13.11	
	Final	12.94	26.22
Marshfield Invitational	First	12.99	
	Final	12.96	
Intra-city		12.98	25.12
Columbus Dual		13.03	26.80
Conference	First	12.96	25.92
	Final	12.94	25.20
Regionals	First	12.89	25.94
	Final	12.88	25.89
Sectionals	First	12.98	25.95
	Final	12.88	25.84
State	First	12.89	25.87
	Final	12.88	25.88

If I eliminate the wind assisted and the muddy track times, my average times were 12.97 in the 100 and 25.87 in the 200. What strikes me

-9-

now as I review these times is the inconsistency. While my best time in the 100, 12.88, won me Class A First Place in the State Meet (just .04 away from the state record), my worst time, 13.11, would not have qualified me even to run in the state meet.

When I asked Jackie Slater, the University Women's Track coach which times to compare, she suggested both the average and the best times. She said it's easy to have an accidental bad day, but it's quite difficult to have an accidental good day. She suggested that anyone who consistently runs the 100 under 12.9 can be competitive in the conference. She said that one of her goals as a coach of sprinters is to find consistency. "Just looking at your high school times, I would say that, with hard work, you could really help us." She went on to say, ho ver, that I should look at the times from other sprinters in the conference and reach my own conclusions. She reminded me to keep in mind that I can expect my times to improve somewhat over high school just because I will have matured one more year and I would have one more year of coaching and practice.

Using the records of the National Association of Interscholastic Athletic Association, and of the Conference of Wisconsin State Universities, I did an analysis of the times put in by 100-meter and 200-meter women sprinters.

Other Sprinter Times

Coach Slater provided me with the results of the 1988 Wisconsin Women's Intercollegiate Athletic Conference Track and Field Meet, held May 6 and 7, 1988, at Simpson Filed, Eau Claire, Wisconsin:

100-meter Dash Finals			200-meter Dash Finals		
1. Sandy Squier	LX	12.63	Sandy Squier	LX	26.01
2. Patty Boehlen	OSH	12.92	Lisa Campion	OSH	26.28
3. Kathy Krzesinski	WW	13.05	Kathy Krzesinski	WW	26.34
4. Sue Kittle	RF	13.15	Lori Jesse	OSH	26.36
5. Lori Nelson	OSH	13.23	Maria Dixson	WW	26.68

100-meter Dash Finals			200-meter Dash Finals		
6. Shelly Ranum	LX	13.26	Gia Esposito	LX	26.72
7. Lynn Wurtinger	OSH	13.32	Sarah Meyer	OSH	27.48
8. Maria Dixson	WW	13.41	Lori Nelson	OSH	27.48
9. Denise Stilen	LX	13.43	Beckie Sherwood	SP	27.54

Coach Slater also provided me the results of the NAIA Women's Outdoor Track and Field National Championships:

100-meter Dash Finals		200-meter Dash Finals	
1. Carol Bailey, Concordia NE	11.54	Airat Bakare, Azusa Pacific	23.71
2. Comfort Igeh, Wayland Bap.	11.80	Carol Bailey, Concordia NE	23.76
3. Marcia Brown, Wayland Bap.	11.85	Wanda Clay, Prairie View	24.20
4. Ann Kiecker, Moorhead State	11.86	Lori Ewig, Simon-Fraser	24.46
5. Vickie Aoko, Wayland Baptist	11.90	Sheron Wegener, West. OR	24.61
6. Pattie Harris, Prairie View	11.99	Comfort Ngeh, Wayland B.	24.65

Since I am interested in knowing how I would do against the competition in our conference, I compared my times with those from the conference meet finals. My average time in the 100 last year was 12.96. The average time in the conference finals was 13.15. If I were able to run as well as I have (or improve), I would probably be better than average in the 100.

My best time, 12.88, however, is not as good as the winning time at the conference meet, 12.63. From this analysis, I conclude that, although I probably would not often finish first, I might realistically expect an occasional second in meets with conference schools.

Unless I improved tremendously, however, I could not expect to compete at the nationals. The last place runner at the NAIA nations ran the 100 in 12.01, nine-tenths of a second better than my best time. Over a short distance like the 100, nine-tenths of a second is light years.

To my surprise, it appears that I could be more competitive in the 200. The average time in the 200 at the conference meet finals was

26.68. My average time last year in high school was 25.87, eight tenths of a second faster than the conference average. In 1988, at least, I think that I could have won the 200 meter dash at the conference meet. And although I couldn't yet compete at the nationals, I was surprised to see that the difference between my best time (25.12) and the last place finisher at the nationals (25.03) might be closed with maturity and practice.

Subconclusion

By comparing my high school times with the WWIA Conference and the NAIA National times, I learned that I am probably "good enough." I am not likely to go to nationals, but I could be competitive in the conference.

Although I should be satisfied on this point, I still want to investigate my potential for improvement. I know I am not going to be satisfied to do only as well each year as I did the year before. I want to investigate my potential to develop even greater speed.

Do I Have Potential to Develop Greater Speed?

Although I had some success as a high school sprinter, the times I ran then would not make me a consistent winner in college. It would be necessary for me to improve. Each of the seasons I ran track in high school I was able to progress over the year before. Now, however, I am afraid that I might have peaked. If I have, I probably should not try track in college. In order to find out whether or not I have still untapped potential, I used two strategies. I analyzed my body size and type, the composition of my muscles, the percentage of fat in my body, and other related physical elements which, according to coaching literature, are predictors of success in sprinting. In addition, I was curious if there were significant features of my running style which, with good coaching and practice, could be improved to make me faster.

Through the materials I found in my library search, I discovered three basic methods I can use to test my potential as a sprinter. First, I can measure my "explosive strength," one of the key characteristics of successful sprinters. I can also see where I am now on the "performance curve" for women sprinters. And finally, with the help of Coach Slater, I can examine my running techniques to see if I might be able to improve my times by working on technique.

To my surprise, body size, height, and relative limb length are not reliable predictors. In an article, "How To Predict Sprint Potential," P. Siris and his colleagues reports,

> Contrary to many other track and field events, the anthropometric measurements have no great importance in sprinting. Top performances have been achieved by tall as well as short athletes. (14)

Several other sources confirmed Siris on this point, so I abandoned body size and type as a predictor for my potential to improve.

In spite of the development of new tests and techniques for measuring explosiveness, the old familiar "Sargant" jump and reach test is still considered the most reliable and valid (Viitasalo, 9). In the Sargant test, the subject stands next to a wall which has distances above the floor marked on it. The subject stands flatfooted and reaches as high on the wall as he or she can. Then, from a standing start, the subject jumps and reaches as high on the wall as he or she can. The difference between the flatfooted reach and the jumping reach equals the test result. Many high school students are administered this test in high school physical education classes.

I also had performed the test in high school, but I had forgotten the results. With the help of a friend, I performed the test for this research project during the first week in October. I jumped ten times, and the differences between my standing reach and my jumping reach ranged from 18.5 to 25 inches. The average difference was 23 inches, about six inches more than the average of women my age.

Age and years of training are additional factors which might affect my potential to improve as a sprinter. I am now eighteen years, six months, and I wanted to find out where I am on the typical "perfor-

-13-

mance curve" for sprinters. P. Siris and other researchers from the Soviet Union studied Olympic sprinters from all over the world, and concluded that the average age for Olympic champions and finalists in women's sprinting events has remained quite constant during the last four Olympics—23.6 years in the 100 meter, and 23.8 years in the 200 meter (13).

Siris and his colleagues also conducted longitudinal studies which track the performance curves of elite women sprinters. The curves for the 100 meter and the 200 meter are exactly the same:

First Success—17 to 19 years of age

Optimal Performance—20 to 22 years of age

Top Performance—23 to 25 years of age

(14)

I should be able to expect improvement for at least three more years. So far, the evidence seemed to show that I could expect my performance to improve if I continued in track. As one more test, however, I wanted Coach Slater to examine my techniques and see if I can improve my times by polishing technique. Although my high school coach tried often to get me to change my starting style, I confess I didn't listen. Now I feel that I am more willing and ready to learn.

I made an appointment with Coach Slater to show her a videotape of my 100 meter race in the conference meet. My then-boyfriend had taped the race and gave it to me as a present. He had overcranked the whole thing, so playing the tape back at normal speed shows it in slow motion.

Coach Slater watched the tape twice, taking notes. Then we looked at the tape together, stopping it when she wanted to point out areas where I could improve technique. She said my starts were a disaster—the blocks were too close together and set at the wrong angles. My head was turned up too high and I had too much weight on my hands. No wonder my high school coach nagged me about my starts. She told me that I had to get my arms into the race more, especially getting out of the blocks and over the first twenty meters. "Of course nobody has perfect technique," she said, "but I see no reason why you shouldn't be able to cut at least five tenths of a second off your times just by working on technique."

Subconclusion

I find the results of this section exciting, and if I considered only them, I would definitely go out. I am pleased to learn that, if I go out, I can expect to improve as I mature, and as I work on technique. I am still worried about my health, however.

How Will My Health Be Affected?

I realize now that I can be competitive in the WWIA Conference and help my school team. My next worry has to do with injuries and long term health. Last year, while participating in track, I suffered a painful stress fracture of the calcaneus (heel bone). I don't want that to happen again. I have also heard rumors that rigorous training can affect a woman's hormonal system, slowing up or even shutting down her menstrual cycles. My grandmother even told me that, when I'm ready to have a baby, I will have trouble giving birth because my hips will be too narrow because of all the running I do. If I go out for track, will I get injured again? Will my long-term health be affected?

Risk of Injury

When I injured my foot, my family doctor thought that it might get better if I just put a special pad in my shoe and took it easy. When the injury got worse instead of better, he sent me to a specialist—Dr. Burton Wimmer, an orthopedist who specializes in sports injuries. In spite of my objections, Dr. Wimmer, installed a "walking cast" on my foot and ankle. I hobbled around on it seven weeks.

As part of his treatment, Dr. Wimmer lectured me about sports injuries. He advised me to examine the causes and conditions which lead to the injury so that I might learn from my past experiences. He had me write an essay describing as well as I could remember what led to the injury. He asked me especially to mention anything different about the way I trained, ate, slept, or felt in the days leading up to the injury. Although I didn't take the essay too seriously at the time, I got it out again when I began this project.

The essay I wrote for Dr. Wimmer mentions that during the two weeks before my injury was diagnosed, because I was preparing for the sectionals and then the state meet, my workout sessions were longer than they had been during the year. My training routine also changed. Until then, I had been devoting only about half of my workout to speed work—cycles of full-speed sprinting. When I realized I had a chance for state, I added 30 minutes to each workout, and devoted most of that additional time to sprinting work.

When Dr. Wimmer read my essay, he told me that my injury fit the pattern exactly. "Runners, especially women, develop stress fractures when they suddenly go from a reasonable training program to an excessive one, and then top it off with competition. If I had known what you were doing, I could have predicted your injury. Nine out of ten stress fractures I see fit this pattern." He encouraged me to learn more about how injuries develop so that, if I ran competitively again, I could avoid injury. "To top it off," he said as I was about to hobble out on my cast, "by adding that extra sprinting practice, you probably did nothing to improve your times." That left me wondering.

Everything I have since read and heard about stress fractures confirms Dr. Wimmer's analysis. In the August, 1987 issue of The Physician and Sportsmedicine two orthopedists, Dr. Richard H. Alfred and Dr. John A Bergfeld, make a similar point: "Patients who have stress fractures almost always have a history of high-intensity training, and they frequently have abruptly increased their training regimen in the recent past" (83).

The university women's track coach, Jackie Slater, told me that she also had suffered stress fractures when she "ran through the pain" in an important race. "From that little bit of stupidity, I had four (yes, four!) stress fractures. I am somewhat of an expert in stress fractures" (personal interview). She assured me that the university track coaches were very aware of injury hazards and dedicated to preventing them by using well designed training programs. "That doesn't mean we can guarantee an injury free program for you, however. It simply means that we always put the health of our athletes above winning."

Two weeks ago I visited Dr. Wimmer for my final visit. I asked him if my foot will be more vulnerable to injury again. He told me that, if anything, the calcaneus in that foot would be stronger than in my other foot. He assured me that I could resume full scale workouts whenever I wanted to. He warned me, however, to always keep in mind the golden rule—moderation. "As long as you don't let either the training or the prospect of another victory become obsessions, you should be able to participate in track without serious injury."

To check Dr. Wimmer's assertions, I wanted to find out exactly how many college women sprinters were injured each year. Coach Slater did not think specific data would be available for our conference, but she did give me the name of a physician, Dr. John P. Albright, at the University of Iowa Hospitals, who is in charge of the "Big Ten Injury Surveillance Survey." According to Dr. Albright, the "Survey" notes "any injury severe enough for the athlete to lose time from practice or competition." He said that, "In contrast to the other sports we track, and even in contrast to other track and field events, sprinting has a very low ratio or injuries to participants." I asked him if he could be more specific, and he dug more deeply into his files. Finally he came back to the phone: "In the last five years, from all of the ten schools, we have had nine injury reports for women sprinters." I asked him what kind of injuries they were. He told me he didn't have that information handy, but he remembered that most of them were "muscle pulls, 'shin splints,' that kind of thing." I asked him if stress fractures were common. "No," he said. "Not with sprinters. We see that more with distance runners" (Telephone interview).

According to the "Survey," only about two sprinters a year in the ten schools of the Big Ten have injuries severe enough to miss practice or a race. If each school has ten sprinters, that makes the injury ratio about two out of one hundred—2%. I consider those acceptable odds.

Subconclusion

From the reading I have done and from my talks with Dr. Wimmer, Dr. Albright, and Coach Slater, I have learned that I should be able to avoid the kind of injury I had last year. My high school coach had warned me those last couple weeks to take it easy, but I had ignored her just as much as I had ignored her suggestions that I work a little harder earlier in the year. I think that I have learned something from my pain. Now I will be more receptive to the guidance of coaches and trainers. For this criterion, therefore, I conclude that I will be able to run varsity track without much greater fear of injury than I would have if I continued to run only for fun.

Long-term Health Affects

Ever since I joined the track team in junior high school, my grandmother has been urging me to take it easy, and sometimes she comes right out and says I should "quit that foolishness." My grandmother is what some might call a "lady." She wears a hat whenever she's out in the sun, and she talks non-stop (between puffs of her Salem cigarette!) about how it's bad for you to swim after lunch, sleep late in the morning, breathe through your mouth, drink coke, and eat fruit without peeling it. Among the other warnings, she told me that it wasn't "natural" for a woman to exercise so strenuously. She told me that, if I continued to run track, I would not be able to have children and my bones would deteriorate when I got older.

Although I just laugh at my grandmother, I have had some unusual (for me) menstrual irregularities during the track season. I decided to check out some of grandmother's claims. Through my reading I discovered that Richard M. Malina is one of the authorities on this subject. His views are featured in an article called, "Maturation and Strenuous Training in Young Female Athletes," published in Physician and Sports Medicine, June, 1987. The author of the article, David Zimmerman, interviews Dr. Malina and asks him, "Should female athletes reduce training levels to avoid problems with menarche and menstruation." Dr.

Malina answers, "For the vast majority of youngsters who are involved in sports, training is an important adjunct to normal growth and maturation" (221).

Although Dr. Malina believes strongly that training—as long as it's not excessive—is healthy and important, he does agree that women athletes need to continue to "maintain training at some level" throughout their lives, not just as children and young adults. He points out that some athletes expect to eat as much after they stop training as they ate while they were training (222). Both Dr. Wimmer and my family doctor agree that participation in track will definitely be better for my health in the long run than no training at all.

Other experts have been slightly more alarmed. Gary Barrow and Subrata Saha from the Department of Orthopaedic Surgery at the Louisiana State University Medical Center investigated the relationship between, "Menstrual irregularity and stress fractures in collegiate female distance runners." When I began the article I thought, "Yes. I missed a couple of periods and I had a stress fracture. They are going to explain the connection." After I checked the details of their report, however, I realized that I was not the kind of person their investigation identified as at risk. First, I am not a distance runner. Second, according to their definition of "menstrual regularity," I would be classified as regular. Last spring I went sixty days between menses, and another time, forty-five. I was well within their definition of "regular (10 to 13 menses/year)" (210). Finally, they report that a significant number of the women they observed with menstrual irregularity also suffered from eating disorders—anorexia and bulimia (211). I have never had any symptoms of those disorders. In short, I conclude that I am far from being the kind of person they worry about.

Subconclusion

I am satisfied that running track will not harm my health later in my life. I have found no evidence to support my grandmother's assertions that I would not be able to have children or that my bones will disintegrate. In fact, some evidence suggests that the opposite if true, but only if I maintain physical conditioning after I stop running in competition. As I age and as I cut back in exercise, I will also need to cut back in my calorie intake—no more hot fudge sundaes.

Will I Be Able to Afford the Time?

As a first semester freshman, I have to work very hard to do well in my classes. In high school I could get better than average grades with only an hour or two a day devoted to classwork. Now I spend at least three hours a day and sometimes four or five when I'm preparing for a big test or a paper is due. In addition, I work six or seven hours a week in the university mailroom. I seriously wonder if I can afford the additional time required for participation in varsity track.

How Much Time Do I Spend Now?

Usually when I run, I jog slowly through Putnam Park, back to school on the neighborhood streets, up the 122 wooden steps to the upper campus (about two miles total), four times around the football practice field at an 80 second per quarter-mile pace, and end up with a final lap as fast as I can run it. I walk slowly back to the gym to cool down, then I change into my swimming suit and swim laps for fifteen or twenty minutes more. On alternate days I spend about the same amount of time in the weight room. Counting shower and change time, I spend about one hour and fifteen minutes a day on my work-outs—seven and one-half hours per week.

How Much Time Does Varsity Track Require?

During my interview with Coach Slater, I asked her to describe the track team workout and meet schedules. She gave me a copy of the 1988–89 schedule of meets, and we looked at it together.

UNIVERSITY OF WISCONSIN—EAU CLAIRE
Tentative 1988—89 Women's and Men's Track Schedule

Day, Date	Opponent/Meet	Site	Time
INDOOR			
Sat. 1/23	Northwest Open	Minneapolis, MN	10:00 am
Sat. 1/30	Domino's Pizza Open	Mankato, MN	10:00 am
Sat. 2/6	UW-Stout	Eau Claire, WI	12:00 noon
Sat. 2/13	Eric Liddal Games	Bethel, MN	9:00 am
Sat. 2/20	St. Thomas/UMD	Eau Claire, WI	1:00 pm
Sat. 2/27	St. Cloud State	St. Cloud, MN	12:00 noon
Fri.-Sat.,	NAIA		
Feb. 26—27	Indoor Nationals	Kansas, City, MO	TBA
Fri.-Sat.,	WSUC Indoor		
March 4—5	Championships	La Crosse, WI	TBA
Fri.-Sat.,	NCAA Division III		
March 11—12	Indoor Championships	Smith College, MA	TBA
OUTDOOR			
Sat. 4/9	Coleman Open	Stevens Point, WI	12:00 noon
Wed. 4/13	Twilight	Menomonie, WI	6:00 pm
Sat. 4/16	Blugolds Invitational	Eau Claire, WI	11:00 am
Fri.-Sat.,	Carleton		
April 22—23	Invitational	Northfield, MN	TBA
Fri. 4/29	UW-ST/UW-SU	Eau Claire, WI	3:00 pm
Fri.-Sat.,	WSUC Outdoor		
May 6—7	Championships	Eau Claire, WI	TBA
Sat. 5/14	Last Chance	La Crosse	TBA
Wed.-Sat.,	NCAA Division III	Northfield, MN	TBA
May 25—28	Outdoor Championships		

She pointed out that the first indoor meet took place in January, and the last outdoor meet was in early May (unless I qualified for nationals). Informal conditioning workouts had already begun in September, but official team workouts would not begin until after Thanksgiving. The five-day-a-week team workouts begin at 3:30 and wrap up on time for most people to be showered and dressed by 5:30. "We run that schedule from the fourth Monday in November until the second Friday in May," Coach Slater said.

So far the time requirements didn't seem so overwhelming. I was already spending seven and a half hours per week. Though the track team workouts were longer than mine by about 45 minutes each, I worked out six days a week to their five. If I joined the team I would have to devote an additional 2.5 hours a week. I think I could handle that without difficulty.

I see more problems with the meets. Looking at the schedule, I can see that almost every Saturday during the second semester would be devoted to track. In some cases, the meets require travel of several hundred miles and staying overnight. Coach Slater pointed out that only those athletes who qualify go to the NCAA Championships, so probably this year at least, I wouldn't have to worry about those weekends. She smiled at me when she said it, and it was the closest she came during our interview of flat-out recruiting me. The way she described the atmosphere and the excitement of the 1988 Nationals at Smith College almost pushed my decision out of the realm of reason. At that moment I wanted to "show her" that I could make it to Nationals.

When I got back to my room, I tried to write down everything I do on Saturdays now. What would I miss if I spent them at track meets? I sleep late. I wash clothes. I clean my room. If the weather is nice, I play outside—touch football, swim, go for a bike ride. Since it's the season, I go to the school football game if it's at home. I party. Once a month I go home for the weekend.

Time spent studying is conspicuously missing from my list of Saturday activities. Clearly the meets would not interfere with my performance in classes, but I would have to find other times to do my laundry and clean my room. Once I got involved in track, I don't think I would miss the other activities very much. I might miss going home, but I do not consider that a major factor.

Subconclusion

I was surprised to discover that going out for track would remove only about two hours from the productive time of my work week. I would lose time on the weekends, but most of that time I now spend on rest and recreation (I'll examine the consequences of that loss in section VI). Although I might miss out on some fun, I am now confident that my grades would not suffer.

Psychological, Emotional, and Mental Satisfaction

When I was twelve, I got in an argument with my Sunday school teacher. I think about it often. She had been reading to us from St. Matthew, Chapter Five. I recall listening with only half an ear until she got to the part where Jesus says, . . . "whosoever shall smite thee on thy cheek, turn to him the other also. . . . Love your enemies, bless them that curse you, do good to them that hate you . . ." I just couldn't believe it—When someone hits you, you should invite them to hit you again?!? My personal ethics at that age were closer to an "eye for an eye." When I told the teacher how ridiculous an idea "turning the other cheek" was, she suggested that this lesson might be especially for people like me, people who always fought back, never forgave, always had to be first. That was the first time anyone had ever told me I might be too competitive. Since then other people (my parents, my brother, friends) have also told me that I am "competitive." I wonder sometimes if I am TOO competitive, and I wonder how that relates to participation in track.

Over the years I have come to appreciate the power of cooperation and the importance of forgiveness. But I know enough about myself to realize that I don't like to lose and that I don't take it well. Considering that negative tendency in my personality, I wonder if varsity track will make it worse, or whether track can help me learn to cope with loss and pay more attention to cooperative goals.

In his book, Coaches Guide to Sport Psychology, Rainer Martens describes three important psychological needs that "athletes seek to fulfill

-23-

by participating in sports" (23). Although he mentions others, these are the most basic:

> To play for fun, which meets the need for stimulation and excitement.
> To be with other people, which meets the need to affiliate with others and belong in a group.
> To demonstrate competence in order to meet the need to feel worthy (23).

Self-worth

Of these three, the psychological need for self-worth is the one most clearly satisfied for me by track. For the last six years, my self-worth has always been enhanced, perhaps even dependent on, my ability to run fast. Whenever I feel depressed I go out and run a few sprints. Sometimes it's enough to imagine myself running fast, faster than everyone around. That's why I worry about subjecting my self-worth to the inevitable realization that I am not always able to be the fastest in a race. If I run in college, I will have to adjust my sense of self-worth to accept being second or third sometimes.

Last year, I came in second in a 100-meter race only once. The meet was a dual meet with a local private high school, our last meet before the conference meet. I had beaten their fastest sprinter twice only five days earlier in an invitational meet. When she crossed the tape ahead of me, I was taken completely by surprise. I literally could not believe it. I was used to people coming up to me, congratulating me. I took it for granted. This time I was left standing alone. I didn't know what to do. I felt intense shame. I saw the coach coming toward me. I didn't want to see her and I could feel tears coming, so I turned and sprinted across the infield and behind the bleachers on the other side of the field. I crawled under the bleachers and sat there in the dark with hot tears sluicing down my cheeks.

I sat there until the call for the 200. I ran, but I finished second, my worst time on the 200 all season. This time I wasn't surprised and I

-24-

continued running directly into our locker room. I threw my stuff in a corner, changed into my street clothes and left without even a shower. My parents were amazed when I came home, but I wouldn't talk with them or anyone else. The next day (a Friday) I told my mother I was sick and stayed home from school.

Even though that happened only six months ago, I find it hard to understand why I behaved like that. It seems so immature and selfish. I like to think I am not like that now, but maybe I would be again if I were involved in competition.

On the Saturday morning after the meet, about 10:00, the coach came to see me. I was still in bed, but my mother woke me and the coach came right in with her. She sat right down on the edge of the bed. At first she just harangued me about being a coward, a quitter, a crybaby, etc. etc. Then she calmed down a little and told me some interesting news. The girl who beat me had never been beaten herself until I beat her at the invitational meet the Saturday before. My time in the race I lost would have been fast enough Saturday, but on Thursday, the girl who won had run her best time ever—a new record for her school, in fact.

The coach also pointed out that the team points for the meet had been very close. "If you hadn't been sitting under the bleachers feeling sorry for yourself, you might have noticed that our team really needed the points you could have earned us in the 200." The responsibility to the team I should have felt then was now sweeping over me. "As it was," she said, "you were lucky to pull out second." I began to cry again, but this time she didn't call me a crybaby. Instead she said, "We've got to learn from our losses, get stronger through what we gain from our mistakes. Come see me before practice on Monday and we'll see what we can do to turn your loss (and your tantrum) into a growing experience."

On an intellectual level, I have learned my lessons. I know that I will not win every race, that I have to learn how to accept defeat, that I have to think of the team needs as well as my own. On an intellectual level, I also know that not going out for track is already an acceptance of defeat which should have an impact on that part of my self-worth,

-25-

which depends on my running speed. The defeat, however, would remain hypothetical, nothing nearly as visceral and clear as coming in second in an actual race.

Fun

Another of the needs that Martens lists is "fun . . . the need for stimulation and excitement." Without hesitation I know that I miss the excitement very much. If this were the only factor, I would definitely go out. Working out on my own, with no competition to prepare for, I get very bored and often get distracted. I sometimes quit in the middle of a workout to stop at a garage sale or to talk with a friend. At the slightest excuse I will cancel a workout to play in a pickup volleyball or basketball game. I know that I am not the kind of person who can get much fun out of running one more mile than the day before. I love a flesh and blood challenge, an opponent, someone to beat.

Sometimes I am shocked and surprised at myself. For example, last Wednesday, as I was taking my leisurely jog through the park, I heard another jogger coming up behind. I glanced back and saw that it was Shane, a guy I know from the weight room who is always bragging about his running. I picked up my pace a little so that when he came up along side I was going almost as fast as he. I let him go by and noticed that he was blowing pretty hard—he must have been near the end of his workout. I let him get about twenty yards ahead and then I turned on a little speed and blew by him. He was a little startled, but he tried to catch up. I was feeling strong, so as he gained a little, I accelerated a little, keeping him just close enough so he wouldn't give up right away. I could hear him suffering behind me, but I was starting to suffer a little myself. I knew that I had about a quarter mile left at this pace, or an eighth of a mile at full-kick.

I didn't think he had enough left to follow my full kick, and I knew my turn-off was only about 300 meters ahead, so I kicked and heard him stumble farther and farther behind. When I got to my turn-off up the steps, he was no where in sight. I could hardly make it up the steps and into the locker room, but I felt great. I had beaten the twerp. I canceled the rest of my work-out, showered, and stopped at the dairy bar for an ice-cream cone.

No doubt about it—I love the excitement of winning. For me at least, recreational running does not provide me with opportunities for competition. Not many people jogging in the park are as willing to race as Shane had been.

Affiliation

Someone hearing about my "hiding under the bleachers" episode might conclude that I am not a good team member, and, if that's all they knew, they would be right. That example might show that my need for other people is not very strong, or that my affiliation needs are not well fulfilled by participation in track. Other than that one meet, however, I believe I functioned well as a team member. In fact, I consider my need to be with people who share my interests one of the most satisfying parts of participation in track, the one I miss the most (more about this in section VI).

Theresa Mueller and I were co-captains of the women's track team during our senior year. She threw the discus and put the shot. She's been one of my best friends since sixth grade. I called her at her school in Madison and asked her to answer my questions as frankly as she could. After explaining my research project to her, I asked her if she could think of specific examples which illustrate that I either liked or disliked being with the other members of the team. Although I had trouble getting her to be specific, once she understood the need for hard evidence, she provided several specific examples which showed, in her judgment, that I loved being with the people.

Here are a few samples:

> Paula worked twenty minutes a day for two weeks to help Melinda Meyers learn how to start out of blocks (although that might have been simply to get out of her own starting practice).
>
> During meets Paula always cheered her teammates, congratulated them when they did well, comforted them when they didn't.

-27-

185

Paula practiced for and ran in the 400 meter relay in every meet except one.

Paula won the "Most Valuable Track Athlete" of the year, a choice made by a secret ballot of all the members at the end of the season.

When I reminded Theresa about the time I cried under the bleachers, she paused, seemed to reflect, and cautiously said, "Well, yes, you were a great teammember as long as you were the big cheese and winning all the time. I'd love to see what you're like when you have to scramble to come in third."

Until her final comment, my interview with Theresa had been reassuring. I don't think I have enough information to know how I will respond in a subordinate role. I do believe, however, that through this research I have become much more realistic in my expectations and alert to the hazards of a negative reaction to defeat.

During my library search, I discovered a significant body of psychological literature which investigates the relationship between general personality characteristics and sports participation/achievement. One especially interesting article, "The Relationship of Competitiveness And Achievement Orientation to Participation in Sport and Nonsport Activities," describes SOQ (Sports Orientation Questionnaire), an instrument designed to examine "the competitiveness and general achievement orientation" among participants and non-participants in competitive sports, non-competitive sports, and nonsport activities (139-50)

Using SOQ (developed by Diane Gill, University of North Carolina at Greensboro), the authors attempt to find out if those people who seek out athletic competition have certain attitudes in common in contrast to those who seek non-competitive activities. They conclude that the SOQ discriminates quite well between those who participate in competitive sports and those who don't. I asked coach Slater about this kind of questionnaire, and she responded by saying that she learned more about the athletes she coached by talking with them and, in general, getting to know them as whole people. Like Coach Slater, Rainer Martens suggests in his book that "sport-specific personality tests tell you less about the needs of your athletes and how to motivate them than effective communication"(23). But Coach Slater suggested that, if I wanted to, I could arrange to take a questionnaire like the SOQ by going to the university counseling center.

Although the SOQ is a new instrument and not yet generally available, I was able to take the questionnaire through the counseling service. I answered the questions on the SOQ, and waited for the counselor to score the results. I discovered that I had a significantly above average score on the "general achievement orientation" scale. The counselor, Barbara Satchel, told me that these results suggest I would probably "eagerly approach competitive challenges"—something I already knew.

She told me not to take the results too seriously, however, and asked me to describe my research project for her. As usual with counselors, she wouldn't give me any advice and kept asking me questions instead of giving answers. When I saw her glance at the clock, I got up to leave. She walked me to the door and said, "I am very confident that you will reach the best decision for yourself. You are going about it in exactly the right way—keep looking for as much information as you can. But don't put off the decision too long. Track practice begins right after Thanksgiving" (office consultation).

Subconclusion

Using Doctor Martens' list of three psychological needs served by participation in athletics—fun, affiliation, and a sense of self-worth—helps me see whether going out for track would be good for me or not. To some degree, the satisfaction I derive from each depends on the answer to a crucial question: "Will I be able to handle not always being best?"

The key, I believe, will be whether or not I can adjust my expectations to this new situation. From the results of section one in this paper, I know that with good coaching and hard work, I will win an occasional race, but more often, I will be second or third. If I can accept that, I believe that I will have fun and enjoy affiliation with my team members.

-29-

If I do not go out for track I will be essentially abandoning success in track as a way to support my sense of worth. Perhaps that will make it easier for me to find self worth through other activities. If I go out, and achieve as the results of section one in this paper suggest, I will have to depend less on being first to support my sense of self-worth. When I talked this over with the Dr. Satchel, she responded by asking "Wouldn't that be more mature, more healthy?" I suppose. But I am not absolutely sure I can. For this criterion, I can reach only a qualified conclusion: Unless I am more mature than I was last year, track would not be good for my sense of self-worth.

What Will Track Do to My Social Life?

At this stage of my life, I need people. I am the middle child of five children, and I am used to having people around all the time. Some of my neighbors in the dormitory complain all the time about the lack of privacy and the presence of so many people, but I enjoy it, perhaps too much. Sometimes, however, even a social creature like me feels lonely among all of these people. If I'm gone, no one seems to notice; fifteen other women fill in the gap. I am completely accepted, but I don't feel special in any way.

I wonder how participation in track will affect my social life. If every Saturday during the second semester is tied up with track, will I miss out and be forgotten? For some of the Saturday meets the team will be leaving at 6:00 A.M. That will mean I'll have to get to bed by ten or eleven on Friday nights, just when the action really begins. Although I know that college training rules are not as strict as they are in high school, I still will want to use "moderation" in order to stay in shape and perform well. Will I become a "party-pooper?"

On the other hand, perhaps I will make friends with other members of the track team and do more socially with them. I remember that some of the bus rides to meets in high school were fun even though the school busses bounced around and the coaches scolded if we got too rowdy. Perhaps among the members of the track team I will be special—even if I always come in third.

-30-

To find the answers to these questions, I looked up people on the women's track team in the university yearbook. I called three and each agreed to talk with me. Sheri Albertson, a junior hurdler who will be in her third year on the team, said, "Sure, you lose a little contact with your wing mates your freshman year. During the season you become a little like those girls who go home every weekend to see an old boy-friend. People do tend to forget you and leave you out of things."

Dorene Westman agreed, but she pointed out that "You have to think long-range on college friendships. Most people move out of the dorm af-ter their freshman or sophomore year, and the intense friendships you make with dorm wing-mates often melt like summer romances. What you have in common that first year is your 'Freshmanness.' As you ma-ture you want to be with people who share other more important goals than meeting some hunk on the street [Water Street—a nearby street devoted to places for students] or winning the chug contests."

I still enjoy going with a gang of girls to "look for hunks on the street," but perhaps, like Doreen, I will grow out of those interests. Both Doreen and Sheri told me that both the women's and men's track teams plan social events, both formal and informal. "Although you miss out on a few dorm related activities," Sheri said, "you get in on all the track parties. That's more satisfying because you know you're there because you belong, not because you happen to be living in Towers West."

Subconclusion

Even though I sometimes feel like "just a number," I basically like my social life now. I sense already, however, that dorm wing friendships are based more on chance than on shared attitudes and interests. With a couple of exceptions, I know that for most of my wingmates, I'm just someone who happens to be around ready to do things with. I feel that way about most of the other girls myself. Eventually I will want more. I'm still not sure that track will provide it for me, but both Doreen and Sheri assured me that, if I made half an effort, I could make friends and have a good time in track.

The evidence for this section does not seem conclusive. In terms of importance, however, "social life" was last on my list, and so a strong conclusion one way or another in this section will not sway my decision significantly.

Summary

Before I make my final decision, I would like to review the subconclusions for each criterion.

After comparing my high school times with the times of the sprinters who ran the 100- and 200-meter races in the university conference, I have concluded that I can be competitive. Probably I will not win often, but I am confident that I could finish in the top three of most meets. The evidence also suggests that my college times should be better than my high school times if I work hard on technique, and if my performance curve follows the normal pattern.

My stress fracture last Spring did more to discourage me from running track than anything else. If the evidence had lead me to believe that I had a good chance of an injury again, I would have stuck with recreational running. I am convinced now, however, that I can train and compete in varsity track without injury. For me, the most convincing evidence came from Doctor Albright and the "Big Ten Injury Surveillance Survey."

I am also relieved to learn that my grandmother was wrong about the long term health effects. If I were a long distance runner and I suffered from an eating disorder too, my grandmother might be right, but I am a sprinter and I like my three square meals a day—even breakfast! I am aware now, however, that I need to exercise systematically all my life, and as I cut down on training, I need to cut down on calorie intake. Even working out as I do now, I have gained seven pounds over my racing weight. I learned that I'll need to work all my life to keep a balance between my eating and my exercise.

I was surprised to discover how small the differences in time commitment are between the time I now spend working out and the time I would spend working out with the track team—about two hours a week. I continue to worry, however, about all the weekends I would spend travelling to track meets, participating, and resting before and after. Of all my criteria, I find this one the most clearly pushing against my going out.

I have concluded that I really do love the stimulation and excitement of competitive track. I don't enjoy working out by myself for no special reason than staying in shape. I also realize I get more satisfaction out of being with people who share significant goals than with people who just happen to be there. I think I can have deeper, more lasting friendships with other track members.

Although when I go running now, I never have the satisfaction of victory, I also never have the bitter disappointment of defeat. I know that I have not handled defeat well in the past, and I am not completely certain I can handle it well now. Since I will no doubt experience defeat more in college track than I did in high school, I'd better be ready to accept it. I hope that my analysis of this question will help me accept defeat when it comes, but I cannot with any certainty say I will. The evidence on this criterion appears to point away from varsity track.

Track will definitely separate me sometimes from my existing friends. I won't have as much time, especially on weekends, to fool around with my wingmates. Although I think I would gain deeper friendships on the track team, I would still regret losing contact with the other girls on my floor. The evidence here is not conclusive.

Conclusion

After reviewing my subconclusions, I could see clearly that most of the evidence points to going out for track. I think I can compete. I am confident I won't be injured again and that my long term health will not be affected. I don't like the idea of being tied up every weekend, but I guess I need to make some sacrifices. I'm still worried about how I'll react the first time I come in third or fourth, but I have adjusted my expectations and am preparing myself for defeat. Win or lose, I know I love the excitement and challenge of a race. I will be working with others for clear and significant goals. I will have a clear role. I like that. I have decided to go out for the varsity track team.

-33-

When I finished the rough draft of this paper, I called Coach Slater and told her my decision. She said, "Welcome aboard. First practice will be 3:00 Monday after Thanksgiving. Stop by my office this week to start on the paperwork. We'll need an official physical, insurance information, and biographical details for our roster"

I am out for track.

Works Cited

Albertson, Sheri. Telephone interview. 1 Nov. 1988. A veteran of the varsity track team, Sheri described the social activities sponsored by the track team.

Albright, John P. Telephone interview. 19 Oct. 1988. An orthopedic surgeon on the University of Iowa Hospital faculty, Dr. Albright maintains the "Big Ten Injury Surveillance Survey."

Alfred, Richard H. and John A. Bergfeld. "Diagnosis and Management of Stress Fractures of the Foot." Physician and Sportsmedicine Aug. 1987: 83–89. A technical description of the causes and treatments of stress fractures among athletes, including the specific type I suffered last spring.

Barrow, Gary and Subrata Saha. "Menstrual Irregularity and Stress Fractures in Collegiate Female Distance Runners." American Journal of Sports Medicine 16 (1988): 209–16. A complex analysis of women distance runners who suffer both menstrual irregularity and stress fractures. They conclude that most such women also suffer from eating disorders and thus inadequate diet.

Gill, Diane L., David A. Dzewaltowski, and Thomas Deeter. "The Relationship of Competitiveness and Achievement Orientation to Participation in Sport and Nonsport Activities." Journal of Sport and Exercise Psychology 16 (1988): 139–50. A report on the field testing of the Sports Orientation Questionnaire (SOQ) which was developed by Diane Gill, one of the authors. They conclude that the instrument is valid and reliable, especially on the "general competitiveness" scale.

Lammers, Joyce. "1988 Meet Reports—Sprints and Relays." Records of all heats and final races (with official times) maintained by my high school track coach for the 1988 outdoor season.

Martens, Rainer. Coaches Guide to Sport Psychology. Champaign, IL: Human Kinetics Publishers, Inc, 1987. Recommended to me by both Ms. Slater and Ms. Lammers, this textbook provides information about the psychological side of sports performance—handling stress, imagining good performances, improving motivation, and effective communication among team members and coaches.

Mueller, Theresa. Telephone interview. 1 Nov. 1988. Co-captain of my high school track team, Ms. Mueller provided me her perspective about my relationships with other team members.

National Association for Interscholastic Athletics, "Results," Women's Outdoor Track and Field National Championships, date and place. NAIA National Championship times for the top eight places in both the 100-meter and 200-meter races.

Satchel, Barbara. Personal interview. 15 Oct. 1988. A Counselor in the UWEC Counseling center, Ms. Satchel arranged for me to take the SOQ, and then she explained the results.

Siris, P., P. Gaidarska, and K. Racco. "How to Predict Sprint Potential." Modern Athlete and Coach Oct. 1986: 13–15. Translated from Russian (no translator identified), this article is a summary of years of research with young athletes in the Soviet Union. Remarkably technical in its approach to evaluating sprint potential.

Slater, Jackie. Personal interviews. 4, II, and 19 Oct. 1988. UWEC track coach, Ms. Slater provided me with information about the university's program and about the meets in which the team participates. She also provided me with information about running injuries, and an analysis of my high school sprinting technique.

Viitasalo, Jukka T. "Evaluation of Explosive Strength for Young and Adult Athletes." Research Quarterly for Exercise and Sport 59 (1988) 9–15. Professor of Sports Physiology at the University of Jjvaskyla, Finland, Professor Viitasalo uses scientific techniques to measure "explosive" strength.

Westman, Dorene. Telephone interview. 28 Oct. 1988. A veteran member of the UWEC track team, Ms. Westman provided me with insights into the social life of a track team member.

Wimmer, Burton, Office Consultation. 22 Oct. 1988. An Orthopaedic Surgeon at the Marshfield Clinic, Marshfield, Wisconsin, Dr. Wimmer treated my stress fracture last spring and during my last visit, he signed me off as completely healed. He also provided me information about the causes of my injury and advice about how to avoid similar injuries in the future.

Wisconsin Women's Intercollegiate Athletic Conference. "Sprints: Heats and Finals." 6 and 7 May 1988. The results of the Conference Track and Field Meet held at Simpson Field, UWEC, Eau Claire, Wisconsin.

Zimmerman, David. "Maturation and Strenuous Training in Young Female Athletes." Physician and Sportsmedicine June, 1987: 219–22. This article features an extended interview with Richard M. Malina, a widely recognized authority on this topic. During the interview, he analyzes the existing research on the effects of rigorous training by young women.

Additional Works Consulted

Books

Crawford, Terry and Bob Bertucci. Winning Track and Field Drills for
    Women Champaign, Il.: Leisure Press, 1985.

Gambetta, Vern, ed. Track and Field Coaching Manual Champaign, IL:
    Leisure Press, 1981.

Glover, Bob and Murray Weisenfeld. The Injured Runner's Training
    Handbook New York: Penguin Books, 1985.

Wisconsin Interscholastic Athletic Association. 65th Annual WIAA Year-
    books Reviewing 1987–88 Stevens Point, WI: WIAA Press, 1988.

Periodical Articles

Chow, John W. "Maximum Speed of Female High School Runners."
    International Journal of Sport Biomechanics 3 (1987): 110–27.

Henschen, K. P., S. W. Edwards, and L. Mathinos. "Achievement Motiva-
    tion and Sex-Role Orientation of High School Female Track and
    Field Athletes Versus Nonathletes." Perceptual and Motor Skills 55
    (1982): 183–87.

Nutter, June and William Thorland. "Body Composition and Anthro-
    pometric Correlates of Isokinetic Leg Extension Strength of Young
    Adult Males." Research Quarterly for Exercise and Sport 58 (1987):
    47–51.

SHOULD I CONTINUE TO WORK

TOWARD A BACHELOR OF SCIENCE IN NURSING,

OR SHOULD I RETURN

TO WORK AS A 3-YEAR DIPLOMA REGISTERED NURSE?

A Documented Paper

by

LuAnn Fletcher

Presented to

Tim Hirsch

English Composition 110

on

November 23, 1987

This paper was prepared for an English Composition class. It is used here by permission of the author. Some of the names of people and places have been changed to protect their right to privacy.

Outline

THESIS QUESTION Should I continue to work toward a B.S.N. or should I return to work as a 3-year Diploma R.N.?

   I. INTRODUCTION.
- **A.** Why is this question relevant to me?
- **B.** What is my present situation?

  II. WHAT ARE THE DIFFERENCES BETWEEN A B.S.N. AND A DIPLOMA IN THE WORKPLACE?
- **A.** Will having a B.S.N. provide more job flexibility?
- **B.** Will having a B.S.N. mean a higher salary?

 III. WILL HAVING A B.S.N. BE MANDATORY TO MAINTAIN PROFESSIONAL STATUS AS AN R.N.?
- **A.** What is the probability of this occurring?
- **B.** When would it occur?
- **C.** What would my status be if it occurs?

 IV. WHAT EFFECT WILL THE NURSING SHORTAGE HAVE ON JOB FLEXIBILITY AND THE MANDATORY B.S.N. PROPOSAL?
- **A.** Is the shortage real and if so how long will it last?
- **B.** Will the shortage effect job flexibility?
- **C.** Will it prevent or delay the mandatory B.S.N. proposal?

  V. WILL HAVING A B.S.N. ENHANCE MY NURSING SKILLS?

 VI. WILL THE SHORT-TERM PERSONAL SACRIFICES RESULT IN LONG-TERM PERSONAL GAINS?

 VII. SUMMARY: What have I discovered?

VIII. CONCLUSION: What have I decided?

       QUESTION: Should I continue working towards a B.S.N. or should I return to work as a 3-year Diploma R.N.?

Why is This Question Important to Me?

I am 45-years old and a college freshman, a difficult but interesting situation to be in after having been employed as a registered nurse for the past 24 years. The transition from a position of authority and responsibility to the position of merely following orders has been stressful. It has brought me to the decision, "Do I want to continue in college or return to work?"

After having a successful and varied career as a 3-year Diploma R.N. for over two decades, complacency and job security had taken hold. Then slow but escalating rumors began to break that shell. The two largest nursing organizations—the American Nurses Association and the National League of Nurses—were proposing that a bachelors degree be necessary to maintain professional status as an R.N. Neither ignoring the rumors nor denying their existence made them go away and reluctantly I started to contemplate my career future. Since I enjoy working and have potentially 20 years of employment remaining I felt threatened. By the spring of 1987 I had consolidated my thoughts into two questions. 1) Would I need a B.S.N., even if it were not mandatory, to retain credibility in the nursing profession? 2) Could I, at 45 years of age, succeed in college?

I decided to answer the second question first, enrolled in summer session in June of 1987, and earned a 4.0 grade point average. I am now at mid-term of my second semester and am maintaining a "B" average. Thus, I can dispense with this question.

Facing the question of the need for a B.S.N. was difficult. I truly did not want to know the answer but reality forced me. In fairness to myself, I also find, I must face another question—is the upheaval of my life going to be worth the end results?

What is My Present Situation?

Since June of 1987, I have been enrolled at the University of Wisconsin at Eau Claire's R.N. completion program with my earliest graduation date being June of 1989. At the end of the required course work I will have a Bachelor of Science in Nursing.

I am on a two-year educational leave of absence (June, '87–June, '89) from my position as a Nursing Consultant with the Wisconsin Division of Health. I have decided not to return to that specific job due to my dissatisfaction with the working conditions, but I will retain my LOA (Leave Of Absence) status to preserve my seniority rights in case I choose to return to state service in another capacity.

As I consider my options of either continuing to work toward a B.S.N. or of returning to work as a 3-year Diploma R.N. I seek answers to the following questions: Will having a B.S.N. provide me more flexibility than I would have as a 3-year Diploma R.N., thus allowing me to choose the position I want at a higher salary? Will having a B.S.N. be mandatory to maintain professional status as a Registered Nurse? Will this occur during my career life and if so, how will it affect me? Is the nursing shortage real and if so, how will it affect the mandatory B.S.N. proposal and job flexibility? Will having a college degree afford me gains in areas other than professional?

What are the Differences Between a B.S.N. and a 3-Year Diploma in the Workplace?

In researching this question I attempted to determine if a B.S.N. would allow me more opportunities than a 3-year Diploma to secure a position in a field of nursing of interest to me at a higher salary.

To begin, I went to the classified ads of a national nurses' magazine to get a broad picture. In the May 1987 American Journal of Nursing classified ads there were twenty-two nationwide job announcements. Of these, eleven stated that only an R.N. license was required and supplied no job description. Two required a B.S.N. and specified the jobs as a psychiatric nurse and a clinical coordinator. Nine faculty positions required a masters degree (744–45). The August 1987 issue of the same journal contained 25 employment announcements. Thirteen required an R.N. license, four called for a B.S.N. and eight called for a masters degree.

-4-

There were no specific salaries quoted for any of these positions (1109–10).

The classified ads I examined show that some advertised positions specifically require a B.S.N. While 24 positions were open for R.N.s, six additional were available for B.S.N.s. Since I already qualify for the R.N. positions, it's clear that I could increase by 25% the number of positions open to me by earning the B.S.N.

"Chicago Story," an article by Catherine Ballman, reports that Rush Presbyterian/St. Lukes Medical Center in Chicago is one of the first hospitals to require a B.S.N. for employment. In Ballman's interview with Janet Moore, R.N., Associate Vice President at Rush Presbyterian, Moore states that "The policy for requiring B.S.N.s has felt the cold glare of publicity and heated skepticism from nursing and hospital administration who said it wouldn't work." Moore concludes, however, that the experiment has been successful (1342).

Ballman comments that Rush Presbyterian offers the B.S.N.s flexible hours and both clinical and academic appointments with salaries starting at $22,256 and ranging to $40,179.

Ballman's article continues with an interview with Patricia Baker, Director of Personnel at Humona Hospital, Hoffman Estates, who states, "degrees are not required, although to move into management we prefer a B.S.N., but it depends on the person." (1342).

I did several phone interviews to identify, locally, the trend toward having a B.S.N. versus a 3-year Diploma, and to estimate the salary differences between the two. Sandra Everett, Employment Assistant at Holy Cross Hospital in Clear Water, revealed that B.S.N.s and 3-year Diploma R.N.s, working as staff nurses, have the same responsibilities and receive the same salaries. She stated, however, that Holy Cross prefers B.S.N.s for managerial positions. These administrators receive higher salaries than do staff nurses. I asked Ms. Everett if she thought the day would come when Holy Cross Hospital would require a B.S.N. and she replied that "we have no plans to do so, but if other hospitals required it we would follow suit."

According to Phyllis Homes, Clinical Director at Grace Hospital in

Eau Claire, no distinction is made—either in job responsibilities or salary—between a B.S.N. and a 3-year Diploma R.N. when hired as a staff nurse. They do, however, prefer B.S.N.s for supervisory positions that are compensated at a higher salary.

Rapid River Valley Nursing Home's Director of Nurses, Helen Neibauer, stated that they have no specific positions for B.S.N.s and concluded with the information that she is a 3-year Diploma R.N. and is Director of Nurses. She also revealed that salaries for both B.S.N.s and 3-year Diploma R.N.s are identical at her facility.

Jean Willets, Director of Nurses at Signet County Health Care Center, Signet, Wisconsin, stated that "not all my head nurses are B.S.N.s but all my B.S.N.s are head nurses." She also stated that being a head nurse provided the advantages of working only the day shift.

In general, both the administrators interviewed by Ballman and the ones I talked with suggest that B.S.N.s have a slight advantage over R.N.s in opportunities for supervisory positions.

Jean Willets provided me with the following wage scale for the Signet County Health Care Center. She pointed out that the scale is determined by educational background.

Head nurses	$10.63 to $12.12 in 3 yrs.
B.S.N.s	$10.05 to $11.54 in 3 yrs.
3-yr. Diplomas	$ 9.52 to $11.01 in 3 yrs.

The June 1986 <u>American Journal of Nursing</u> had the results of an August 1985 survey conducted by the U.S. Bureau of Labor Statistics. The survey covered 23 major metropolitan areas. Here I reproduce a list of average hourly wages for different positions in the Minneapolis–St. Paul area:

Staff Nurse	$12.70
Head Nurse	$15.47
Supervisor	$15.94
Clinical Specialist	$15.12
Director of Nurses	$16.36 to $18.63
	(746–47)

The Illinois Nurses Association, according to Ballman, negotiated a contract including pay scales differentiated for B.S.N.s and non-B.S.N.s. The final results were as follows:

Diploma R.N.s	$21,320 to $24,939 per year
B.S.N.s	$22,000 to $25,958 per year
	(1346)

From another interview with Marjie Townsend, R.N., recruiter for Mercy Hospital, Ballman reports that B.S.N. salaries start $728.00 higher than those of non-B.S.N.s (1348).

Barbara Stevens, R.N., PhD., and Joanne Disch and Paula Fieldstein offer two differing views on the value of education as it relates to monetary compensation. Stevens quotes an article by Mennemeyer and Gaumer in the Journal of Human Resources, which concludes that the longer education required to become a B.S.N. is not compensated by sufficient wage hikes to replace lost wages (126). Disch and Feldstein take the opposite view, believing that a worker's productivity is the result of education, experience, and skills and that the difference in income in professions is due to these factors. They also believe that educational training would not be worthwhile without higher wages (25).

Based on the information gathered it appears that 3-year Diploma R.N.s and B.S.N.s have approximately the same chances to be a staff nurse although a slight edge may be held by the B.S.N. For managerial and supervisory positions the evidence points to the B.S.N. having more opportunities with these positions garnering higher salaries. Therefore, I must conclude that having a B.S.N. would provide more job flexibility and higher wages.

Will Having a B.S.N. Be Mandatory to Maintain Professional Status as an R.N.?

As I stated in the introduction, there are attempts to make a B.S.N. mandatory to retain professional status as an R.N. After regarding myself, and being regarded, as a professional for 24 years, this proposal has created a great deal of anxiety for me. It would be helpful to me in this decision to know if and when having a B.S.N. will be required and what my status as a 3-year Diploma will be.

Doris Blaney, in her article in the Journal of Nursing Education states that the American Nurses Association has supported the B.S.N. since 1960. She continues with the information that the 1984 resolution of the American Nurses Association House of Delegates included a deadline of 1995 for every state to require the bachelors degree as the educational background for a professional nurse license (182 & 185).

The news section of the August 1987 American Journal of Nursing stated that at the National League of Nurses June, 1987 convention an important issue of discussion was about having two titles and two separate examinations for B.S.N.s and Diploma R.N.s. The end result would have the B.S.N.s as registered professional nurses and the Diploma R.N.s as registered associate nurses. The articles goes on to say that a vote was postponed due to evidence that it would have been defeated. NLN leaders are quoted as having said, "our members are clearly not ready to proceed with it." (1091)

Barbara Stevens regards the proposal as essential if nurses are to be recognized as professionals. She states that nurses must pay their "academic dues." (125)

Sarah Hilman of the Wisconsin Nurses Association assured me that neither my license nor my scope of practice would be limited. However, she feels that the job market will limit my opportunities with a 3-year Diploma,because the industry prefers B.S.N.s.

At this time North Dakota is the only state in the union requiring that nursing education programs be baccalaureate, according to Nursing Success (27).

After researching this area I feel confident that even if the mandatory B.S.N. requirement is passed, it will affect only people just entering the profession. Thus my license, professional status and scope of practice would be jeopardized only slightly.

What Effect Will the Nursing Shortage Have on Job Flexibility and the Mandatory B.S.N. Proposal?

Recently, many reports claim a nationwide nursing shortage. I attempted to find out if there was a shortage, and if so, how long it would last. Would it have any effects on job flexibility? Would it prevent or delay the proposed requirement for a B.S.?

Who Needs Nurses, by Curron, Minnick, and Moss reports statistics from a December 1986 survey conducted by the American Organization of Nurse Executives. The results of the survey showed vacant R.N. positions in hospitals as having doubled since 1985. The survey concluded that in December 1986, 13.6% of R.N. positions were vacant as opposed to 6.3% in a September 1985 survey by the American Hospital Association (444).

In the news section of the August 1987 American Journal of Nursing, three sections were devoted to the nursing shortage. The first was a paragraph revealing the National League of Nurses Statistics on the declining number of accredited Diploma schools. In 1976 there were 390; today 232 (1094). Another news item reported on the closing of Boston University's Nursing School due to dwindling enrollments and competition from less expensive schools (1095). The last reported on the Nursing Shortage Reduction Act, the first national legislation aimed at the growing problems of filling R.N. vacancies. Senator Ted Kennedy is quoted as saying, "The national nursing shortage has reached crisis proportions," as he introduced the bill which would provide five million dollars in fiscal year 1988 to help relieve the shortage (1094).

Ballman interviewed Linda Harty, R.N., the staffing coordinator and nurse recruiter for Louis A. Weiss Memorial Hospital in Chicago. Harty, when asked if B.S.N.s were preferred, said "reality forces me to say that this isn't a realistic pursuit at this time because the number of students enrolled in B.S.N. programs is declining. Our ability to recruit experienced nurses is diminished in the kind of market with that kind of requirement." (1340) Ballman also interviewed Barbara Prieb, R.N., Vice President of Nursing at Columbia Hospital in Chicago, who indicated that 35 of their 350 full-time R.N. positions were vacant. Prieb said, "We

-9-

would love to have a B.S.N. requirement, but considering the local market we accept any level." (1338)

Jean Willets stated, "I was attempting to have an all R.N. staff but I'm using Licensed Practical Nurses just to staff."

Willets, Helen Neibauer and Phyllis Homes all felt that the current nursing shortage is definitely a deterrent to the passage of the mandatory B.S.N. proposal.

The research reveals that there is a serious nursing shortage and with the number of nursing schools, both 3-year and B.S.N., declining, the shortage will last for some time. Although the nursing shortage has created vacant positions that institutions may be forced to fill with non-B.S.N.s, it appears that they still prefer B.S.N.s. The nursing shortage may delay the mandatory B.S.N. proposal, but this is not conclusive.

Will Having a B.S.N. Enhance My Nursing Skills?

With 3 years of formal nursing education coupled with 24 years of continuous and varied experience, in both staff and supervisory positions, I feel that my nursing skills are both current and competent. An important question is whether the course work required to receive a B.S.N. will improve the nursing skills I already possess.

According to Jean Willets there are definite differences between 3-year nurses and B.S.N.s. The 3-year nurse, she feels, knows basic nursing care while the B.S.N. is a better writer, thinker, has better management skills and "can see the whole picture." She stated that she felt so strongly about the differences that she persuaded the administration to allow her to develop separate job descriptions delineating the expectations of the two levels.

Grace Hospital's Phyllis Homes believes that 3-year nurses have better technical skills at first, but that the B.S.N.s quickly come up to their level due to better comprehension. She also believes that the B.S.N. has a better background in nursing theory and is better able to "pick-up" on problem patients.

Helen Neibauer, a 3-year R.N., stated that "3-year R.N.s are better at

-10-

assessing patients and better at working with nurses' aides," while "B.S.N.s are trained for management, not patient care."

Vivian DeBack and Marsha Merkowski, a research team that conducted a survey for the National Institute of Education, titled "Developing a Professional Competency Mode for Nursing Education." (275) Some of the findings:

> Nurses with bachelors degrees demonstrated more nursing competence compared with associate or 3-year diploma colleagues (283).
>
> The more educated nurses acted more independently—took more responsibility for judgment, even at the risk of incurring disapproval (281).
>
> Experience and education, in combination, seem to provide the nurse with greater ability to consider the total concept of the nursing situation and what it requires as opposed to simple reliance on routine practice (284).

Doris Blaney, in her article in the Journal of Nurses Education, discusses the finding of a 1983 study by the National Commission of Nurses on nursing education. The study found patient care so advanced that more nurses with masters degrees are needed with a B.S.N. being the first step toward this goal (1984).

From the information gathered, I conclude that 3-year nurses and B.S.N.s have approximately the same knowledge of technical skills, but the evidence suggests the similarities stopping there. According to my sources, the B.S.N. is more competent overall, demonstrating better conceptualization of the total picture, more confidence in judgments, and better management abilities.

Will the Short-term Personal Sacrifices Result in Long-term Personal Gains?

As I stated in my introduction, I am finding that adjusting to college is difficult for many reasons. The demands on my time are significant, my income is zero, most of my time is spent with people twenty years younger than I, and I am in a position of no authority. However, there are days when I enjoy what I am doing very much and feel some dissatisfaction over achievements made. I am interested in knowing if the personal sacrifices will result in long-term personal gains.

Carol Mishler, in her article "Adult Perceptions of the Benefits of a College Degree," reports on a survey of adult graduates of the University of Wisconsin system, three to five years after graduation (224). One of the categories of the survey was "Other Gains Achieved from a Degree." According to Mishler, most of those surveyed (441, with 64% responding) felt they had made significant progress in "personal achievement and self-satisfaction." (218) The following table taken from her article shows her results in the nine areas examined.

Survey Question	% Favorable
Sense of personal achievement and self-satisfaction	90%
Intellectual curiosity	76%
Understanding your own abilities, limitations, interests	66%
Ability to think analytically	58%
Ability to learn and work on your own	55%
Ability to carry out work duties and responsibilities	51%
Appreciation and use of fine arts and humanities	45%
Ability to write well	45%
Ability to speak well in public	35%
(224)	

Mishler reports that the adults were asked one final question, "Would you do it again?" They were also asked to write a comment supporting their answer. She reveals that 85% of the responses said they would definitely do it again and that none answered simply "no." Approximately 150 comments were received—130 positive and 22 negative. Of the 150 positive comments, 43 indicated satisfaction and accomplishment gains, 18 stated they enjoyed learning and college and 10 commented on the value of knowledge. Of the negative comments, 9 out of 22 expressed dissatisfaction with their particular major (225).

-12-

Mishler also comments on a 1982 survey of students age 25 who dropped out of college. The three leading reasons were job obligations, family obligations and financial problems (29). Mishler concludes with the statement, "Although the adults received their degrees later in life than their younger counterparts, it seems clear that most benefitted greatly from the college experience and the possession of a bachelors degree. Thus benefits appeared in both their working lives and their personal lives" (227).

A sense of personal achievement and self-satisfaction seems to be the prevailing theme of the section. The evidence appears conclusive that personal gains were attained, and regarded as very important by those surveyed.

Summary

Before reaching a conclusion I will review what I have learned from re-searching my criteria. First, I have learned that having a B.S.N. would allow more job flexibility, leading to a greater range of working conditions, and, more often than not, higher wages.

Secondly, I discovered that as a 3-year Diploma R.N. neither my license, professional status nor scope of practice will be limited by a mandatory B.S.N. requirement.

I am now convinced that the nursing shortage is real and will continue for a number of years due to the declining number of nursing schools and enrollments. There are no hard facts to estimate whether the shortage will affect the mandatory B.S.N. proposal, but there will be more vacant R.N. positions available providing a degree of flexibility for job choices.

Next, I found that technical skills for a 3-year Diploma R.N. and a B.S.N. are similar, but there are differences in other areas. A B.S.N. would give me better ability to comprehend the total picture, better managerial and writing skills and a broader nursing theory base.

Finally, I discovered that attaining a degree would probably lead to a feeling of personal achievement and self-satisfaction.

-13-

Conclusion

From the information I have gathered researching my criteria I feel I can now make an informed decision to my question: Should I continue working towards a B.S.N. or should I return to work as a 3-year Diploma R.N." The evidence makes it clear that I should continue to work towards a B.S.N. Although this is a difficult conclusion to accept because of the problems intrinsic to a college student in my position, it is clear that I will emerge from the B.S.N. program with the satisfaction of knowing that I made the right choice.

Works Cited

"ANA's Change in Nursing Education." Nursing Success Mar. 1986: 27. The news item stated that North Dakota is the first state to require nursing education to be at the Baccalaureate level after Jan. 1, 1987.

Ballman, Catherine. "The Chicago Story." American Journal of Nursing 87.10 (1987): 1338–46. The article contained information on the trend toward preferring B.S.N.s, advantages of B.S.N.s and salary differences.

Blaney, Doris. "An Historical Review of Positions in Baccalaureate Education in Nursing as Basic Preparation for Professional Nursing Practice 1960–1984." American Journal of Nursing 86.5 (1986): 182–85. This article gave me insight on the beginning of the B.S.N. Proposal by the American Nurses Association—where it is now and why the association favors it.

"Boston U Set to Shut Down Its School of Nursing." American Journal of Nursing 87.8 (1987): 1095. This news item was about the declining number of nursing schools and students.

-14-

"Classified Advertisements." American Journal of Nursing 87.5 (1987): 740–41. These ads provided nationwide information on preferences for B.S.N.s.

"Classified Advertisements." American Journal of Nursing 87.8 (1987): 1109–10. These ads gave me some idea of the preference for B.S.N.s nationwide.

Curan, Connie, Ann Minnick and Joan Moss. "Who Needs Nurses?" American Journal of Nursing 87.4 (1987): 444–47. This article provided information on the percentage of vacant R.N. positions.

De Back, Vivien and Marcia Merkowski. "Does the Baccalaureate Make a Difference?" Journal of Nursing Education Sept. 1986: 275–84. This article outlines differences between B.S.N.s and nonB.S.N.s.

Disch, Joanne and Paul Fieldstein. "An Economic Analysis of Comparable Worth." Journal of Nursing Administration June 1986: 25. This article relates wages to education.

Everett, Sandra. Employment Assistant at Holy Cross Hospital, Signet, WI. Telephone interview 22 Oct. 1987. Information on hiring preferences, salary differences—promotional opportunities.

Hilman, Sarah, R.N. M.S.N. Official with Wisconsin Nurses Association. Telephone interview 9 Nov. 1987. Provided information on stability of my R.N. license and WNA's work toward a mandatory B.S.N.

Homes, Phyllis, R.N. M.S.N. Clinical Director at Grace Hospital, Clear Water, WI. Telephone interview 22 Oct. 1987. Information on differences in 3-year R.N. versus B.S.N.—salary differences, hiring preferences, promotional opportunities and opinion on nursing shortage affecting B.S.N. proposal.

"Kennedy Bill Seeks Long-term Solutions to Nursing Shortages." American Journal of Nursing 87.8 (1987): 1094. This article gave me insight into the reality of the nursing shortage.

"League Postpones Action on Entry Level Plan." American Journal of Nursing 87.8 (1987): 1091–92. This news item dealt with the National League of Nursing attempt to pass the mandatory B.S.N. proposal and its defeat.

Mischler, Carol. "Adult Perceptions of the Benefits of a College Degree." Research in Higher Education 19.3 (1988): 213–29. This article gave me information about personal gains from a college degree.

Neibauer, Helen, R.N. Director of Nurses at Rapid River Nursing Home. Telephone interview 22 Oct. 1987. This interview provided information on hiring preferences, salaries, differences between 3-year R.N.s and B.S.N.s and any effects of nursing shortage on mandatory B.S.N. proposal.

"New Survey Points to Cities Where Salaries are Highest (San Francisco) and Lowest (Buffalo)." American Journal of Nursing 86.6 (1986): 742–47. This article provided information on salaries for different levels of nursing.

Ostberg, John. Member of Wisconsin Bureau of Regulation and Licensing. Telephone interview 9 Nov. 1987. Information on the stability of my R.N. license.

Stevens, Barbara. "Does the 1985 Nursing Education Proposal Make Economic Sense?" Nursing Outlook May–June 1985: 124–27. This reading provided insight into why a B.S.N. is needed. It is cost efficient.

"Tri-Council Sees Single Scope of Practice." American Journal of Nursing 87.6 (1987): 868. This article outlined the possibility of separate technical and professional licenses for nurses.

"Twin Cities Lose Diploma School." American Journal of Nursing 87.8
(1987): 1094. This brief news item provided information on the declining number of diploma schools.

Willets, Jean, B.S.N. Director of Nurses at Signet Co. Health Care Center,
Signet, WI. Telephone interview 22 Oct. 1987. Information on differences in 3-year R.N. versus B.S.N.—salary differences, promotional
opportunities and hiring preferences and opinion on nursing shortage affecting B.S.N. proposal.

212

WHERE SHOULD I TAKE
MY DAUGHTER FOR DAY CARE?

A Research Paper
by
Elizabeth Ryan

Presented to
Tim Hirsch
English Composition

on

November 23, 1988

THESIS QUESTION: Should I keep my daughter at her present day care or should I find a different one?

  I. INTRODUCTION

      A. Why is this question important to me?

      B. What are my "givens?"

      C. What "criteria" are important to me?

  II. WHAT ARE THE DIFFERENT TYPES OF DAY CARE?

  III. WHAT ARE THE RULES AND REGULATIONS GOVERNING THE DIFFERENT TYPES OF DAY CARE?

      A. Who regulates the day cares?

      B. What are the ratios of adults to children?

      C. What are the differences in training for the providers?

  IV. WHAT INFORMATION DO I NEED FROM EACH DAY CARE I LOOK AT?

      A. What type of day care?

      B. What is the education of the provider?

      C. What type of program structure is followed?

      D. What age range of children is served?

      E. What food arrangements need to be made?

      F. What is the ratio of adults to children?

      G. Is there any other information relative to this particular day care?

  V. WHAT DIFFERENCE WILL MY CHILD'S RACIAL HERITAGE MAKE?

      A. Will the provider take non-white children?

      B. Has the provider dealt with a racial minority before?

      C. Are there any non-white providers in this area?

  VI. WHAT ARE JESSICA'S SPEECH NEEDS AND ARE THEY BEING MET?

      A. What is Jessica's current level of speech?

      B. What methods are being used to correct her speech delay?

      C. How important are age-appropriate activities to her speech delay?

D. Will the provider work with a child with a speech delay?

    1. Does this provider have any experience with speech delay in children?

    2. Are the provider's speech patterns a good model?

E. What causes frustration in the child and what should I watch out for?

VII. OF WHAT IMPORTANCE IS SEPARATION ANXIETY IN CHILDREN?

    A. Do a parent's feelings about day care make a difference?

    B. Does the amount of time spent each day in a day care make a difference?

    C. How will a change in providers affect a child in reference to separation anxiety?

    D. How is my daughter doing where she is presently located?

VII. ARE THERE ANY OTHER AREAS OF CONCERN I WANT TO EXAMINE?

    A. Who would meet Jessica's bus?

    B. Who takes care of the children when the provider is ill?

    C. Where is the day care located and what is the cost associated with the travel to and from care?

    D. What is the cost of the day care?

IX. SUMMARY

X. CONCLUSION

Imagine being transported from where you live now to a strange land, filled with strange-looking people, different smells, and unusual food. You cannot understand a word you hear. You do not know a soul. Would you feel insecure?

Add to the above scenario the fact that the person involved was nine-months old when this traumatic experience occurred. This is how our youngest child, Jessica, started her life with our family.

This fall, after being out of school for 18 years, I returned to college. This required me to place Jessica in day care for the first time since her arrival from Korea three years ago. She is having a hard time adjusting to the change. Every day when I kiss her goodbye, the tears cascade down her cheeks and the sobs shake her entire body. She calls after me "No Mama, no." I thought the care I chose for her was good, but now I have second thoughts. Maybe there is a better place for her. The importance of this question became obvious to me when I realized the effects my concern about Jessica had on my concentration in class.

The Givens

Last November, I decided to return to college. Some of the reasons I made this decision at this time were: job burn-out, a need for personal fulfillment, and a strong desire to get my degree. I have my family's backing. I felt the timing was as good as it would get until 1991. In 1991, Jessica will enter first grade.

The child care I chose for my youngest child is not working as well as I had hoped. Jessica, only three and a half years old and Korean by birth, starts crying as soon as she sees the Children's Center where I presently take her for day care. This makes it very hard for me to leave and go to classes. Most children her age could tell a parent what the problem was, but Jessica has a speech delay making it very hard for her to communicate her feelings. Rather than make a hasty decision, however, I will leave her where she is until I finish my research.

Jessica's mornings are filled as she goes to an Early Childhood Intervention Program with other children who also have speech difficulties. This program offers both group and individual speech therapy. Jessica takes a bus to and from this program and this bus must be met at lunch time. Therefore, convenience as well as reliability are important in deciding where she goes each afternoon. Unfortunately, I have no relatives in the area to help out.

The cost of day care is also a factor as I must cover the cost with my student loan. Since these funds are limited I cannot afford to hire a person to come into my home.

As time goes on, Jessica seems to be doing better at her present day care, once she is past the initial separation each day. In fact, a few times she has even finished whatever she was doing when I arrived, before she was willing to leave.

The Criteria

First I need to explore the different types of day care available. I want to find out what regulations, if any, apply to each type.

After identifying the different types of day care I intend to compare the following criteria: How reliable are each of the available providers? Who cares for the children when the primary provider is sick? How are each of these options monitored? Some other areas to explore are the ratio of adults to children, the age range served and the flexibility of the programs.

After finding the differences, I need to address how these differences will answer the following questions: Are the activities age-appropriate for Jessica? What effect will Jessica's speech delay have on the activities the provider offers? Does the provider have the time, interest, and commitment to try to understand Jessica's speech? Will Jessica become frustrated when she is not understood?

Separation anxiety is another concern. Will a change in providers be helpful or harmful in the long run? Has there been any improvement where she is presently in care? Will the provider consider Jessica's crying a disruption? How will her crying be dealt with?

A value judgment must be made on how well a particular provider

-5-

217

will react to a crying child. Will the pressure and disruption lead to another change in providers? Who can the provider count on when Jessica's needs have to be met?

Other needs to be considered are the location of the day care and who will meet Jessica's bus. If I must meet the bus, can it be done without interruption of my classes? What is the cost of day care? Can I change the hours of care if I need more or fewer hours of care in a particular week?

While researching this topic, I want to protect the confidentiality of the personal information I discuss; therefore I will refer to all providers I interview in numerical order (provider 1, provider 2, and so on) rather than by name.

Types of Day Care

To find out about the types of day care and the regulations governing them I spoke with Nancy McCarthy, a Day Care Licensing Specialist who works for the state of Wisconsin. She talked to me about some of the differences in types of day care and then sent me several printed resources to find the types of day care and the regulations covering them. Two of the resources are pamphlets; one is entitled "Your Day Care—is it Legal?" by the Division of Community Services. The second one is called "To: Parents Subject: Choosing Child Care," published by the Department of Human Services. The remaining two resources are excerpts from Wisconsin administrative code, each under its own cover. The first one is "Wisconsin Administrative Code HSS 55 Licensing Rules for Family Day Care Centers." The second one is "Wisconsin Administrative Code HSS 55 Licensing rules for Group Day Care Centers." Both of these are published by the state of Wisconsin, revised in 1988. The following paragraphs are paraphrased or summarized from these sources. All included essentially the same information.

There are four types of day care: "Non-regulated," "County Certified," "State Licensed Family Day Care," and "State Licensed Group Day Care Center."

"Non-regulated" day care is just what its name implies; it is not regulated. The only law it must abide by is that there can be no more than three children per adult in care at one time. However, unless someone reports a person for having more than three children, no one will investigate the day care. Most non-regulated day care is provided by people with little or no training. There seems to be no required structure to the day in these day care facilities. The children may be left to play as they wish with the toys and other materials available.

The "County Certified Day Care" has some regulations. For instance, they also can have only three children per adult. Certification also offers the provider some benefits. The provider is eligible for participation in a USDA Food Program. They can also collect money from the county for children in their care whose families receive AFDC. Certified programs tend to give some structure to the child's day as this structure and its benefits are introduced to the provider during the ten hours of training required to become certified.

"State Licensed Family Day Cares" is home-based, regulated day care for up to eight children per adult. There are strict state laws concerning the operation of the Family Day Care. The Family Day Care is also eligible for the USDA Food Program and County money for care of children receiving AFDC.

The "Wisconsin Administrative Code" includes the following limits for the number of children a State Licensed Family Day Care provider can accommodate:

Under the Age of 2

Max Number in Group	Ages 2 to 6	Over 6
0	8	8
1	7	8
2	5	7
3	2	5
4	0	4
		(64)

A "State Licensed Day Care" is generally more structured with a variety of activities, such as free time, story time, music, art and outside play. However, this varies from one day care to another.

A minimum of forty hours of training are required to obtain a license, and then fifteen hours of training each year thereafter to keep the license. During this forty hours of training, the provider learns the laws under which she must operate, ideas for projects, and the structure encouraged for family day care.

In addition to limiting the number of children in the facility, there are rules governing the minimum space per child (35 square feet), building standards, health and fire standards and required forms which must be kept current. The provider is also informed of the right of a representative of the state of Wisconsin to make surprise visits to the day care in addition to the two yearly regular visits and the two yearly inspections by the fire department. Family Day Cares are required to have a second adult available within five minutes in case of an emergency. There is a thirty-six page booklet available spelling out all the rules and regulations governing State Licensed Family Day Cares.

The last type of care is "State Licensed Group Day Care." There are many rules concerning this type of care which can be found in the booklet "Wisconsin Administrative Code HSS 55 Licensing for Group Day Care Centers." These day care centers must meet all of the requirements governing Family day care centers, as well as some additional requirements. For instance, the building must have water sprinklers every 150 feet of hallway that the children use (87). There must be a fenced play area outside with a minimum of 75 square feet per child (92). There are requirements for the number of sinks and toilets available for the children's use (91). There must also be a written program plan posted for parents to refer to (92).

The training is much more intense for group day care providers. The primary provider (hereafter referred to as the teacher) MUST have a minimum of two years post-secondary Early Childhood Education and 80 hours of experience in a licensed day care. The secondary provider (hereafter referred to as the assistant) is required to have 80 hours of training. Both are required to complete an additional fifteen hours of training yearly (Wisconsin Code, 87).

Group day care can have a larger total number of children in each group, but they must also have more adults to keep the ratios at what state laws require. I will limit my areas of concern to group care for three- to five-year-old children as there are slightly different requirements for different age groups, and this is the age group of my daughter. The ratio of adults to children for three- to four-year-old children is one to ten with a maximum of twenty children in a group. (85) The ratio for four- to five-year-old children is one to thirteen with a maximum of twenty-four children in a group (Wisconsin Code, 85).

Group day cares are also required to have a written statement indicating the center's policies, philosophy, and disciplinary policy. They are also required to have bound log books for records of medicine given to children at the center, injuries that happen while a child is at the center and any unusual injuries the child brings to the center. Monthly reports are written and accessible to Health and Social Service personnel who are responsible for issuing and renewing state licenses. These reports are checked for compliance with Wisconsin State Statutes.

Group day cares must have a Director who oversees all teachers and assistants, makes sure they post and follow a planned schedule and comply with state rules and regulations. The Director is in charge of all issues related to the children's health and the well-being of the children. The individual child's records are confidential and are only allowed to be seen with the parents' permission, by people directly involved with the child. The Director must provide qualified substitutes when needed. The director must also see to it that the teachers and assistants are free of all non-classroom duties during the hours of operation in compliance with state law (Wisconsin Code, 86). The Director must see to it that the center's equipment is in good repair and that there are materials which reflect an awareness of cultural and ethnic diversity. Because Jessica is non-white, this is especially important.

The following is a chart from page 85 of the "Wisconsin Administrative Code" book showing the allowed ratio of adult to children by age groups.

-9-

Age of Children	Ratio of Adults to Children	Maximum Number of Children Per Group
Birth to 2 years	1 to 4	8
2 to 2½ years	1 to 6	12
2½ to 3 years	1 to 8	16
3 to 4 years	1 to 10	20
4 to 5 years	1 to 13	24
5 to 6 years	1 to 17	32
6 years and over	1 to 18	32

I asked Nancy McCarthy to tell me about the USDA Food Program. She said that the Federal Government set up guidelines for nutrition of children. Day care providers who qualify and follow these guidelines receive money to help pay for the meals and snacks they provide to children in their care. These guidelines are the same ones used in the hot lunch programs in elementary schools.

Interviewing the Providers

I interviewed six family day care providers and one group day care. Each of these day cares is unique in many ways, reflecting the individuals providing the care. I will be comparing these day cares in several areas: 1) type of day care, 2) education of the provider, 3) the structure followed, 4) age range of the children, 5) ratio of adults to children, 6) food arrangements, and 7) other information which comes up. I will use these same seven day cares again later when looking at other important issues. There were eight providers on the original list; one has already been dropped from consideration for reasons I will discuss later.

Provider 1 is in the process of acquiring county certification. She had no formal background in child education. Her day care is somewhat structured as she uses a lesson plan part of the day, she says, but also allows time for free play. The age range she serves is two- to four-year-old children, but she also said she cares for a ten-month-old right now. The adult-to-child ratio would be one to four in the morning and two to

-10-

six in the afternoon when her mother, who is a student in special education, comes over to help. These ratios are above those allowed for by certification and do not include any new children who would be entering at this time. In regard to meals, she said she provides all food except the afternoon snack.

During a phone interview and a follow-up personal interview in her home, Provider 2 stated that she is finishing up the requirements for her state license and that she has a degree in elementary education. As of yet she has no children in her care because she just started to provide day care. Her plan is to use a structured approach and limit television watching. The age range she wants to serve is from birth to five years of age, and because of this large range, she is not sure exactly how many children she will have until she knows their ages as they enter. She intends to be at the full number allowed by law which can be found on the chart on "numbers and ages of children in family day care," given earlier in this report. She will provide all meals and snacks and will follow the guidelines established by the USDA Food Program.

While interviewing Provider 3 on the phone she stated that she is county certified and, in addition to the ten hours of required training, has a college degree in child care. She stated she is not strong on structure because of the large age range of the children she presently cares for. The ages of these children are from eight weeks to two years. The ratio of adults to children is one to three, so adding another child would take her over the limit for a certified provider. She said she provides all the food but is not on the USDA Program.

Provider 4, who is a non-regulated provider, she said that she felt her background as a mother make up for her lack of formal education. She offered to provide references from the parents of children for whom she provided care. She said that she primarily wants the children she cares for to be happy, so she reads to them and plays with them, but she has no specific structure set up. She will accept children from two to five years old, and she will accept no more than two children in addition to her own child. The ratio of adults to children would be one to three after adding the one child she is hoping to add. In her program,

-11-

parents bring the lunches for their child but she would provide the snacks.

In my telephone interview with Provider 5, she stated she is "non-regulated and [has] no plans of changing that." She has no background education in child care and the only experience she has had is babysitting as a teenager and now as a mother of a two-month-old infant. She said "I plan to be totally unstructured and have made no plans or bought any material for the children I will take in yet." The age she will take care of will be three years or older and there will be three children in addition to her own. She said she has not thought about meals yet. One further comment she made was, "We do not smoke and I will not take care of children of smokers."

From my telephone interview with Provider 6, I found she has plans to become county certified and then state licensed. She believes in a mixture of structure and free time activities. "Children must have free time," she claims. She intends to have all the children be between four and five years old with an eventual total of five children: "Six people fit around my table nicely." She stated that the only formal education she has had regarding children is the certification training she is taking right now.

However, she did work with a Learning Disabled group while she was in high school. When I went to her home for a second interview, I saw the area she has decorated for the children and furnished with child-size equipment and other materials. When she is "full," by her standards, her adult to child ratio will be one to five. She provides the meals and just learned about the USDA Food Program and intends to look into using it when she gets her certification.

The seventh provider I spoke with works for a State Licensed Group Day Care Center. The initial contact was made by telephone and I spoke with the Director. She explained that in addition to the state's requirements, the center went further in their own requirements. The teachers all have a minimum of a four-year degree in some type of early childhood education and the assistants have a wide range of experience from four-year degrees to current University of Wisconsin—Eau Claire students in education or nursing.

The Director sent me a copy of the center's philosophy. In part, this booklet states that their philosophy is based on a "high quality early childhood program which is developmentally appropriate" (3). The center feels that there are two dimensions of developmental appropriateness: 1) age—which is based on knowledge of the typical development of children within the age span of a given group. 2) Individual appropriateness—which is based on the fact that each child is a unique person with individual patterns, timing of growth, personality, learning style and family background. The booklet goes on to state that "both the curriculum and the adults interacting with the children must be responsive to these differences while also offering a challenge to children" (4).

After talking with the Director and reading the booklet, I went to the center and spoke with the teacher in the room where my child would be. The following information came from the interview I had with the teacher. She has a four-year degree in Early Childhood Education and a Masters Degree she received by doing a thesis on "Handicapped Children in the Day Care Setting." The area the children are in has been set up especially with children in mind. It includes a loft, computer, and a wide assortment of materials. There is a large fenced-in area where the children go outside to play twice each day, weather permitting. The adult to child ratio is at a maximum of two to twenty, but often there are extra assistants in the room helping with the children. The day I was there, four adults and eighteen children were present.

These are the seven day care situations I choose to look at and they cover all four different types of day care that were mentioned in the area of my paper on types of care.

A Non-white Child in the Day Care Setting

When doing my outline I did not include the section dealing with racial heritage until the end. After interviewing providers I felt that I needed to address this issue earlier on. The importance really became apparent when, during my first telephone interview, the provider hung up when I stated that my daughter is of Korean heritage. As I mentioned earlier, this provider is not one of the seven I am considering. In thinking over this aspect of my child's needs, I decided that although I do not feel that a provider has to offer material or experiences to enhance Jessica's nationality, the provider MUST NOT be uncomfortable dealing with someone who is racially different.

After speaking with the providers I have included in this research I can make some general comments covering all but providers four and seven. Provider four is of Korean heritage and has Korean-American children herself, and the seventh provider, the group day center, has children of different racial backgrounds. The remaining five providers all stated that they had no problem with taking in a non-white child, but also stated that they did not have any experience with a minority or a handicapped child. Among these five, only one knows personally anyone who belongs to a minority race. While at the group day care I observed that there were several non-white children in the group where Jessica would be. The races represented include White, Japanese, Chinese, Native American, Black, and Israeli. I could see from observation that the teacher is very comfortable with all the children. Watching through an observation window, I have seen her hold, hug, play with, and comfort each and every child.

In addition to the one who hung-up on me, only one other provider forced me to question whether she would be comfortable with a non-white child in her care. I was so uncomfortable I did not conduct a second interview with her. In our telephone conversation, Provider 1 referred to the "abnormality of the Hmong people in our society," saying "Well, I guess that's just how they were brought up." Several other times she said in references to the Hmong, "Those kind of people; you know what I mean." Hmong are considered to be Asian, as of course are Koreans. What the major difference to her is, I do not know, and in fact do not wish to find out. The provider also said during our conversation that "It would be good for the other children in our care to see someone different from themselves." My family's belief is that people are the same on the inside, just a different color on the outside.

As part of my outline I wanted to look into the possibility of a minority as a provider. The Department of Health and Social Services were not aware of any state licensed providers who fit this requirement. However, as you already know, I did find one during my telephone interviews.

At this point in my research, I concluded that I would not use a provider who could not comfortably deal with a non-white person. For this reason I have have eliminated Provider 1 from further consideration.

Speech Needs and Ways to Meet Them

Jessica has a "speech delay." For this section of my paper, I wanted to learn more about what it is, what the current methods of treating this type of delay are, and what a day care provider can to do to support the treatment.

Jessica spends four mornings a week at Putnam Heights School in the Early Childhood Education Program. She entered this program at three years of age because she was tested at being at least thirty percent deficient in speech and language. She has been in a speech program since she was almost two years old. Her speech delay is in the areas of articulation and sequencing. Dr. James Coplan, who is with the Department of Pediatrics at the University of New York, in his report "Unclear Speech," described articulation as the clarity and formation of sounds, words, and sentences (449). Sequencing deals with putting the sounds and words made into the correct order and the proper length of the utterances.

In speaking with Penny Hanson, a teacher at Putnam Heights School with a degree in Early Childhood Education, and Lu Ann Shea, a speech therapist at Putnam Heights School, I was informed that they concur with the findings of Help Me Say It, a book by Carol Barach, and Assistant Professor of Speech Pathology and Audiology at the University of Tennessee.

The current belief in education of speech correction is mostly to working to increase the number of sounds made and to reinforce them with modeling. Children with speech problems should not be punished for incorrect speech, nor should they be made to feel ashamed, dumb or inferior to their peers. Adults working with these children must be consistent in the approach they use. Therefore, it is very important that a

-15-

provider for Jessica be in complete agreement with the form being used to work with her. This provider must frequently model the correct speech patterns that most people for granted (Barach, 157–59). At this point the issue of age-appropriate activities must be considered on all levels of development, not just in the area of speech. It is therefore very important that activities offered be at the correct age level, not her current speech level.

In this area I want to look at the likelihood of age-appropriate activities a provider is likely to offer Jessica as well as the speech patterns of those providers. Information from developmental testing and an M-Team review (described below) indicate that Jessica's spoken language age is a full twelve months behind her actual age. In the area of receptive language she has also been tested as below her actual age. Receptive language is understanding what other people say to her. Also, Jessica needs to be challenged in other areas of development such as fine motor skills, gross motor skills, listening skills and cognitive development. Challenge is needed in these areas to keep these skills at current age level and not allow them to fall behind because of concentration on speech.

An M-Team review is a group of professionals concerned with a child's needs. Jessica's M-Team consists of a classroom teacher, speech therapist, physical and occupational therapists and both of her parents. Parents are a part of this team approach because, as stated in the forward of "Help Me Say It," "the most critical factor in the outcome of speech therapy is parental support and effort" (xi).

When I spoke with each of the providers on the telephone and explained Jessica's speech delay and how it was being handled all of them expressed a willingness to work with the teachers and me to provide a consistent approach. Now I will be able to evaluate the individual age-appropriateness of each day care and any possible interference to language development that might be there.

Having eliminated Provider 1, I will start with Provider 2. Although she has an elementary education degree, this provider did not have any experience with speech problems and felt her personal communication was poor. This is a woman looking to provide a service; however, her

-16-

thoughts on day care were disordered and many times she did not speak in complete sentences. I did go to her home for a personal interview.

I asked my husband to accompany me to get a second opinion. This second interview did nothing to change my first impression of her speech patterns and my husband had the same impression.

Provider 3 has excellent speech skills. She used standard grammar, she articulated clearly, and she spoke in complete sentences. She spoke to Jessica on a child's level and even understood several words Jessica said. The ages of the children she now cares for are two one-year-olds and an eight-week-old infant. This leads me to wonder if, in spite of good intentions, the age-appropriateness would not be even lower than Jessica's speech age.

Oh for no speech problems! This woman would be excellent for Jessica if only speech was not an issue. I am referring to Provider 4 who is also of Korean heritage. I am not sure that the accented English she speaks would be a good speech model. Since language is the area I am looking at in this section, I must keep only this aspect in mind during this evaluation. I intend to ask the speech therapist's opinion on this matter. I think this provider would keep activities on an age-appropriate level as her son is also three years old and does not appear to be behind in his activities.

I spoke with Lu Ann Shea, the speech therapist, and she agreed that at this time a good speech model is very important in the development of Jessica's speech. This is consistent with my thoughts that accented speech would not be the best for Jessica.

Provider 5 stated in our telephone interview that she has had no experience with children with speech delays. Her speech patterns are clear and grammatically correct. So far, she has no children in her care except her own two month old, but states that she would offer age-appropriate activities.

Provider 6 has clear speech patterns, speaks in complete sentences, and related well with Jessica. She told me what they did when she was growing up with her brother, who stuttered. The approach they used is very close to how we are handling Jessica's delay. The age of the group Jessica would be with is a little older than her. I feel this age difference

-17-

would be an advantage, as Jessica would be challenged and have good peers to model her language after.

The seventh provider is the group day care center. The center has dealt with other children with speech delays and has one other child now, in part time care, with a speech problem. (More details are unavailable due to the confidentiality of records.) I have not been able to speak with his mother as we arrive at different times. It would have been interesting to ask her for an opinion of how the center is handling her son's speech. The age level of the group Jessica would be in is the same as her own. Watching the children, they do not seem to have a problem relating to Jessica, nor she to them.

Another aspect of speech is watching out for frustration on the part of the child. In the book Help Me Say It, the author warns of being "overly critical of a child's speech" (151) and the importance of "reinforcing speech lessons at home" (129, 152). In my opinion, to paraphrase the author and her respected references, parents are encouraged to reinforce the speech lessons the child is learning at school, and to continue to encourage all other areas of growth. However, the author repeatedly cautions parents to be careful not to overwhelm the child or allow her to become frustrated. Frustration generally results from failure of important adults to take time to understand the child (153).

The professional people who presently work with Jessica say they are seeing a little frustration. Most agree that they think we will see more as she continues to increase her vocabulary unless there is a sudden increase in clarity.

Looking over the information in this area of my research I find that clear speech is very important to the future of Jessica's development. For this reason I am eliminating Provider 2, as I do not feel her communication skills meet the needs of my child. I am also eliminating Provider 4 because, as stated earlier, the speech therapist agreed that accented speech is not a good idea at this time in Jessica's speech development. I am also eliminating Provider 3 on the basis of peer interaction. Although she states the activities would be age-appropriate, I feel the children are too young. Older children would provide better speech models.

Separation Anxiety

Much of the information I have found regarding separation anxiety agrees with an article by noted researchers on family living, Ellen Galinsky and Judy David. In their article, "Say Goodbye to Guilt," they say that parents must feel good about where and with whom they are leaving their child. If a parent is uneasy the child will sense it. A child will play on a parent's guilt feelings. Nancy Balaban, Director of the Infant and Parental Development program at the Bank Street College of Education Graduate School, in her book Learning to Say Goodbye, stated "sometimes we may feel that it is not the child but the parent who is having a trouble separating" (12). Evelyn B. Thompson, Ph.D., who is currently a Professor of Biobehavioral Sciences at the University of Connecticut, in her book Born Dancing, agreed with the above statement when she wrote "the less anxious and guilty you feel about working, the easier your baby will adjust" (199). The general feeling I have from reading the book, Learning to Say Goodbye, is that parents need to deal with separation in a matter-of-fact way, trying to be consistent with as few changes as possible. "Consumer's Guide to Child-Care," a pamphlet from the Wisconsin Department of Health and Social Services, recommends that parents "avoid care hopping; changing care is confusing and disruptive to a child." This advice is repeated often: "Consistency, it is important, but do not be afraid to change care if it is in the best interest of the child."

From what I have read, I conclude that a change in care-givers needs careful consideration. Change is encouraged if it is to the benefit of the child, but not something to be done without a lot of research for a good, stable and long-lasting arrangement. A statement by John Bowlby, Chairman of the Staff Committee of the School of Family Psychiatry and Community Mental Health in London, is quoted in Eleanor E. Maccoby's book Social Development as saying "Children should be allowed to remain with their accustomed caretaker under all possible circumstances" (88). He also says that "continuity of an attachment relationship is the most important consideration in making decisions about children's lives" (98). In his book Attachment and Loss, Bowlby states, "It is com-

-19-

mon for children ages 2 to 4 to have problems separating from their mother" (205–6). T. Berry Branzelton M.D., a well known and respected pediatrician who is an Associate Professor at Harvard Medical School and Chief of the Child Development Unit at Boston Children's Hospital Medical Center, in his book, To Listen to a Child, seems to agree with John Bowlby's views when he writes "Crying can serve many purposes—anger, protest, a call for help or just letting off steam. After the crying period is over, the emergency will have been met, someone is likely to have responded and everyone feels better" (57).

When I chose this question for my research, I made a chart on which to the length of time Jessica cried when dropped off at her present day care. I started this chart on September 22 and continued to record information until October 28. To start with, I was just recording the amount of time Jessica cried, but a pattern emerged—I thought she was crying longer for one of the care providers at the day care than the other. I started to keep track of who I left Jessica with. To record this information I used my watch, staying out of sight to prevent another bout of crying if she were to see me again. The charted information and some results follow:

Date	Crying Time (Minutes)	
9 / 22	10	
9 / 23	.9	
9 / 26	3	
9 / 27	12	
9 / 28	5	
9 / 29	5	
9 / 30	4	

10 / 3	4	
10 / 4	Dad dropped her off.	
10 / 5	3	
10 / 6	5	
10 / 7	2	
	(Noticed who I dropped her off with seemed to make a difference.)	PERSON (A OR B)
10 / 10	3	A
10 / 11	5	B
10 / 12	4	B
10 / 13	1.5	A
10 / 14	2	A
10 / 17	2	A
10 / 18	5	B
10 / 19	4	A
10 / 20	3B	
10 / 21	1	A
10 / 24	Did not use day	
10 / 25	care these two days.	
10 / 26	3	B
10 / 27	2	A
10 / 28	1	A

I totalled the number of minutes of crying for each person and divided this total by the number of times I left Jessica with them to get an average number of minutes of crying for each person.

Person A: 16 minutes ÷ 8 times left = average time 2 minutes.
Person B: 20 minutes ÷ 5 times left = average time 4 minutes.

This result leads me to think that the pattern I hypothesized probably does exist.

At this point I decided I should talk to the teacher and get her opinion of what she saw as far as Jessica's crying. She stated that although Jessica is still crying, it is not too bad, and it does not seem to be lasting as long. The teacher feels this is Jessica's way of expressing her sadness at my leaving. The teacher then stated "I hold her for a few minutes and then she is just fine; we have no more crying the rest of the time she is here." Jessica's teacher feels she fits in well and plays nicely with the other children. Jessica has her favorite friends by whom she likes to sit at lunch, snack, and art time, but will sit elsewhere if someone asks her to.

Direct observation has shown me that the other children come over to Jessica when she arrives and comfort her. I have heard "It's OK, your Mom will be back." One day I even heard "My Mom's at school with your Mommy." Jessica returns this care to other children later in the day by helping them pick up their toys or helping them with their shoes, according to the teacher.

As for how a new provider will handle Jessica's crying, it is hard to tell. As all are looking for children, no one would say anything negative. I do know from experience that different people handle Jessica's crying in different ways where she is at now, and it makes a difference on how well she settles down. Because of this observation, I feel there would also be a personal difference in how a new provider would handle it.

There was a lot of information available on separation anxiety. Two things seem to come forward to me as the most important areas I personally need to deal with. The first is to trust my feelings on how I would feel about my child being in a particular person's care. For this reason, I am going to eliminate Provider 5, as my intuition tells me there are potential problems with her. She may, in the end, turn out to be a good provider, but I am not willing to risk my child's future on that possibility. I get the feeling she is taking in children for the money, and that they will get very little of her time. Her own baby will definitely come first, and if there is any time and energy left the other children will get some. The second thing I feel is that there seems to be an improvement in the crying time when I leave Jessica with person A. Until I make a final decision on where to place Jessica, I will arrange my schedule so I can get Jessica to the day care during the time that person A can be there to receive her.

Other Areas of Concern

Other areas that need to be addressed, but of lesser importance, include meeting the bus, what happens when the provider is ill, the cost of care and the location of the day care. At this time there are only two out of the original seven providers remaining to consider.

First I need to consider how I would meet Jessica's bus. Now she rides a bus from Putnam Heights School four days a week to her present day care. I must meet this bus, which limits the times I am free to take classes. I asked Provider 6 if it would be possible for her to meet Jessica's bus at her home. Her response was that she felt it would be a problem because of the timing, which is lunch time, and that this would require her to either dress all of the children to go out to meet the bus or to leave them alone inside while she went outside. She did not like either of these choices and said I would have to get Jessica to the house some other way.

My choice here seems to be to meet the bus at the provider's house or to pick Jessica up at Putnam Heights and drive her to the provider's home. There are some advantages to my picking Jessica up at the school as this would mean she would not have to ride the bus. There is a large difference in the amount of time she might have to spend on the bus depending on the location of the care facility. This time difference

ence could be as little as ten minutes or as long as fifty. I will explore this further when I look at the location of care.

Another concern I have is what happens when the provider is sick or for some other reason is unable to provide care. I found that with all the home-based day cares, the problem of alternative care was left to the parents to resolve. They all said that they would give me as much notice as possible, but that I needed to find alternative care. I could find out that morning that I needed care for that afternoon. With a State Licensed Group Day Care, this is not a problem. By state law they are required to provide a qualified substitute to replace all missing employees. In fact, the group day care I presently use has a person who spends a short amount of time with each group every day so that the children already know her if she is needed to substitute.

I have put together a chart listing mileages and travel time for the two remaining providers. After I include this chart I will use it to make some comparisons on the amount of time I will need care and the cost of both care and transportation.

Day of Week	Drop-off Time	Pick-up Time	Total (Hours)
Provider 6			
Monday	7:45 A.M.	4:15 P.M.	8.5
Tuesday	11:45 A.M.	4:30 P.M.	4.75
Wednesday	11:45 A.M.	3:00 P.M.	3.25
Thursday	11:45 A.M.	4:30 P.M.	4.75
Friday	11:45 A.M.	3:00 P.M.	2.25
			24.50
Provider 7			
Monday	8:30	3:30	7.0
Tuesday	11:45	3:45	4.0
Wednesday	11:45	2:15	2.5
Thursday	11:45	3:45	4.0
Friday	11:45	2:15	2.2
			20.0

The hourly cost of Provider 6 is $1.50. The total number of hours of care needed would be 24.5 hours per week. The 24.5 hours include travel time. $1.50/hour × 24.5 hours = $36.75 per week with a semester total of $36.75/week × 16 weeks = $520.00 per semester.

The cost of Provider 7 is $1.60 per hour; however, I would need only twenty hours per week because there is less travel time involved (see above chart). The total would be $1.60/hour × 20 hours = $32.00 per week and $32.00/week × 16 weeks = $520.00 per semester.

This section has revealed a very surprising fact to me: the cost of transporting my child to a less costly provider a further distance, compared to a more expensive but conveniently located provider, adds up to a lot of extra mileage, especially if I must also transport Jessica after she finishes school in the morning. I find it astounding that the cost of just the extra mileage is as much as the actual cost of day care. I strongly feel, however, that despite the cost, the most important consideration must still be the quality of the care.

Having found the extra cost of transportation, I must now consider that any provider I could afford to use would either have to be near my home, near campus or near Putnam Heights School. Secondly, if it is not a short walk to the provider from campus, the provider must be willing to meet the bus.

As far as the actual cost of day care is concerned, Provider 6 has a lower hourly rate but because of the extra hours the total is more. However, the difference $36.75 − $32.00 = $4.75 per week and $4.75 × 16 = $76.00 per semester is not very great. This would not stop me from using her if it only came down to that cost.

Summary

There are four different types of day cares that range from no direct regulation to a strict set of rules and regulations to follow. Although the ratio of adults to children ranges from one to three in a non-regulated to one to ten in a group day care center, the training required increases considerably with the number of children served.

I found seven day cares, some of each, to consider as possible places for my child. There was a wide range of personnel differences in the seven day cares. By process of elimination, at the end I was only considering two.

Only the group day care has arrangements for someone to replace the provider when she needs time off.

As far as racial differences, most providers were willing to take a non-white child in, but only the group day care had any experience in the area.

The quality of speech that Jessica is exposed to is directly related to her projected levels of improvement. The degree to which the day care provider actively participates is a crucial factor in her overcoming her speech delay.

As far as separation anxiety, I found a lot of information that reinforces my belief that a parent is the best judge of what their child needs. Sometimes as a parent we must make choices without a perfect reason to explain why we ruled something out.

Changes in providers should be done with caution with the best interest of the child in mind. Continuous care by the same provider is very important to help the parent and child feel good about care.

In the other area of concern, the location of care became a more significant consideration because extra travel costs can add up very quickly. On the other hand, the hourly rate has less of an impact on the total cost than I originally anticipated.

Conclusion

Having completed this research I have reached the decision to keep Jessica where she is presently in care. My reasons for this are to follow.

1. By charting her crying I can see that the actual time she cries is less than when I started.
2. The ratio of adults to children is the same, if not even higher at certain times of the day.

3. The children at the center where she is at are of the same age and I believe she will receive age-appropriate activities there.

4. The teacher where she is at has had some experience with children with speech delays.

5. From the reading I have done it seems that unless there is a very good reason, it's best not to change providers.

6. This research has made me look at what is happening where Jessica is and to look into the possibility that there may have been a better place for her. However, I did not find a better place and as an added benefit, I am more comfortable leaving her now.

Although I will continue to use the same day care that I am presently using, I will make two changes. The first is that I have changed Jessica's arrival time so I can leave her with person A. Even though she cries with person A, it is for a shorter amount of time and I like the way this person handles the crying. Secondly I am cutting the total hours of both Putnam and the day care to no more than six hours per day. The reason for this is that some of the reading I did stated that more than six hours may not benefit the child and, in fact, it may detract from the best of care. This will mean some adjustments in my study times, but, in the long run, I believe I will feel better. I do not want my being in school to harm my child.

Works Cited

Books

Balaban, Nancy. Learning to Say Goodbye. New York: Plume books, 1987. This book deals not only with separation anxiety in children but also their parents. There also was a section on choosing child care.

Barach, Carol. Help Me Say It. New York: Harper & Row, 1983. This book deals with recognizing speech problems and the current methods of treatment. This book explains the approach we are taking to our child's speech delay.

-25-

Bowlby, John. Attachment and Loss. 2 vols. New York: Basic Books, 1969, vol. 2. In his research this author points out how common separation problems arise with young children.

Brazelton, T. Berry. To Listen to a Child. Reading, MA: Addison-Wesley Publishing, 1984. Doctor Brazelton looks at various reasons why children cry when separated from their parents. He does not feel it is always because of a bad day care arrangement.

Maccoby, Eleanor. Social Development. New York: Harcourt Brace Jovanovich, 1980. This book provided several valuable references. It dealt with the need for consistent care givers early in a child's life.

Thoman, Evelyn. Born Dancing. New York: Harper & Row, 1974. This book deals with guilt feelings of parents leaving their child, and encourages parents to find good care and then keep it as long as possible.

Booklets

The Children's Center Handbook. Eau Claire, WI: University of Wisconsin—Eau Claire, 1987. This handbook explains the rules and regulations the center operates under.

Wisconsin Administrative Code HSS 55 Licensing Rules for Family Day Care Centers. Madison: Wisconsin State Division of Community Services, 1984. This booklet contains the complete set of rules for Family Day Cares.

Wisconsin Administrative Code HSS 55 Licensing Rules for Group Day Care Centers. Madison: Wisconsin State Divison of Community Services, 1984. This booklet contains the complete set of rules governing group day care centers.

Interviews

Evans, Maire. Personal interview, 22 October 1988. As Director of the Children's Center, Ms. Evans gave me a lot of information concerning the day to day operations and the background on the teachers.

Hansen, Penny. Personal interview, 3 November 1988. Ms. Hansen is my daughter's teacher at Putnam Heights School. Ms. Hanson has a degree in Early Childhood Education and has been working with Jessica for the last ten months. We discussed Jessica's overall development and what is seen as future needs. We also discussed if she has seen any changes since Jessica started spending afternoons in day care.

McCarthy, Nancy. Telephone Interview, 17 October 1988. Ms. McCarthy is a Day Care Licensing Specialist for the State of Wisconsin. In our conversation we discussed the various types of day care and the rules and regulations governing them.

M-Team. School Consultation, 4 November 1988. This is a team of professionals that work with Jessica. This team, along with her parents, evaluated her progress since the last M-Team meeting, and set up the future goals for speech therapy. This time we also discussed what they felt was important in a day care setting.

Provider 1. Telephone Interview, 29 October 1988. I spoke with this provider on the set-up of her day care, her background and other areas of concern to my research.

Provider 2. Interview, 29 October 1988. I conducted two interviews on the same day, one on the phone and the other at her home where she provides day care. In addition to answering my questions about her day care, I also viewed where my child would be if I used her as a provider.

-27-

Provider 3. Interviews, 29 October 1988, 1 November 1988. These interviews were used to obtain answers to my questions concerning how she ran her day care, and to see the actual day care.

Provider 4. Interviews, 29 October, 3 November 1988. These interviews were conducted, one on the telephone and the other in her home, in order to obtain an understanding of what she felt was important to offer children in her care.

Provider 5. Interviews, 29 October, 3 November 1988. The first interview by telephone gave me the basic answers to questions on the operation of her day care. The second one gave me a chance to see her day care and to ask more questions.

Provider 6. Interviews, 29 October, 5 November 1988. These interviews provided me with good insight into the working of her day care and what she felt was important for children in her care.

Provider 7. Personal Interviews, 27 October, 15 November 1988. These were two formal interviews to obtain information about the day to day activities of the day care. At other times when I picked my daughter up and there were a few minutes to spare, we also talked concerning my daughter's personal adjustment.

Savolainen, Richard. Telephone Interview, 28 November 1988. Mr. Savolainen is the Principal of the Putnam Heights School. We discussed the reasons why children attend only half-days at the Early Childhood Program.

Shea, Lu Ann. Personal Interview, 4 November 1988. Ms. Shea is Jessica's speech teacher at Putnam Heights School. We discussed Jessica's progress, program, needs and consistency with her speech program. We also discussed the effects of using a day care provider who speaks with a Korean Accent.

Magazine Articles

Coplan, James. "Unclear Speech: Recognition and Significance of Unintelligible Speech in Preschool Children." Pediatrics, 2 September 1988: 447–52. This article looked into the forms of speech problems and current trends in treating them.

Galinsky, Ellen and Judy David. "Good News for Working Mothers: Say Goodbye to Guilt," Family Circle, 9 September 1988: 106–7. The main idea of this article was finding good day care so that parents did not have to feel guilty when leaving their child.

Pamphlets

Consumer's Guide to Child Care. Child Care Information Center. This pamphlet deals with what to look for when going to see a day care and it stresses that, even if you do not see anything wrong, if you are uncomfortable for any reason to not use this day care.

Your Day Care: Is it Legal? Wisconsin State Division of Community Services. This is just a short overview of the basic differences in types of day care and the number of children each is allowed by law to care for.

Additional Works Consulted

Books

Tips on the Care and Adjustment of Vietnamese and other Asian Children in the United States. Washington D.C.: U.S. Department of Health, Education and Welfare, 1974.

Caplan, Frank; editor. The Parenting Advisor. Garden City, New York: Anchor Press-Doubleday, 1977.

Mecham, Merlin J. and Mary Louise Willbrand. Language Disorders in Children. Springfield, Illinois: Thomas Press, 1979.

Melina, Lois. Raising Adopted Children. Cambridge, Philadelphia: Harper & Row Publishers, 1986.

Pamphlets

I'll be back for you. Wisconsin State Department of Health and Social Services. n.d.

To: Parents Subject: Choosing Child Care. Wisconsin State Department of Human Services. n.d.

Tips on Selecting the 'Right' Day Care Facility. American Academy of Pediatrics. n.d.

CHAPTER EIGHT

ADDENDA

EVALUATION FORM ONE

EXPLANATION OF EVALUATION CRITERIA

EVALUATION FORM TWO

QUICK GUIDE TO DOCUMENTATION—MLA STYLE

FORMS FOR COMMONLY USED SOURCES—MLA STYLE

QUICK GUIDE TO DOCUMENTATION—APA STYLE

FORMS FOR COMMONLY USED SOURCES—APA STYLE

EDITING CHECKLIST

ANNOTATION WORKSHEET

PROCESS LOG FORM

	On Time	Thorough	Resourceful
SELECT QUESTION Due date: _____ Ready by: _____	1 2 3 4 5	1 2 3 4 5	1 2 3 4 5
ESTABLISH GIVENS Due date: _____ Ready by: _____	1 2 3 4 5	1 2 3 4 5	1 2 3 4 5
IDENTIFY CRITERIA Due date: _____ Ready by: _____	1 2 3 4 5	1 2 3 4 5	1 2 3 4 5
DEVELOP AN OUTLINE OF QUESTIONS Due date: _____ Ready by: _____	1 2 3 4 5	1 2 3 4 5	1 2 3 4 5
KEY THE OUTLINE FOR INFORMATION NEEDS Due date: _____ Ready by: _____	1 2 3 4 5	1 2 3 4 5	1 2 3 4 5
IDENTIFY SOURCES—INDEX BASED SEARCH Due date: _____ Ready by: _____	1 2 3 4 5	1 2 3 4 5	1 2 3 4 5
SELECT THE MOST VALID AND RELIABLE SOURCES Due date: _____ Ready by: _____	1 2 3 4 5	1 2 3 4 5	1 2 3 4 5
SUPPLEMENT WITH REFERRALS Due date: _____ Ready by: _____	1 2 3 4 5	1 2 3 4 5	1 2 3 4 5
TAKE NOTES Due date: _____ Ready by: _____	1 2 3 4 5	1 2 3 4 5	1 2 3 4 5
WRITE THE FIRST DRAFT Due date: _____ Ready by: _____	1 2 3 4 5	1 2 3 4 5	1 2 3 4 5
DELINEATE EVIDENCE LEVELS Due date: _____ Ready by: _____	1 2 3 4 5	1 2 3 4 5	1 2 3 4 5
INTRODUCE BORROWED MATERIAL Due date: _____ Ready by: _____	1 2 3 4 5	1 2 3 4 5	1 2 3 4 5
PREPARE WORKS CITED/WORKS CONSULTED Due date: _____ Ready by: _____	1 2 3 4 5	1 2 3 4 5	1 2 3 4 5
REACH CONCLUSIONS Due date: _____ Ready by: _____	1 2 3 4 5	1 2 3 4 5	1 2 3 4 5
CREATE A LEAD Due date: _____ Ready by: _____	1 2 3 4 5	1 2 3 4 5	1 2 3 4 5
PROVIDE A COMPLETE ATTRACTIVE PACKAGE Due date: _____ Ready by: _____	1 2 3 4 5	1 2 3 4 5	1 2 3 4 5

Explanation of Numbers on Scale: 1 = failing   4 = good
                                   2 = inadequate   5 = excellent
                                   3 = acceptable

EXPLANATION OF EVALUATION CRITERIA

Your work on each of these steps will be evaluated as failing, inadequate, acceptable, good, and excellent, according to the following criteria: On Schedule'? Thorough? Resourceful?

The first of these criteria, *on schedule,* is the only one which can not be modified by additional or revision work. If you have the work completed on time, your rating on this criterion will be "excellent." If you have most of it done except for one little fragment, your ranking will be "good." The more you have yet to do, the lower the ranking. If you are uncertain about due dates, check with your teacher or check your class schedule. No excuses of any kind will be considered.

For the remaining criteria, you have an opportunity to improve your ranking. For example, if your rating on thoroughness is inadequate, you may ask for a reassessment when you have done a more thorough job. Each day you go beyond the scheduled date for initial assessment, however, the more rigorous become the assessment standards. For example, if your index-based search is rated "inadequate," and the day after the initial assessment you are ready for a reassessment, your chances for a higher rating are much better than they would be if you took three weeks. In short, remedy any deficiencies as soon as possible.

To score well on *thoroughness,* do everything you possibly can to complete every detail. Anticipate as much as you can what else you might be expected to do. Think of yourself as one of the best students in class, and do everything you think the other "best" students will do in order to be thorough.

To be thorough, take care with details. Be patient and willing to spend extra effort if necessary to make your work outstanding.

The research process requires the use of many resources for each stage of the process. To do well on the criterion of *resourcefulness,* you will be expected to use the available resources with skill and precision. If you do not know how to use a certain tool, you will teach yourself or find someone to teach you. You will be inventive in finding new tools and using old ones in new ways. To be resourceful, you need to "work smart," be clever, use your intelligence. Again, ask yourself what the best students in class will do. If you find it impossible to think of yourself as among them, commit yourself to make up for it by scrambling a little harder.

At any time, if you do not understand why your work was rated as it was, contact your teacher. Do not brood in silence. This evaluation instrument is intended to help you learn the research process, never to punish.

<u>**Evaluation Form Two**</u>

Name _____

A. Selection and Clarification of the Question
 Level of significance to self and/or society
 Clarity of the question
 Clarity of the conclusion
 Quality of insights represented in the question

B. Approach to the Question
 Organization of the paper
 Outline
 Delineation of evidence levels
 Clarity of criteria

C. Research
 Thoroughness of the search
 Validity of the sources
 Honesty of transcription
 Balance among sources

D. Quality of the Writing
 Paragraphs (ordered, developed, unified)
 Sentences (coherent, standard syntax, variety)
 Diction (standard usage, precise)
 Style (general character)

E. Format and Editing
 Title page, outline margins, documentation forms, works cited
 Spelling, typing punctuation
 Overall appearance
 Assigned sequence (Did you have each step completed on time?)

COMMENTS:

QUICK GUIDE TO DOCUMENTATION—MLA STYLE

Introduce Borrowed Material in the Text

By introducing borrowed material in the text of your paper, you help your audience a) assess the reliability of the source and the validity of the information, b) see clearly what you borrowed and what you contributed yourself, and c) find the full citation for the source among the "Works Cited/Consulted."

> SAMPLE: Since the beginning of our history, American cities and towns have been in competition with each other for residents, businesses, and visitors. That's why any effort to "rate" communities draws so much attention. The people of 17th Century Salem thought it was their city St. Matthew had in mind when he wrote, "Ye are the light of the world. A city that is set on an hill cannot be hid" (5,13). In the introduction to their latest edition of *Places Rated Almanac*, Boyer and Savageau anticipate the usual controversy and encourage their readers to use the *Almanac*'s data to make their own choices (2).
>
> Popular magazines and scholarly journals have picked up the challenge. Writing for the *Journal of Geography*, Thomas Bell suggests that the *Almanac*'s limitations "should be viewed by instructors as opportunities to hone the critical, evaluative skills of their students" (285). Others apply their own criteria. Psychologist Donald Routh, for example, created "A Places Rated for Pediatric Psychology" (113–19). And *Psychology Today* selected the twenty-five best and the twenty-five worst U.S. cities judged on the criterion of stress (Levine 53–58).
>
> Naturally each city considers itself the "best" in its own unique way. A typical publication of the Eau Claire Chamber of Commerce includes a large shot of the photogenic Chippewa River (*Eau Claire, Wisconsin Visitors Guide*, front cover). Another Chamber publication, *Eau Claire: A City for All Seasons*, tries to make something positive out of extreme seasonal variations in temperature (21–22). Even a one page "Community Profile" mentions the advantages of "four distinct seasons." When I asked the Chamber president, if he liked winter, he said, "You betcha!" (Anderson, personal interview)

Provide a "works cited" or "works consulted" page

Using information from the text, your readers will be able to find the full citation in your "works" page. Sample:

Works Cited

Anderson, Oscar. Personal interview. 3 May 1989.

Bell, Thomas L. "Places Rated Almanac: Flawed but Pedagogically Useful."
Journal of Geography 83.6 (1984): 285–89.

Boyer, Richard, and David Savageau. Places Rated Almanac: Your Guide to
Finding the Best Places to Live in America. New York: Prentice Hall, 1989.

Greater Eau Claire Area Chamber of Commerce. Eau Claire Wisconsin: Visitors
Guide. Eau Claire, WI: n.p., n.d.

———. Eau Claire: A City for All Seasons. Eau Claire, WI: Modern Communications, 1989.

———. "Community Profile." A single page handout. n.d.

Levine, Robert. "In Search of Eden: City Stress Index: 25 Best; 25 Worst." Psychology Today Nov. 1988: 53–59.

Routh, Donald K. "A Places Rated Almanac for Pediatric Psychology." Journal
of Pediatric Psychology 13.1 (1988) 113–19.

FORMS FOR COMMONLY USED SOURCES— MLA STYLE

Books

1. By a single author:

Martens, Rainer. *Coaches Guide to Sport Psychology*. Champaign, IL: Human
Kinetics Publishers, 1987.

2. By two or three authors:

Boyer, Richard, and David Savageau. *Places Rated Almanac: Your Guide to
Finding the Best Places to Live in America*. New York: Prentice Hall,
1989.

4. Prepared by an agency, association, or other organization:

American Psychological Association. *Publication Manual of the American Psychological Association*. 3rd ed. Washington: American Psychological Association, 1983.

5. Prepared by an editor, compiler:

Caplan, Frank., ed. *The Parenting Advisor*. Garden City, NY: Anchor Press-Doubleday, 1977.

6. In a second or later edition:

Gibaldi, Joseph, and Walter S. Achtert. *MLA Handbook For Writers of Research Papers*. 2nd ed. New York: Modern Language Association, 1984.

7. Edited, translated, or introduced by someone other than the author:

Rolvaag, Ole Edvart. *Giants in the Earth*. Trans. Lincoln Colcord. New York: Harper & Row, 1927.

Periodicals

1. An article from a journal with pagination by issue (and, in this case, more than three authors):

Horowitz, Stephen M., et al. "Association between Job Stress and Perceived Quality of Life." *College Health* July 1988: 29–34.

2. An article from a journal with continuous pagination:

Bell, Thomas L. "*Places Rated Almanac*: Flawed but Pedagogically Useful." *Journal of Geography* 83.6 (1984): 285–89.

3. A signed article from a monthly magazine:

Levine, Robert. "In Search of Eden: City Stress Index: 25 Best; 25 Worst." *Psychology Today* Nov. 1988: 53–59.

4. A signed article from a daily newspaper.

Lindquist, Eric. "Circle Wisconsin draws tourists to state." *Leader Telegram* [Eau Claire, WI] 28 Jan. 1990: D-1.

5. An unsigned article from a magazine or a newspaper:

"America's Best Colleges: What's Behind the Rankings." *U.S. News & World Report* 16 Oct. 1989: 58 + .

Other Formats

1. Pamphlets, brochures, booklets:

Greater Eau Claire Area Chamber of Commerce. *Eau Claire Wisconsin: Visitors Guide*. Eau Claire, WI: n.p., n.d. [Note: "n.p." is the abbreviation for "no publisher named, and "n.d." is the abbreviation for "no date provided."]

2. Personal letter to author:

Anderson, Oscar. Letter to author. 5 May 1989.

3. Personal interview:

Anderson, Oscar. Personal interview, 3 May 1989.

4. Notes from a jacket or cover:

Albertson, Chris. Jacket Notes. *Say Amen, Somebody*. New York: DRG Records SB2L 12584, 1983.

5. Feature length film, play, broadcast:

Wilder, Thorton, *Our Town*. New York: Coward McCann, 1938.

6. Lecture, Speech, or concert:

Lynn, John. "Life on the Mississippi." Chippewa Falls Public Library. 26 February, 1990.

QUICK GUIDE TO DOCUMENTATION—APA STYLE

Introduce Borrowed Material in the Text

By introducing borrowed material in the text of your paper, you help your audience a) assess the reliability of the source and the validity of the information, b) see clearly what you borrowed and what you contributed yourself, and c) find the full citation for the source among the "References."

Sample: Since the beginning of our history, American cities and towns have been in competition with each other for residents, businesses, and visitors. That's why any effort to "rate" communities draws so much attention. The people of 17th-century Salem thought it was their city that St. Matthew (5, 13) had in mind when he wrote, "Ye are the light of the world. A city that is set on an hill cannot be hid." In the introduction to their latest edition of *Places Rated Almanac*, Boyer and Savageau (1989, p. 2) anticipate the usual controversy and encourage their readers to use the *Almanac*'s data to make their own choices.

Popular magazines and scholarly journals have picked up the challenge. Writing for the *Journal of Geography*, Thomas Bell (1985, p. 285) suggests that the *Almanac*'s limitations "should be viewed by instructors as opportunities to hone the critical, evaluative skills of their students." Others apply their own criteria. Psychologist Donald Routh (1988, pp. 113–19) for example, created "A Places Rated for Pediatric Psychology." And *Psychology Today* selected the twenty-five best and the twenty-five worst U.S. cities judged on the criterion of stress (Levine, 1988, p. 53–58).

Naturally each city considers itself the "best" in its own unique way. A typical publication of the Eau Claire Chamber of Commerce includes a large shot of the photogenic Chippewa River (*Eau Claire, Wisconsin Visitors Guide*, front cover). Another Chamber publication, *Eau Claire: A City for All Seasons*, (1989, pp. 21–22) tries to make something positive out of their extreme seasonal variations in temperature. Even a one page "Community Profile" mentions the advantages of "four distinct seasons." When I asked the Chamber president, if he liked winter, he said, "You betcha!" (Anderson, 1989, personal interview).

References

Anderson, O. (1989, May 3). Personal interview.

Bell, T. L. (1984). Places rated almanac: flawed but pedagogically useful. Journal of Geography, 83 (6), 285–289.

Boyer, R., & D. Savageau (1989). Places rated almanac: Your guide to finding the best places to live in america. New York: Prentice Hall.

Greater Eau Claire Area Chamber of Commerce (no date). Eau Claire Wisconsin: Visitors Guide. Eau Claire, WI: Author.

_____ (1989). Eau Claire: A city for all seasons. Eau Claire, WI: Modern Communications.

_____ (no date)."Community Profile." A single-page handout.

Levine, R. (1988, November). "In search of Eden: City stress index: 25 best; 25 worst." Psychology Today, pp. 53–59.

Routh, D. K. (1988). A Places rated almanac for pediatric psychology. Journal of Pediatric Psychology, 13, 113–119.

FORMS FOR COMMONLY USED SOURCES— APA STYLE

Books

1. By a single author:

Martens, R. (1987). *Coaches guide to sport psychology.* Champaign, IL: Human Kinetics Publishers.

2. By two or three authors:

Boyer, R. & D. Savageau (1989). *Places rated almanac: your guide to finding the best places to live in america.* New York: Prentice Hall.

3. Prepared by an agency, association, or other organization:

American Psychological Association (1983). *Publication manual of the american psychological association.* (3rd ed.) Washington, D.C.: Author.

4. Prepared by an editor, compiler:

Caplan, F. (Ed.). (1977). *The parenting advisor*. Garden City, NY: Anchor Press-Doubleday.

5. In a second or later edition:

Gibaldi, J. & W. S. Achtert (1984). *MLA handbook for writers of research papers*. (2nd ed.) New York: Modern Language Association.

6. Edited, translated, or introduced by someone other than the author:

Rolvaag, O. E. (1927). *Giants in the earth*. (L. Colcord, Trans.) New York: Harper & Row. (Original work published in 1927)

Periodicals

1. An article from a journal with pagination by issue (and more than six authors):

Horowitz, S. M., et al. (1988, July). Association between job stress and perceived quality of life. *College Health*, pp. 29–34.

2. An article from a journal with continuous pagination:

Bell, T. L. (1984). *Places Rated Almanac*: flawed but pedagogically useful. *Journal of Geography, 83* (6), 285–89.

3. A signed article from a monthly magazine:

Levine, R. (1988, November). In Search of Eden: city stress index: 25 best; 25 worst. *Psychology Today*, pp. 53–59.

4. A signed article from a daily newspaper:

Lindquist, E. (1990, January 28). Circle Wisconsin draws tourists to state. *Leader Telegram* [Eau Claire, WI] D-1.

5. An unsigned article from a magazine or a newspaper:

America's Best Colleges: What's behind the rankings. (1989, October 16). *U.S. News & World Report*, pp. 58+.

Other Formats

1. Pamphlets, brochures, booklets:

Greater Eau Claire Area Chamber of Commerce. (no date). *Eau Claire Wisconsin: Visitors Guide*. Eau Claire, WI.

2. Personal letter to author:

Anderson, O. (1989, May 5). Letter to author.

3. Personal interview:

Anderson, O. (1989, May 3). Personal interview.

4. Notes from a jacket or cover:

Albertson, C. (1983). Jacket Notes. *Say Amen, Somebody.* New York: DRG Records SBL2L 12584.

5. Feature length film, play, broadcast:

Wilder, T. (1938). *Our Town.* New York: Coward McCann.

6. Lecture, Speech, or concert:

Lynn, J. (1990, February 26). Life on the Mississippi. Chippewa Falls Public Library.

EDITING CHECKLIST

HAVE I INCLUDED ALL OF THE REQUIRED PARTS?

☐ Title page?
☐ Full sentence outline?
☐ Text with division headings?
☐ Annotated Works Cited Page and Works Consulted Page?
☐ Preliminary Drafts and other working materials?

HAVE I PROVIDED APPROPRIATE DOCUMENTATION?

☐ Introduce borrowed material in the text?
☐ Parenthetical citations where needed?
☐ Quotation marks where needed?
☐ Legitimate use of summary and paraphrase?
☐ Format of Works pages complete and consistent?

DO ALL OF MY PUNCTUATION MARKS DO WHAT I WANT THEM TO DO?

☐ Commas, semi-colons?
☐ Dashes, colons, parentheses?
☐ Periods, question marks, exclamations?
☐ Quotation marks, possessives?
☐ Italics, underlinings, bold print?
☐ Upper and lower case?

ARE MY SENTENCES CLEAR?

- ☐ No fragments?
- ☐ No run-ons?
- ☐ No misplaced or dangling modifiers?
- ☐ Parallel elements grammatically parallel?
- ☐ Pronoun references clear?
- ☐ All elements in agreement?
- ☐ Tenses and moods consistent?

ARE MY SENTENCES STRONG?

- ☐ Primarily active voice?
- ☐ Action verbs outnumber linking verbs?
- ☐ Forms of the verb, "to be," limited?
- ☐ Variety in the use of subordinators?
- ☐ Sentences linked to one another by references?
- ☐ Adjectives and adverbs carefully distributed?
- ☐ Sentences pass the "Read Aloud" test?

IS THE DICTION PRECISE AND THE USAGE APPROPRIATE?

- ☐ Exactly right word choice?
- ☐ Appropriate level of usage?
- ☐ Standard inflections?
- ☐ The most specific words possible?
- ☐ Unnecessary jargon avoided?
- ☐ Consistent tone?

DOES EVERYTHING FOLLOW THE FORMAT GUIDELINES?

- ☐ All spelling/typographical errors corrected?
- ☐ Typewriter or printer ribbon dark enough?
- ☐ Consistent spacing for text, titles and headings?
- ☐ Margins at specified width?
- ☐ Page numbers complete and in order?
- ☐ All stray marks removed?
- ☐ Check the spelling of your teacher's name?
- ☐ Appropriate cover, folder, or fastenings?

ANNOTATION WORKSHEET

For each of the sources you wish to consult and/or cite, prepare one of these "Annotation Worksheets." In addition to providing a record of essential bibliographical detail, this sheet will help you remember the context for any information you cite and help you judge its validity and reliability. In addition, this work sheet will help you prepare the annotation required for every cited or consulted source.

1. Record below a complete citation (Using the MLA forms) as it will appear on your "works cited" or "works consulted" page.

2. Write a sentence or two about the author. What is his/her occupation, position, education, experience? In your judgment, is the author qualified and reliable?

3. As far as you can tell, what was the author's purpose for writing the article, doing the research, offering the interview?

4. To what audience is the work addressed? (Is it endorsed for the general public, for scholars, policy markers, teachers . . . ?)

5. Does the author have a bias? What is it? Does he/she make assumptions? What are they? How were you able to tell?

6. What methodology did the author use to collect information? (direct observation, interviews, polls, laboratory experiments, other?)

7. What conclusions did the author reach?

8. Does the evidence support the conclusions? Why or why not?

9. To what degree does this source agree with others you have used? Disagree?

10. Has the author provided you with any supplementary resources—additional sources, charts, maps, photographs, recording, . . . ?

This worksheet is adapted from "Preparing An Annotation," created by Eugene Engeldinger, Reference Department, Wm. D. McIntyre Library, University of Wisconsin—Eau Claire, August, 1988.

PROCESS LOG

ENTRY #					
DATE	TIMES BEGIN	END	SLIPPAGE TIME (Subtract)	TOTAL TIME ON TASK	STAGE OF RESEARCH ENGAGED

WORKSITE	TOOLS USED	PROGRESS	PROBLEMS

COMMENTS/OBSERVATIONS/PLANS FOR NEXT SESSION

KEY TERMS

Annotation: Information which you provide about a citation—its contents, and its value to your project. Annotations may be as short as two sentences or as full as several paragraphs.

APA Style: The forms of documentation and manuscript preparation recommended by the American Psychological Association.

Audience: The specific person or persons we have in mind when we undertake a writing project. The audience is different for each writing task.

Backup Copy: An additional electronic copy of what you have written. The devices (usually disks) on which information is stored are vulnerable to damage. If you have no "backup" you could lose weeks of work in seconds.

Bibliography Card: A note card on which you record a single citation along with its call number or other guide to the item's location. Useful in the initial stages of research to help you locate and sort your sources, and later, to help you provide documentation.

Board of Directors: A metaphoric description of your research paper audience.

Boolean Logic: A strategy of logic which permits users of data base indexes to narrow a search. If one begins with a broad term ("Athletes," for example) the data base will find hundreds of sources. On a system with a Boolean "and" feature, one can add additional terms to Athletes ("College" and "Women," for example), and the system will supply only items in which all of the terms appear.

Borrowed Information: Any words, information or concepts we borrow from other sources. If you were not familiar with the information before you located it, it is borrowed information, and you have an obligation to give credit to its source.

Call Number: An index code number assigned to each item in the library. Essential to the organization, storage, and retrieval of materials.

Card Catalog: A comprehensive index with library holdings entered on note cards cross referenced by Subject, Title, and Author. Until recently, the standard comprehensive index for libraries.

CD ROM: An abbreviation for "Compact Disc, Read Only Memory." Used for data-based specialized indexes.

Chicago Style: The forms of documentation and manuscript preparation recommended by the University of Chicago Press.

Citation: Information about a specific source usually including author, title, publisher, date, and location.

Cite Your Sources: Same as "Document Your Sources."

Cognition: A technical term for the process of thinking.

Comprehensive Index: The library's main index—the card catalog or on-line data base—with entries for every item in the library.

Conclusion: The comprehensive, evaluation level decision which culminates the written presentation of the research. The answer to the overall research question.

Copy Machine System: Alternative or supplement to Note Card System. Employs library copy machines to duplicate complete sources or parts of sources.

Criteria: Standards of judgment selected by the researchers as the basis for a search for information, and for the decisions (once information becomes available) they want to make. Conditions, circumstances, or factors relevant to making a valid judgment. For example, to choose one breed of dog over another, I might select as my standards of judgment such factors as bird hunting ability, ability to live outside, probable costs of care and feeding.

Delineate: To make clear distinctions between one level and another. Thus, "to delineate evidence levels" means to make a clear distinction between evidence on one level and evidence on another level.

Dewey Decimal System: One of the standard classification systems for comprehensive indexes, it is used to organize, store, and retrieve library materials. The other standard system is the Library of Congress Cataloging in Publication System.

Direct Quotation: Word for word presentation of borrowed information. Must be documented.

Discourse Community: Technical term used by composition theorists to describe the group of people who make up the audience for a specific piece of writing. A Discourse Community is a group of people who shares assumptions about research and scholarly writing.

Document Sources: The process of introducing and identifying the sources of borrowed information. The specific forms differ slightly from style to style.

Draft: The stage in the writing process during which you attempt, for the first time, to move ideas and information in your head onto paper in a form you hope will lead to a final draft.

Elaborate: During revision, to add detail, explanation, or other elements of development.

Electronic Slate: A metaphoric description of the way words are stored in word processors. While markings of chalk store the words on a slate chalkboard, the words in a computer are stored as electronic signals.

Empirical: Direct observation through one's senses.

Empirical Method: A strategy for collecting information by direct observation. Includes isolating and controlling selected variables, and directly observing results, often with the help of specialized instruments.

Enlarge: During revision, to add entire sections, paragraphs, or other major elements.

Exhortations: Efforts to persuade or encourage someone to do well.

Givens: All of the known conditions relevant to the research question which probably will remain the same during the research process. For example, I might know that I want a dog, that I hunt quail and pheasant, that the dog must live outside, that I have a fenced in space of 40 feet by 20 feet, and that I have $200 a year to spend on it.

Hardware: The mechanical and electronic equipment used for computing.

Holistic: An evaluation strategy designed to consider the work as an entity. Generally most valid if the work evaluated is one of a group.

Human Subject: Anyone you interview from whom you elicit personal information about traditionally confidential areas.

Index-Based Search: A search for sources which primarily makes use of library indexes, especially those organized by subject.

Index: Any classification system designed to help users gain quick access to specific material or information from among much.

Indexing System: Specific classification system, for example, the Dewey Decimal System.

Inference: Reaching a judgment from incomplete information.

Informed Consent: A procedure used by interviewers (and other researchers) to make certain that "human subjects" know the risks they face by participating in the research project.

Interactive: In interviews, the process of listening carefully to the people you interview, of following up leads they provide, and of becoming an alert, active participant.

Introduce Sources in the Text: Introducing the name of the author and/or the title of the work directly in the text of the paper immediately before paraphrasing, summarizing, or quoting.

Kinds of Information: The general categories of information a researcher needs. For example, Paula needed information about the short and long-term health effects of competitive sprinting.

Lead: Opening paragraph or two which draws the audience into the text of the paper by using techniques drawn from narrative writing.

MLA Style: The forms of documentation and manuscript preparation recommended by the Modern Language Association.

Note Card System: Traditional strategy for recording, sorting, and arranging borrowed information. Employs 4" x 6" or 5" x 8" note cards, one for each segment of information you want to record from your sources.

On-Line Data Base: A computerized comprehensive index stored on a data base with access gained by patron-operated terminals.

Paraphrase: Translating into your own language information you have borrowed. Must be documented.

Parenthetical Citation: Publication information enclosed by parenthesis included in the text to help the reader find the source on the "Works Cited" page.

Periodical: Any publication which is issued on a schedule of regular intervals— newspapers, magazines, journals, and so on.

Persuasion: Writing which attempts to convince the audience that the writer's assertions are true.

Plagiarism Technical: Out of sloppiness or ignorance, presenting borrowed information in a poorly paraphrased form, or without complete appropriate documentation. A lapse of skill and/or effort, but probably not moral judgment.

Plagiarism Intentional: Intentionally presenting borrowed materials as your own. An ethical and moral violation of Western intellectual traditions.

Primary Trait: An evaluation strategy during which the evaluator examines specific components of the work and assigns a score for each "trait."

Process: All of the activities (often organized into steps or stages) which one goes through to complete a specific project.

Procrastination: Putting off until sometime later a task which could just as well be attended to now. A common pattern of behavior among students because they often work without direct supervision.

Purpose: What we hope to achieve by writing. Usually the purpose is a specific response from a specific audience.

Question Approach: Research which begins with a need to find an answer to an important question. The researcher looks for information to answer the question.

Rearrange: During revision, to move large or small segments of writing from one place to another.

Referral Based Search: A search for information which follows up referrals from authoritative sources already located—bibliographies, notes, and works cited.

Refine: During revision, to reshape sentences, clarify diction, and, in general, do whatever is necessary to improve the quality of the writing.

Release: Procedure and/or form for securing permission to use material provided during an interview, concert, or speech, especially if it is audio or video recorded.

Relevance: Connection or relationship. In order to be valid, research information needs to have "relevance," a clear relationship to the question.

Reliable: Producing the same results when observed again. Evidence may be "unreliable" if the results are not consistently the same.

Report: Writing which provides as much information as possible on a limited topic, usually in the form of paraphrase and summary.

Save: The signal sent to a word processor if you want to keep what you have written. The words entered into a word processor are stored in a temporary state. If the user wants to keep them, he or she must signal the word processor to ''Save'' them.

Slippage: Time (and sometimes other things like money) lost to distractions, broken equipment, anything which takes one away from ''time on task.''

Software: The electronic programs which enable computer hardware to organize and shape information. Most programs are designed for specific computing tasks. Word Processing programs, for example, enable users to devote a computer to writing processes.

Specialized Index: An index to materials in only specific sources, generally related to specialized information—periodical indexes, government document indexes, and so on.

Specific Source: A specific magazine article, a specific book, an interview with a specific person, and the like.

Stylus: A device which permits humans to transfer the words in their brains to words on a page—a pencil, a computer keyboard, a piece of chalk.

Subconclusion: Intermediate, evaluation level judgments reached at the end of each major section of the research. The answer to one of the ''criterion based'' subquestions.

Summary: A general description of borrowed information, especially useful to provide a context for more specific paraphrased or quoted information. Must be documented.

Summary: A recapitulation of all of the subconclusions.

Survey: Quick read-through to estimate an item's value to your research project.

Taxonomy: An annotated list. Thus a ''taxonomy of information'' is a list of information levels with definitions, explanations, and examples.

Thesis approach: Research which begins with a general statement assumed to be true at the beginning of the project. The researcher looks for information to support the initial thesis, modifying it if the evidence is clearly contrary. Usually research which uses a thesis approach culminates in a persuasive final paper.

Time on task: The actual amount of time devoted to work on a project. Total time engaged in the process minus slippage.

Topic Approach: Research which focuses on the exploration of a limited topic of interest to the researcher. Using primarily library resources, researchers learn as much as they can about the topic. A topic approach usually leads to a report paper.

Type of Source: General category of source materials—books, magazines, interviews, and so forth.

Valid: Having direct relevance to the outcome of a research question. Evidence may be "invalid" if it does not deal directly with the issues under investigation.

Word Processor: A combination of hardware and software set up for writing—composing, revising, editing, and printing.

Work-Avoidance: Anything we do to escape the discomfort of work—sharpening pencils, eating, drinking, playing games, watching television, and the like.

Working Bibliography: A list of all the sources which, from index citations, appear to have potential for specific information needs. As you examine these sources you will add others by referral, and some you will cut.

Works Cited: In the MLA style, a list of citations provided at the conclusion of the paper. Includes only those sources specifically cited in the text.

Works Consulted: In the MLA style, a list of citations provided at the conclusion of the paper. Includes the works which were cited in the text and, in addition, other works which were consulted.

INDEX

E

G

H

I